8·3·77

BURT FRANKLIN: RESEARCH & SOURCE WORKS SERIES
Philosophy & Religious History Monographs 140

A DISSERTATION

CONCERNING

LIBERTY & NECESSITY

A DISSERTATION

CONCERNING

LIBERTY & NECESSITY

CONTAINING REMARKS ON THE

ESSAYS OF DR. SAMUEL WEST

AND ON THE
WRITINGS OF SEVERAL OTHER AUTHORS,
ON THOSE SUBJECTS

JONATHAN EDWARDS

BURT FRANKLIN REPRINTS
New York, N. Y.

Published by LENOX HILL Pub. & Dist. Co. (Burt Franklin)
235 East 44th St., New York, N.Y. 10017
Reprinted: 1974
Printed in the U.S.A.

Burt Franklin: Research and Source Works Series
Philosophy and Religious History Monographs 140

Library of Congress Cataloging in Publication Data

Edwards, Jonathan, 1745-1801.
    A dissertation concerning liberty and necessity.

    Reprint of the 1797 ed. printed by L. Worcester at Worcester.
    1. Free will and determinism. 2. West, Samuel, 1730-1807. Essays on
liberty and necessity. I. Title.
BJ1461.E32 1974   243'.9   73-21786
ESBN 0-8337-1003-6

CONTENTS

1974121

A

DISSERTATION

CONCERNING

LIBERTY AND NECESSITY;

CONTAINING

REMARKS

ON THE

ESSAYS OF DR. SAMUEL WEST,

AND ON THE

WRITINGS OF SEVERAL OTHER AUTHORS,
ON THOSE SUBJECTS.

By JONATHAN EDWARDS, D. D.

PRINTED AT *WORCESTER*,
By LEONARD WORCESTER.

1797.

ADVERTISEMENT.

I BEGAN this Differtation before I faw Dr. Weft's fecond edition of his Firſt Part *publiſhed with his* Second Part : *But on hearing, that he was about to publiſh his fentiments on* Liberty *and* Neceffity *more largely, I fufpended the profecution of my defign, that I might fee what he ſhould further publiſh. Since the publication of the fecond part, I have been neceffarily though reluctantly kept back till this time, from finiſhing what I had begun. At length I fend it forth, requeſting the candour of all who ſhall read it. If ever candour to a writer be reaſonably requeſted, it is fo, on the deep and difficult fubjects brought under confideration in this Differtation.*

The quotations from the Doctor's firſt part, *are made according to the pages of the firſt edition, with which I began. Yet wherever any variation in words, between the firſt and fecond editions, has been noticed ; the fecond edition has been followed in that refpect. When I quote the firſt part the page or pages only are referred to. When I quote the fecond part, I fpecify the part as well as the pages.*

A

DISSERTATION, &c.

CHAPTER I.

Of Natural and Moral Neceffity and Inability.

RESIDENT Edwards, in his book on *the Freedom of Will*, diftinguifhes between *natural* and *moral* neceffity and inability. By *moral* neceffity he tells us, he means, " That neceffity " of conne&ion and confequence, " which arifes from fuch moral cauf- " es, as the ftrength of inclination or motives, and the " conne&ion which there is in many cafes between " thefe and certain volitions and a&ions." P. 21. By *natural* neceffity he explains himfelf to mean, " Such " neceffity as men are under, through the force of " *natural* caufes, as diftinguifhed from what are call- " ed *moral* caufes; fuch as habits and difpofitions of " heart, and moral motives and inducements." Ibid. He further holds, that " the difference between thefe " two kinds of neceffity, does not lie fo much in the " *nature* of the conne&ion, as in the *two terms* con- ne&ed;" that in moral neceffity, " the caufe ——— is " of a *moral* nature, either fome *previous habitual dif-*

A 3

" *pofition,*

" *pofition*, or fome *motive* exhibited to the underftand-
" ing : And the effect is alfo ———— of a moral nature
" ———— fome *inclination* or *volition* of the foul or *vol-*
" *untary action*." P. 22. Alfo he held, that natural
neceffity always " has reference to fome fuppofable
" voluntary oppofition or endeavour, which is infuffi-
" cient. But no fuch oppofition or contrary will and
" endeavour is fuppofable in the cafe of moral neceffi-
" ty, which is *a certainty of the inclination and will it-*
" *felf*, which does not admit of the fuppofition of a
" will to oppofe and refift it. For it is abfurd to fup-
" pofe the fame individual will to oppofe itfelf *in its*
" *prefent act.*" P. 23, 24. And p. 16. " Philofophical
" *neceffity* is really nothing elfe than the full and fixed
" connection between the things fignified by the fub-
" ject and predicate of a propofition. When there is
" fuch a connection, then the thing affirmed in the
" propofition is neceffary————In this fenfe I ufe
" the word *neceffity* ———— when I endeavor to prove,
" that *neceffity is not inconfiftent with liberty*." Ibid.
" Philofophical neceffity is nothing different from the
" certainty that is in things themfelves, which is the
" foundation of the certainty of the knowledge of
" them."

This is the account given by Prefident Edwards,
of the diftinction, which he made between natural
and moral neceffity. Moral neceffity is the certain or
neceffary connection between moral caufes and moral
effects ; natural neceffity is the connection between
caufes and effects, which are not of a moral nature.
The difference between thefe two kinds of neceffity
lies chiefly in the nature of *the two terms* connected
by it. Natural neceffity admits of voluntary, but ineffectual oppofition from him who is fubject to the neceffity ; the immediate effect, produced by that neceffity, may be oppofed by the will of the fubject.
But with refpect to moral neceffity, which is a previous certainty of the exiftence of a volition or voluntary action, it is abfurd to fuppofe, that *in that act* the

will fhould either oppofe itfelf, or the neceffity from which the act arifes.——The diftinction between natural and moral inability is analogous to this. Inability is the reverfe of neceffity.

Now Dr. Weft tells us, that this " is a diftinction " without a difference," p. 8. But if the terms connected in thefe cafes be different, as Prefident Edwards fuppofes ; if in one cafe " the caufe, with which " the effect is connected, be fome previous habitual dif- " pofition, or fome motive exhibited to the under- " ftanding ; and the effect be a volition or voluntary " action ;" in the other, the caufe be neither an habitual difpofition nor a motive exhibited to the underftanding, and the effect be neither a volition nor a voluntary action ; it is manifeft, that there is that very difference in the two cafes, which Prefident Edwards's diftinction fuppofes. To fay, that this is a diftinction without a difference, is to fay, that an habitual difpofition* or a motive, is the fame with fomething, which is not an habitual difpofition or motive ; and that a volition or voluntary action, is the fame with what is not a volition or voluntary action.

But Dr. Weft endeavours to fupport his charge of a diftinction without a difference. Let us attend to what he offers with this view: It is this, " That," according to Prefident Edwards, " the principal, if not the only " difference between natural——and moral neceffity " and inability, is, that in the former cafe, the oppofi- " tion and endeavour againft what does take place, is " overcome and borne down by a fuperiour force; but " in the latter kind of neceffity and inability there is no " oppofition and endeavour, that is overcome by any " fuperiour force. But that Mr. Edwards's moral ne- " ceffity and inability are attended with as much infuf- " ficient oppofition and endeavour, as his natural necef-

A 4 " fity

* Gentlemen may differ in their explanations of that habitual difpofition or bias, which is the caufe or antecedent of volition or voluntary action ; fome fuppofing it to be a certain caft or mould of the fubftance of the foul ; others fuppofing it to confift in a divine conftitution, that volitions of a certain kind, fhall, in a regular manner and on certain conditions, fucceed each other in the mind. But it does not appear, that Prefident Edwards meant to decide this queftion.

"fity and inability ;" p. 8. Whether this, which is here said to be, be indeed according to Prefident Edwards the only or the principal difference between natural and moral neceffity and inability, I fhall not at prefent ftand to difpute. It is fufficient for my prefent purpofe to fhow, that Prefident Edwards's moral neceffity and inability are not, and cannot be attended with as much infufficient oppofition and endeavour, as his natural neceffity and inability.

Natural neceffity may compel a man to that, to which his whole will is entirely oppofed, and againft which he puts forth all the oppofition, of which his ftrength of body and mind admits : As when he is thrown from a precipice or is dragged to prifon. But a man's whole will is never oppofed to the influence of that bias, difpofition or motive, or of any moral neceffity, with which he complies. Whenever any of thefe influences a man to put forth a volition or a voluntary external action, it prevails on his will ; his will therefore confents, though it may be with fome degree of reluctance occafioned by *fome* other bias or motive. Nothing is more common than fuch oppofition between reafon or confcience, and depraved appetite ; between covetoufnefs and ambition ; indolence and a wifh for gain, &c. But whenever any of thefe principles becomes ftronger than its oppofite, the will confents, and the man acts voluntarily under the influence of moral neceffity ; and though he may act with fome degree of reluctance from the oppofite principle, yet no man will fay, that he is compelled to act againft his *whole* will, or even againft his ftrongeft inclination ; for by the very cafe fuppofed, he acts agreeably to his ftrongeft inclination.* But by natural neceffity he is or may be compelled to that, to which every inclination and act of his will, the ftrongeft as well as the moft feeble, is moft directly oppofed. A man dragged to prifon may be compelled to enter it, in direct oppofition to
every

---

* By *inclination, difpofition* or *bias,* I mean fomething diftinct from volition. This diftinction is made by Dr. Weft, p. 13.

every act of his will. This is natural neceffity. But an indolent man, who is influenced to labour by the profpect of gain, is not compelled to labour in oppofition to every inclination or act of his will, but complies with the ftronger inclination and act, in oppofition to the weaker, which would lead him to indulge himfelf in eafe. This is an inftance of moral neceffity.———One difference between natural neceffity and moral, is, that every inclination and act of the will does or may directly oppofe natural neceffity ; but every act of will always coincides with that moral neceffity, from which it arifes, and when there is a ftruggle between different inclinations or propenfities and their acts, the acts of that which prevails, never oppofe the moral neceffity by which they take place.

When Prefident Edwards fays, that no voluntary infufficient oppofition or endeavour is fuppofable in the cafe of moral neceffity ; his evident meaning is, that it is not fuppofable, that an act of the will fhould be oppofed to that moral neceffity, by which it takes place. For inftance, if a man be under a moral neceffity of choofing a virtuous courfe of life, this choice is not oppofed to the neceffity, which is the fource of it, nor is it fuppofable, that it fhould be oppofed to it or at all refift it. The cafe is very different with regard to natural neceffity. A man dragged to execution may in every refpect oppofe with his will, that neceffity, by which he is carried on.

But though a man, who is determined by moral neceffity to choofe a virtuous courfe, cannot *in that act* oppofe that choice or the caufe of it ; yet he may *in other acts* of his will oppofe both this choice and the caufe, and thus in different acts choofe and act inconfiftently. He may from prevailing motives and from moral neceffity, choofe virtue. He may at the fame time from weaker motives and ineffectual temptations, choofe vice, and fo far feel reluctant or indifpofed to virtue. And this weaker choice is no more oppofed to the moral neceffity, which caufes it, than the ftronger
choice

choice of virtue is to the moral neceſſity which cauſes that. In both there is no ſuppoſable oppoſition to their reſpective neceſſities, which are their cauſes. This is true with reſpect to every choice whether ſtronger or weaker, whether prevailing to govern the heart and conduct, or not. Yet there is a mutual oppoſition between the forementioned different acts of choice, the choice of virtue and choice of vice. Indeed theſe two oppoſite choices cannot both prevail, ſo as to govern the heart and life at the ſame time. They may in particular caſes be equal, or ſo nearly equal, that neither of them at that inſtant appears to prevail, and the man " is in a ſtrait betwixt two." In other inſtances they may for a time at leaſt alternately prevail, and exhibit a man of very inconſiſtent conduct. In other inſtances one may generally prevail, and denominate the ſubject a virtuous or vicious man, accordingly as the choice and love of virtue, or of vice, prevails and governs him. Thus we ſhall have all thoſe four modes of inſufficient oppoſition to moral neceſſity, which Dr. Weſt ſays, p. 10, Preſident Edwards allows may take place, and from which he argues that Preſident Edwards's moral neceſſity may be attended with as much inſufficient oppoſition, as his natural neceſſity ; and that therefore Preſident Edwards's diſtinction between natural and moral neceſſity is without a difference. 1. The weaker motives to vice may oppoſe the ſtronger motives to virtue. 2. The man may *now* have ſtrong and prevailing acts, deſires and reſolutions againſt thoſe acts of vice, to which he foreſees he ſhall in certain circumſtances be expoſed, and which he actually indulges, when the foreſeen circumſtances take place. 3. The will may remotely and indirectly reſiſt itſelf, not in the ſame acts, but *in* different acts ; the depraved appetites may ſtruggle againſt the principles of virtue. 4. Reaſon pleading in favour of virtue, may reſiſt the preſent acts, which incline, and perhaps prevailingly, to vice. Nor is there any thing in all this, but what was long ſince obſerved by the poet, and has

always

always been noticed by all attentive obfervers of human nature :

"*Video meliora, proboque ; deteriora fequor.*"

Now, it will not be pretended, that this oppofition of one act of the will, to another, is parallel to the entire oppofition of the will which there is or may be, to natural neceffity ; *e. g.* to falling when a man is thrown down a precipice, or to going to the gallows, when a man is forced thither. In the latter cafe, there is or may be an entire and perfect oppofition of the whole will, to the neceffity. In the former, there is a confent of the will to the neceffity, though there may be a degree of oppofite choice arifing from fome other motive, bias, caufe or neceffity.

Dr. Weft infers from this actual or poffible oppofition of the acts of one propenfity in human nature, to thofe of another, acknowledged by Prefident Edwards, that all thofe acts which admit of this oppofition are neceffary with natural neceffity. If this inference be juft, doubtlefs every act of the human will is neceffary with natural neceffity. If a man choofe virtue, he doubtlefs does or may from temptation feel fome inclination to vice. In this cafe then his choice of virtue is, according to the reafoning of Dr. Weft, the effect of natural neceffity ; for natural neceffity is, according to that reafoning, that which admits of any voluntary oppofition. And as there is no propenfity in human nature, which may not be oppofed by fome other propenfity ; and as the human mind is not capable of any act, which may not be attended with fome degree of reluctance at leaft ; therefore human nature is not capable of any act, which is not neceffitated with a natural neceffity, a neceffity, which is equally inconfiftent with praife and blame, as that by which a man falls, when he is thrown from an eminence.

This oppofition of one propenfity in human nature to another, and of one act of the will to another, is abundantly granted by Dr. Weft : So that if this prove or imply a natural neceffity, he holds that the acts of the will are fubject to natural neceffity. P. 14. " A
" man

" man may *love* a perfon, whom he knows to be utterly
" unworthy of his affections, and may really *choofe* to
" eradicate this propenfion from his mind ; and yet he
" may find this paffion rifing in his breaft, in direct op-
" pofition to his *will* or *choice.* And the fame obferva-
" tions may be made with refpect to every other pro-
" penfion in the human mind. *They may all be in di-*
" *rect oppofition to prefent acts of the will and choice.*
" Were not this the cafe, there could be no ftruggle in
" the mind, to overcome wrong propenfions and vicious
" habits. But common experience will teach us, that
" there is frequently a very great ftruggle in the mind,
" to gain the victory over vile affections." Whatever
diftinction Dr. Weft makes between propenfion and
volition, he will doubtlefs grant, that there may be acts
of the will agreeable to a propenfion, as well as in oppofition to it ; that there may be volitions and actions
agreeable to a vicious propenfion, and yet there may be
a ftruggle of virtuous propenfion and volition in oppofition to the vicious. On the other hand, there may
be a ftruggle of vicious propenfion and volition in oppofition to the virtuous. Dr. Weft will not deny that
love to God, to his law and to virtue, is a voluntary
exercife. Now he who has a degree of voluntary
love to God and true virtue, and a degree of voluntary love to vice, has an oppofition not only of propenfions, but of voluntary acts and exercifes, *i. e.* of
volitions. Yet would Dr. Weft allow, that this love
of virtue, which is oppofed by a degree of love to vice,
is neceffitated by a natural neceffity ? This will follow
from the principle of his argument to prove, that Prefident Edwards's moral neceffity is really a natural neceffity.

Dr. Weft, p. 14, afferts, " that it is abfurd, that the
" will fhould directly oppofe its own prefent acts ;"
and yet in p. 9, he fays, " there may be will and en-
" deavour againft, or diverfe from *prefent acts of the*
" *will.*" Thefe propofitions feem incapable of recon-
ciliation, unlefs on the ground of the diftinction,
which I have made between the will oppofing itfelf

in

in the fame acts, and in different acts arifing from different motives or propenfities.

Prefident Edwards conftantly holds, that natural neceffity and inability are inconfiftent with blame in any inftance. The reafon of this is, that all our fincere and moft ardent defires and acts of will, as well as external endeavours, may be refifted, oppofed and overcome as to their effects. But this is not the cafe in moral neceffity and inability ; therefore they do not excufe from blame. When under a moral neceffity we will to do an action, our ftrongeft defires and acts of will coincide with the moral neceffity, and we voluntarily act agreeably to it. And if we have weaker wifhes and defires oppofing the neceffity and the ftronger defires and acts of our will, which follow from that neceffity, we are not to be excufed from blame on that account, becaufe on the whole we confent to do the action. No man will pretend, that he who is influenced by the malice of his own heart, to murder his neighbour, is excufable in that action, becaufe he has fome weak and ineffectual reluctance arifing from a knowledge of the divine law and from the dictates of his own confcience.

It has been faid by fome of our opponents in this difquifition, that they cannot find out what we mean by moral neceffity, as diftinguifhed from natural or phyfical. If it be not fufficiently plain from his own writings, what Prefident Edwards meant by it, I can only give my opinion concerning his meaning. But concerning my own meanihg I have a right to fpeak more peremptorily, that I mean all neceffity or previous certainty of the volition or voluntary action of a rational being, whatever be the caufe or influence, by which that neceffity is eftablifhed, or the volition brought into exiftence, and however great and efficacious that influence be. When " God's people are made willing in the day of his power," there is doubtlefs a neceffity of their being willing. This neceffity I call a moral neceffity, Againft this willingnefs, or

the

the neceffity, or the neceffitating caufe, from which it
arifes, the will of him who is made willing, does not
and cannot poffibly make entire and direct oppofition. By the very fuppofition he is made willing, his
will therefore coincides with the neceffity and confents to it ; and fo far as it confents, it cannot diffent
or make oppofition.

Some feem to imagine, that the difference between
natural and moral neceffity, is, that the former is the
effect of a ftrong and irrefiftible caufe ; but the latter of a weak one, which may be refifted and overcome ; and that entire oppofition of will is fuppofable
in both cafes ; though with this difference, that in natural neceffity it is ineffectual, but in moral it may be effectual. Whereas the truth is, that let the caufe of
a moral act be what it will, it involves a moral neceffity only, becaufe it is not fuppofable, that the will
fhould be entirely oppofed to it.

The perfons abovementioned object to the application of fuch ftrong epithets as *infallible, unavoidable,*
unalterable, unfruftrable, &c. to moral neceffity and
inability, fuppofing that they imply a natural neceffity inconfiftent with praife and blame. But when our
Lord had given the prediction, was there not an infallible, unavoidable, unalterable and unfruftrable certainty, that Judas would betray his Lord ? And will
it be pretended, that on that account he was not to
be blamed for fo doing ? Yet this action of Judas
was rendered no more unfruftrably neceffary by the
prediction, than it was before, as it was before certainly foreknown. Nor was it more certainly foreknown, than every event and every moral action,
which ever has or will come to pafs. Therefore all
moral actions are unfruftrably certain previoufly to
their exiftence ; and all thofe epithets are as properly applicable to them, as to the treachery of Judas,
after it was divinely predicted.

It has been faid, that till the meafure of influence
implied in moral neceffity, is diftinctly known, it is
impoffible

impoffible to tell, when or how far a perfon is re-
wardable or punifhable. But this is faid, under a
miftaken idea of moral neceffity, viz. that moral neceffity implies a low degree of influence only. Moral neceffity is the real and certain connection between fome moral action and its caufe ; and there is
no moral *neceffity* in the cafe, unlefs the connection
be real and abfolutely certain, fo as to *enfure* the exiftence of the action. And will it be pretended, that
if the meafure of influence be increafed beyond this,
the neceffity ceafes to be moral and becomes natural ?
That if a motive or a malicious temper be barely fufficient certainly and infallibly to influence a man to
murder his neighbour, the neceffity is moral and the
man is blamable ; but if it become more than barely
fufficient for this, fo as to excite him to perpetrate
the action with great eagernefs and with the overflow-
ing of malice, that in this cafe the neceffity is natural and the man entirely unblamable ?———The truth
is, that there is no inconfiftence between the moft efficacious influence in moral neceffity and accountablenefs. Let the influence be ever fo great, ftill the
man acts voluntarily, and there is no fuppofable entire oppofition of will ; and as he is a rational creature, he is accountable for his voluntary actions. The
contrary fuppofition implies, that in order to accountablenefs a man muft have a liberty of *contingence*, and
it muft be, previoufly to his acting, *uncertain* how he
will act. A bare previous certainty of the voluntary
action of an intelligent being is as inconfiftent with
liberty and accountablenefs, as any poffible degree
of influence producing fuch an action. In either cafe
there is an equal confent of the will, and an entire
oppofition of the will is no more fuppofable in the
one cafe, than in the other.

Some infift, that moral neceffity and inability are
always of our own procuring ; and whatever neceffity is not caufed by ourfelves is not moral neceffity.
But moral neceffity is the previous certainty of a
moral

moral action. Now as it was divinely foretold, ages before it came to pafs, that the Jews would crucify our Lord, and that the man of fin would perfecute the faints, &c. &c. there was a moral neceffity, that thofe facts fhould come to pafs : And as this neceffity exifted long before the perpetrators of thofe facts exifted, they did not caufe the neceffity. Therefore according to this account of moral and natural neceffity, it was a natural neceffity, and the Jews and the man of fin were in thofe actions, as innocent as they were in breathing or in any involuntary motion.——Further, as all the actions of rational creatures are foreknown by God, before the authors of them come into exiftence, they are equally certain and neceffary, as thofe which are predicted. But this neceffity, for the reafon already given, cannot be the effect of thofe, whofe actions they are. Therefore either this is not a natural neceffity, or there never was, is now nor can be any crime or fin in the univerfe.

Dr. Clarke in his Remarks on Collins gives a true account of moral neceffity; p. 16. " By *moral neceffi-* " *ty* confiftent writers never mean any more than to " exprefs in a figurative manner, the *certainty* of fuch " an event." And he illuftrates it by the impoffibility, that the world fhould come to an end this year, if God have promifed that it fhall continue another year. Yet in his difpute with *Leibnitz* he gives a very different account of it; p. 289. " That a good " being, continuing to be good, cannot do evil ; or a " wife being, continuing to be wife, cannot do un- " wifely ; or a veracious perfon, continuing to be ve- " racious, cannot tell a lie ; is *moral neceffity*." This laft account implies no other neceffity, than that a thing muft be when it is fuppofed to be ; which is no more than the trifling propofition, that *what is, is.* But the certainty implied in the divine prediction, that the world will continue to a particular period, is a very different matter.——Dr. Weft, if I underftand him, has adopted the laft account given by Dr. Clarke of moral

al neceffity. No doubt he and Dr. Clarke had a right to give their own definitions of moral neceffity ; but Dr. Weft had no right to impute his idea to Prefident Edwards, and then difpute againft it as belonging to him. Dr. Clarke's laft defcribed moral neceffity would exift, if human volitions came into exiftence by a felf-determining power or by mere chance. On either of thofe fuppofitions, *what is*, *is*, and muft be, fo long as it is. But Prefident Edwards's idea of moral neceffity is utterly inconfiftent with volitions' coming into exiftence by chance, or by felf-determination, unlefs felf-determination be previoufly eftablifhed.

In all matters of difpute, it ought to be confidered how far the parties are agreed, and wherein they differ. As to natural and moral neceffity, I believe both parties are agreed, in this, that all neceffity inconfiftent with moral agency, or praife and blame, is natural neceffity ; and that all neceffity confiftent with praife and blame, is moral neceffity. Therefore if all neceffity of the volitions of rational beings, be confiftent with praife and blame ; all fuch neceffity is moral neceffity. But if any neceffity of the volitions of a rational being, be inconfiftent with praife and blame ; then I have given an erroneous account of moral neceffity. Therefore on this let us join iffue. If an inftance can be produced of the volition of a rational being in fuch a fenfe neceffary, as to be on that account the proper object of neither praife nor blame ; I will confefs, that I am miftaken in my idea of moral neceffity. But until fuch an inftance can be produced, may I not fairly prefume, that my idea is right ?——— If it fhould be faid, that no volitions of rational creatures are in any fenfe neceffary, or that they are not previoufly certain ; I recur to the inftances of Judas's treachery, Peter's falfehood, Pharaoh's refufal to let Ifrael go, and to every other voluntary action of a rational being divinely predicted or foreknown.

If any fhould difpute, whether this previous certainty of voluntary actions, be properly called *neceffi-*

B   *ty ;*

ty ; this would be a merely *verbal* difpute, which they who choofe, may agitate to their full fatisfaction. It is fufficient to inform them, that it is what we mean by moral neceffity.

I have already fhown that Dr. Weft grants the mutual oppofition of different propenfions and volitions; it may be further obferved that, though he fo ftrenuoufly difputes againft the diftinction between natural and moral neceffity, and fays it is made without a difference ; yet the fame diftinction is abundantly implied in his book, particularly in his third effay. He there holds forth, that a man may have a *phyfical power* to do an action, and yet *not exert* that power ; that it may be *certain,* there may be *a certainty,* and it may be *certainly foreknown,* that a man will do fomething, which he has a *phyfical* power not to do ; p. 46. That a bare *certainty,* that an agent will do fuch a thing, does not imply, that he had not a power to refrain from doing it ; p. 45. Now by moral neceffity we mean the previous certainty of any moral action. Therefore when Dr. Weft, p. 46, holds, *that there may be a* CERTAINTY, *that a man will do fuch a thing, though he may have at the fame time a phyfical power of not doing it ;* he holds, that there may be the very thing which Prefident Edwards calls a *moral neceffity,* that the man will do the thing, though he may have at the fame time a *phyfical* or *natural* power not to do it.——Thus Dr. Weft makes and abundantly infifts on that very diftinction, which he reprobates in Prefident Edwards, and which he declares to be made without any difference. Indeed it is impoffible for any man to write fenfibly or plaufibly on this fubject, without going on the ground of this diftinction.

It has been inquired concerning Prefident Edwards's moral inability, whether the man, who is the fubject of it, *can remove* it ? I anfwer, yes, he has the fame phyfical power to remove it and to do the action, which he is morally unable to do, which the man, concerning whom Dr. Weft fuppofes there is a certainty, that he will not do an action, has to do the action

and

and fo to defeat or remove the faid certainty. I agree with Dr. Weft, that he has a phyfical power fo to do.

Perhaps after all fome will infift, that natural and moral neceffity are the fame. It is ardently to be wifh-ed, that fuch perfons would tell us, in what refpeĉts they are the fame. We have informed them, in what refpeĉts we hold them to be different. We wifh them to be equally explicit and candid. If they mean, that natural and moral neceffity are the fame in this refpeĉt, that they are or may be equally certain and fixed, and may equally enfure their refpeĉtive confequences or effeĉts ; I grant it. Still they may be different in oth-er refpeĉts, particularly this, that natural neceffity re-fpeĉts thofe events or things only, which are not of a moral nature, while moral neceffity refpeĉts thofe only, which are of a moral nature ; and there may be an entire oppofition of will to the former, but not to the latter. If they mean, that they are the fame as to vir-tue and vice, praife and blame, &c. this is not grant-ed, and to affert it, is a mere begging of the queftion. If they mean, that both thofe kinds of neceffity may arife from *nature ;* meaning by this the fixed proper-ties of beings and the eftablifhed courfe of things and events ; this is granted. Still there may be the grounds of diftinĉtion before mentioned. If they fay, that moral neceffity is *natural* neceffity, becaufe it is or may be *born with us ;* I grant it. But this is mere quibbling on the word *natural.* Though volitions may be the effeĉts of a bias of mind born with us, yet thofe volitions are moral aĉts, and therefore the neceffity from which they proceed, is a *moral* neceffity. A man born with a contraĉted, felfifh difpofition, ftill has a phyfical power to be benevolent, and it is not fuppof-able, that his will or difpofition fhould be entirely op-pofed to felfifhnefs, whenever he is the fubjeĉt of it.

CHAPTER

CHAPTER II.

Of Liberty.

DR. Weſt ſays, p. 16, " By liberty we mean *a* " *power* of acting, willing or chooſing ; and by *a* " *power* of acting, we mean, that when all circumſtan- " ces neceſſary for action have taken place, the mind " *can* act or *not act*." This is not explicit : There is an ambiguity in the words *power, can, not act*. If by *pow- er* and *can*, he mean *natural* power, as it has been ex- plained in the preceding chapter ; I agree that in any given caſe we have a power to act or decline the pro- poſed action. A man poſſeſſes liberty when he poſſeſſes a natural or phyſical power to do an action, and is un- der no natural inability with reſpect to that action. The word liberty ſuggeſts a negative idea, and means the abſence of certain obſtacles, confinement or re- ſtriction. A bird not confined in a cage, but let looſe in the open air, is free ; a man not ſhut up in priſon, is in that reſpect, free ; a ſervant delivered from the control of his maſter, is free ; a man, who has diſengaged him- ſelf from the tie of a civil bond, is in that reſpect free. In all theſe caſes liberty implies ſome exemption, or ſome negation. In a moral ſenſe and with reſpect to moral conduct, a man is free or poſſeſſes liberty, when he is under no involuntary reſtraint or compulſion ; *i. e.* when he is under no reſtraint or compulſion, to which his will does not conſent, or to which it is or may be entirely oppoſed. An exemption from this reſtraint or compulſion, is liberty, moral liberty, the liberty of a moral agent ; and this is an exemption from natural neceſſity and inability as before explained. He who is thus exempted, has a natural power of acting, juſt ſo far as this exemption extends. Even though " all cir- " cumſtances neceſſary for action, have taken place," yet " then the mind can," in this ſenſe, " act" in any

particular

particular manner, or decline that action. For instance, when all circumstances neceffary for Judas's betraying his Lord, had taken place, still he had a natural power either to betray him or not betray him. He was under no compulfion to betray him, to which his will did not confent. He was not, nor could he poffibly be, under any fuch compulfion to *choofe* to betray him. It is a contradiction, that the mind fhould *choofe* to do a thing *involuntarily* and with an entire oppofition of will.

If this be the liberty, for which Dr. Weft pleads, he has no ground of controverfy on this head, with Prefident Edwards, or with any who embrace his fyftem. There is nothing in this inconfiftent with the influence of motives on the will, to produce volition; or with the dependence of volition on fome caufe extrinfic to itfelf, extrinfic to the power of will, or to the mind in which it exifts. What if motives do excite to volition? What if the connection between motive and volition be fuch, that volition never takes place without motive, and always takes place, when a proper motive appears? What if volition be the effect of a caufe extrinfic to the will? Still it is true, that volition never takes place without the confent or with the entire oppofition of the will. The will or mind then is ftill free, as it is exempted from natural neceffity and has a natural or phyfical power to act otherwife.

If it be faid, that it is not fufficient to liberty, that the mind act *with* its own confent, *in the act itfelf;* but it muft in every free act, act *from* its own confent *previous* to the free act; I obferve, that this implies, that in order to any free act, there muft be an infinite feries of free acts following one another. For inftance, the objection fuppofes, that if I now freely choofe to write remarks on Dr. Weft, this free choice muft *arife from* a *previous* confent of my will, or from a previous choice, to write fuch remarks. Again, this previous choice, in order to be free, muft for

B 3   the

the fame reafon arife from another prévious free choice ; and fo on *infinitely*, which is abfurd.

Or if it fhould be faid, that liberty implies not only an exemption from all *natural* or *phyfical* neceffity, but alfo an exemption from all *moral* neceffity ; then, as moral neceffity is nothing but a previous certainty of the exiftence of any moral act, it will follow that any act, in order to be free, muft come into exiftence without any previous certainty in the nature of things or in the divine mind, that it would exift ; *i. e.* no act can be free, unlefs it come into exiftence by *pure contingence* and *mere chance.*

But let us proceed to confider what Dr. Weft fays in further explanation of his idea of liberty.

" To act," fays he, " to will or to choofe, is to be " free." P. 16. If this be liberty, furely Dr. Weft could not imagine, that Prefident Edwards, or any man in his fenfes, ever denied that we are free. It is to be prefumed, that no man ever denied, that we determine, that we will, or that we choofe. However, though I allow all thefe things, yet I cannot allow, that this is a true account of liberty. Will Dr. Weft pretend, that we are never free, but when we are in action ? That we have no liberty to determine, befide when we do actually determine ? That we have no liberty to will or choofe, but when we are in the exercife of volition or choice ? Will he fay, that he himfelf had no liberty to determine to write effays on liberty and neceffity, before he actually determined to write them ? Dr. Weft, in p. 46, holds that there may be a certainty, that a man will do an action ; yet that he may have a phyfical power of doing the contrary. He would therefore doubtlefs grant, that he is at liberty to do the contrary, though he actually does it not ; and this whether the action be external or mental. Befides ; this definition of liberty is wholly inconfiftent with the other favorite one of Dr. Weft, viz. *a power to act or not.* If liberty be a *power*, furely it is not an *action ;* but " to act, to

will

" will or to choose," is an action. Especially if liberty be a power to *not act*, it cannot be *an action*. And if a power of acting, be action ; a power of willing be volition ; and a power of choosing be choice ; then a power of walking or writing, and actual walking and writing is the same thing ; and whoever is able to write, and so long as he is able, is actually employed in writing. Does Dr. West find by experience, that this is true ?

I know there is a class of divines, who have holden, that God is free to good only, because he does good only ; that the saints and angels in heaven are for the same reason free to good only ; that Adam in paradise was free to both good and evil ; that unregenerate sinners and devils are free to evil only ; and that the regenerate in the present life are free to both good and evil. But I presume Dr. West would not choose to rank himself in this class.

Dr. S. Clarke is equally inconsistent in his definition of liberty, as Dr. West. " The whole essence of " liberty," says he, " consists in the *power* of acting. " *Action* and *liberty* are *identical* ideas : And the true " *definition* of a free being, is one that is endued with " a *power* of acting." Remarks on Collins, p. 15. How true it is, that great men are not always wise ! And how surprising, that Dr. Clarke, whom the advocates for self-determination, set up as unequalled in metaphysical acuteness, should contradict himself twice in four lines, in what required so much accuracy, as the definition of liberty ! 1. The whole essence of liberty is here said to consist in a *power* of acting. 2. *Action* and liberty are said to be identical ideas ; and therefore the *power* of action and liberty are not identical ideas, unless the *power* of action and *action* are identical ideas. 3. The true definition of a free being is said to be one that is endued with the *power* of acting. Thus the Doctor ends where he began, forgetful of the middle.

But

But that part of Dr. Weſt's account of liberty, with which he ſeems to be moſt pleaſed, and on which he ſeems moſt to depend, remains yet to be conſidered. It is this, *a power to act or not act*, in all caſes whatever. On this I obſerve, that if by *acting or not acting*, the Doctor mean chooſing or refuſing, I grant, that we have a *natural* power to do either of theſe in any caſe. But refuſing is as real an act of the mind, as chooſing, and therefore is very improperly called *not acting*. I grant, that we have a *natural* power to chooſe or refuſe in any caſe ; but we have no *moral* power, or power oppoſed to *moral neceſſity* : For moral neceſſity is previous certainty of a moral action ; and a power oppoſed to this muſt imply a previous uncertainty. But no event moral or natural is or can be uncertain previouſly to its exiſtence.——But if by a power to act or not act, the Doctor mean a power either to chooſe an object propoſed, or to refuſe it, or to do neither ; this is an impoſſibility. Whenever an object is propoſed for our choice, if there be any medium between chooſing and refuſing, it is a ſtate of perfect blockiſh inaction and inſenſibility or *torpor ;* and this inaction muſt be *involuntary ;* as a *voluntary* inaction implies an act or volition, which is inconſiſtent with perfect inaction. A voluntary ſtate of inaction and torpor is a contradiction in terms : It implies, that the mind is the ſubject of no act at all, and yet at the ſame time is the ſubject of a volition, by which it conſents to inaction. Or if it ſhould be ſaid, that a voluntary ſtate of inaction means a ſtate, to which the mind is indeed reduced by an act of volition, and that the volition having accompliſhed a ſtate of inaction, ceaſes itſelf to exiſt, and thus perfect and univerſal inaction follows ; I obſerve, (1) That ſtill this plea does not rid the matter of the contradiction. The cauſe of the perfect inaction is a volition. This cauſe muſt continue in exiſtence and in operation, till the effect is accompliſhed ; *i. e.* till entire and perfect inaction has actually taken place. And yet ſo long as
this

this caufe continues to exift, it is a contradiction, that perfect and entire inaction fhould take place. (2) Befides this contradiction, if the mind could by an act of volition or by other means be reduced to a ftate of entire inaction and torpitude, this ftate would be utterly inconfiftent with the exercife of any liberty. The man in this ftate can no more exercife liberty, than if he were under ever fo great *natural* neceffity, or than if he were turned into a ftock or ftone. During this ftate he cannot poffibly put forth any act, to aroufe himfelf from this *torpor.* It is in the power of no man, to reduce himfelf to this ftate, with refpect to any object propofed to his choice ; or when he is reduced to it, to recover himfelf from it.

If to this it fhould be objected, that we are entirely indifferent with regard to many objects ; we neither choofe nor refufe them : I anfwer, be this as it may with refpect to objects not propofed for our choice ; it is not true with refpect to thofe, which are propofed for our choice ; and this is all that I have afferted, and all that the fubject requires me to affert ; for Dr. Weft's account of liberty is " a power of act- " ing ; and by a power of acting, we mean, that when " all circumftances neceffary for action have taken " place, the mind can act or not act ;" *i. e.* when an occafion for volition, choice or determination, is prefented ; or when an object of choice, or an object, with refpect to which we are to will or determine, is exhibited.

Mr. Locke's obfervations on this point are very pertinent and convincing : They are as follows ; " A " man in refpect of willing, or the act of volition, when " an action in his power is once propofed to his " thoughts as prefently to be done, cannot be free. " The reafon whereof is manifeft —— he cannot " avoid willing the exiftence or not exiftence of that " action ; it is abfolutely neceffary, that he will the " one or the other, *i. e.* prefer the one to the other, " fince one of them muft neceffarily follow ; and that " which

" which does follow, follows by the choice and deter-
" mination of his mind, that is, by his willing it. For
" if he did not will it, it would not be. So that in re-
" spect of the act of willing, a man in such a case is
" not free : Liberty confifting in a power to act or not
" act, which in regard of volition, a man upon such a
" propofal has not. For it is unavoidably neceffary
" to prefer the doing or forbearance of an action in
" a man's power, which is once propofed to a man's
" thoughts. A man muft neceffarily will the one or
" the other of them, upon which preference or voli-
" tion the action or its forbearance certainly follows
" and is truly voluntary. But the act of volition or
" preferring one of the two, being that, which he can-
" not avoid, a man in refpect of that act of willing is
" under a neceffity.——This then is evident, that in
" all propofals of prefent action, a man is not at liber-
" ty to will or not to will ; becaufe he cannot forbear
" willing."——" A man that is walking, to whom it is
" propofed to give off walking, is not at liberty,
" whether he *will* determine himfelf to walk or give
" off walking, or no. *He muft neceffarily prefer one or*
" *t'other of them*, walking or not walking."——" The
" mind in that cafe has not a power to forbear willing :
" It cannot avoid *fome* determination.——It is man-
" ifeft, that it orders and directs one in preference to,
" or in the neglect of the other." Dr. Weft himfelf
gives up his favourite power of *not acting*, in the following paffage : " As foon as ideas are prefented to
" the mind its active faculty is exerted, and the mind
" continues conftantly acting, as long as it has ideas,
" juft as the act of feeing takes place the very inftant
" the eye is turned to the light, and continues as long
" as the light ftrikes the eye." Part II. p. 9. " The
" mind is always acting." P. 10. If it continue to
act as long as it has ideas, as the eye continues to fee
as long as the light ftrikes it ; then the mind has no
power of not acting, while it has ideas. And I think
it will not be pretended that the mind has a power to

banifh

banifh from itfelf, all ideas at pleafure. This would be a *torpor* indeed ! a torpor of the underftanding as well as of the will ! And if the mind be always acting, it never exercifes the power of not acting.

Doctor Weft thinks it ftrange, that his private correfpondent does not know what the Doctor means by *a power to act or not act;* and the Doctor proceeds to give feveral inftances of it, as of a man, who had been confined in prifon, fet at liberty to go out or ftill to tarry in prifon ; and of an hufbandman, who has the offer of a farm, on certain conditions, and he is at liberty to take the farm or not. But neither of thefe is an inftance of *a power to act or not act;* they are mere inftances of a natural power to act differently, to act one way or another. If the man who has the offer to go out of the prifon, choofe to tarry in it ; he as really acts as if he had chofen to go out. If the hufbandman choofe to decline the farm offered him, this is as real and pofitive an act, as if he had chofen to take it. And the Doctor, though he has attempted to give an inftance of a power to act or not act, has not given one. For this reafon, as well as from the nature of the cafe, I believe it is not in his power to give an inftance of it. If it be in his power, I wifh him to do it. He acknowledges this to be " the " main point, on which the hinge of the whole contro- " verfy turns." A power to act or not act, is his definition of that liberty, for which he contends, and in fupport of which he has written his two books. And if he be not able to give a fingle inftance of fuch a power, it is high time for him to give it up, and the whole controverfy, of which this is the hinge. No wonder Dr. Weft's correfpondent did not underftand what the Doctor meant by this power, if the Doctor himfelf did not underftand it fo far as to be able to give an inftance of it.——*A power to act or not act* muft either mean a power to choofe or refufe ; or a power to act, or to ceafe from all action in either choofing or refufing. If the former be the meaning, it it is no more than we all grant, provided by power be meant *natural* power. But if in this cafe *moral* power be intended, a power oppofed to moral neceffity, which is the previous certainty of a moral action ; this we utterly deny, becaufe it implies, that there is a previous perfect uncertainty in the nature of things and in the divine mind, whether we fhall choofe or refufe the propofed object.——If the laft be the meaning of *a power to act or not act*, as this is a power to fink ourfelves into a ftate of unfeeling and blockifh torpor, I appeal to the reader, whether Dr. Weft, or Limborch, or any other man, has ever had or can have any idea of fuch a power ; or if they have, whether it would be any defirable liberty, or would imply any qualification for moral agency.

I am fenfible, that Dr. Weft tells us, that he has given a definition of " a power to act or not act," and that this definition is, " that there is no infallible con- " nection between motive and volition." But this, which he calls a definition, does not at all relieve the difficulty. If it mean, that when motives are prefented, the perfon can comply with them, or can refufe to comply, or can neither comply nor refufe ; I deny it, declare it to be an impoffibility, and call on Dr. Weft to fhew the poffibility of it. If when he fays, there is no infallible connection between motive and volition, he mean, that the mind may act, whether in choofing or refufing, without motive ; this is contrary to Dr. Weft himfelf.

The Doctor, in p. 86 and 87, Part II, refumes the queftion of acting or not acting, and mentions feveral cafes, which he confiders as inftances of not acting ; *e. g.* when of two objects one is chofen and the other not ; when of the fpots on a chefs-board, A is touched and B not, &c. But not one of thefe is a better inftance of not acting, than there always is, when any one thing is chofen and not another, or in preference to another. Suppofe a man to offer a beggar a fhilling and a guinea, of which he may have

his

his choice, and he take the guinea ; will it be faid, that his leaving the fhilling is an inftance of not act-ing ? Then we never do any thing, without at the fame time not acting ; *i. e.* while we do one thing, we omit many other things, which we might do. If this be what Dr. Weft means by not acting, it is read-ily granted ; but it comes to little or nothing ; it is a mere power to do fome things and to refufe or omit fome other things. This power is confiftent with the moft infallible connection between motives and voli-tions. Whenever under the influence of motives, we do fome things, we certainly have a power to do thofe things, and to omit other things, which in fact we do not.

Dr. Clarke in his Remarks on Collins, p. 6, fays, " All power of acting effentially implies, at the fame " time, *a power* of not acting : Otherwife it is not *act-* " *ing,* but barely a *being acted upon* by that power, which " caufes the action." If he mean by *power, natural* or *phyfical* power, as before explained ; and if by *not acting* he mean, *refufing* or *voluntary forbearing* to act in a certain propofed manner ; 1 agree with Dr. Clarke. But if by *power* to act, he mean fomething oppof-ed to moral neceffity or inability, which is a previ-ous certainty, that the action will or will not take place, in this cafe power to act will be a previous uncer-tainty concerning the exiftence of the action : And in this fenfe of the words, the Doctor's propofition, that a " power of acting effentially implies a power of " not acting," will amount to this merely, that a previ-ous uncertainty concerning the exiftence of an action, effentially implies a previous uncertainty concerning the non-exiftence of the fame action : Which is mere trifling.——If the Doctor mean by *not acting*, entire inaction, I deny that a natural power to act implies a power to fall into entire inaction and torpitude. Nor does an uncertainty whether we fhall act in any par-ticular manner, imply an uncertainty whether we fhall be perfectly inactive and torpid,

Dr.

Dr. Weft, fuppofes *felf-determination* is effential to liberty ; but his account of felf-determination is equally inexplicit, as his account of liberty. " We " ufe felf-determination," fays he, " not to fignify, that " felf acts on felf and produces volition ; or that the " mind fome how determines to will ; *i. e.* wills to " will, or choofes to choofe. But the fenfe in which " we ufe felf-determination is fimply this, that we our- " felves determine ; *i. e.* that we ourfelves will or " choofe ; that we ourfelves act ; *i. e.* that we are " agents and not mere paffive beings ; or in other " words, that we are the determiners in the active " voice, and not the determined in the paffive voice." P. 17.——Now one would expect, that in all this profufion of words, in this variety of expreffion, with the help of three *i. e.*'s. we fhould have a moft clear and explicit account of felf-determination. But the account is entirely inexplicit, and equally confiftent with Prefident Edwards's fcheme of neceffity, as with the oppofite fcheme. He holds, that we ourfelves determine ; but he does not hold, that we are the ef- ficient caufes of our own determinations. Nor can Dr. Weft confiftently hold this ; as this would imply, that our determinations or volitions are effects, which Dr. Weft denies. Prefident Edwards holds, that we ourfelves will or choofe ; that we ourfelves act and are agents : But he does not hold, that we efficiently caufe our own mental acts : Nor for the reafon already given, can Dr. Weft confiftently hold this. Befides, this would imply, that " felf acts on felf and produces " volition," or that " the mind fome how determines to will ;" *i. e.* " wills to will, or choofes to choofe," which the Doctor renounces. Prefident Edwards does not hold, that we are *mere* paffive beings, unlefs this expreffion mean, that our volitions are the effects of fome caufe extrinfic to our wills.* If this be the meaning of it, he does hold it, and the believers in

his

---

* In caufes extrinfic to the will I include both original and acquired tafte, bias, propenfion, or whatever it be called.

his fyftem are ready to join iffue with Dr. Weft, on this point. Though we hold that our volitions are the effects of fome extrinfic caufe, and that we are paffive, as we are the fubjects of the influence of that caufe ; yet we hold, that we are not *merely* paffive ; but that volition is in its own nature an act or action, and in the exercife of it we are active, though in the caufation of it we are paffive fo far as to be the fubjects of the influence of the efficient caufe. This we concede ; and let our opponents make the moft of it : We fear not the confequence. In this fenfe we hold, " that we are determiners in the active voice, " and not *merely* determined in the paffive voice." We hold, that we are determiners in the active voice, in every fenfe which does not imply, that " felf acts on "; felf and produces volition ; or that the mind fome " how wills to will, and choofes to choofe," which Dr. Weft utterly denies ; and " he entirely joins " with Mr. Edwards in exploding the idea, that the " will determines all the prefent acts of the will."

Though we are determiners in the active voice, and not *merely* determined in the paffive voice ; yet our determination may be the confequence of fufficient motive or the effect of fome other extrinfic caufe. We fee, hear, feel, love and hate, in the active voice ; yet we are or may be caufed to fee, hear, &c. And when we are caufed to love or hate, we are indeed the fubjects of the agency or influence of fome caufe extrinfic to our own will, and fo far are paffive : Still the immediate effect of this agency is our act, and in this act we are certainly active. So that we are not *merely* in the paffive voice caufed to love, but we alfo in the active voice *love.* Dr. Weft will not fay, that becaufe a man is influenced or perfuaded by proper motives to the love of virtue, he does not love it at all in the active voice. Yet it is often faid by men of his clafs, that if we be influenced to will or choofe an object, it is no action at all. It is indeed no action in their fenfe
of

of the word, as they mean by action, *felf-determina-tion* : But inftead of taking it for granted, that this is the true fenfe of the word *action*, they ought to fhow the reality and poffibility of fuch an action, and re-move the abfurdities, which are faid to be infepara-ble from it.——To fay, that we are felf-determined or felf-moved, becaufe we ourfelves determine and move, is as improper and groundlefs, as to fay, that a body is felf-moved and felf-determined in its motion, becaufe the body itfelf moves. Extrinfic caufality is no more excluded in the one cafe, than in the other.

The Doctor puts the cafe of his choofing coffee, when that, tea and chocolate were offered him, and all appeared equally eligible ; and fays, " I believe, that " it will be impoffible in this and a multitude of fimi-" lar inftances, to affign any accident or circumftance, " which determines the mind to its choice among things, " which appear equally fit and eligible. Confequently " here is an undeniable proof of the liberty for which " we contend." The liberty for which he here con-tends, is a power to choofe one of feveral equally eli-gible things. If by *power* he mean *natural* or *phyfical* power, I grant, that we have fuch a power to choofe not only one of feveral things equally eligible, if any fuch there be, but one of things ever fo unequally el-igible, and to take the leaft eligible. A man may be under no involuntary reftraint from taking an object ever fo ineligible. But if by power to choofe one of feveral equally eligible things, he mean a power oppof-ed to moral neceffity, it is a previous uncertainty which he will choofe. But there is in this cafe no more pre-vious uncertainty in the nature of things and in the divine mind, than in any cafe whatever.

The Doctor denies, that " any accident or circum-" ftance," or any extrinfic caufe, " determines the mind " to its choice among things which appear equally eli-" gible." If this were granted, though it is not, what would follow ? Doubtlefs either that the choice is de-termined and caufed by the mind itfelf, or that it

comes

comes into exiflence without caufe. But Dr. Weft cannot with confiftency hold either of thefe. To hold that choice or volition is caufed by the mind, is to hold, that it is an effect and has a caufe, which Dr. Weft denies, and has written an effay to prove it. It is alfo to hold, that " felf acts on felf and produces " volition ; or that the mind fome how determines to " will, *i. e.* wills to will or choofes to choofe," and that " the will determines the prefent acts of the will ;" all which are denied by Dr. Weft. On the other hand, that volition comes into exiftence without caufe, though this is maintained by the Doctor, in that he maintains, that " volition is no effect and has no caufe ;" yet it is alfo denied and renounced by him, in that he fays, p. 27, " We cannot be charged with holding, that e- " vents take place without caufe."

In p. 19, he fays, " All who believe there is a De- " ity, muft grant, that he has a felf-determining power : " For he being the firft caufe, his volitions cannot be " determined by any caufe antecedent or extrinfic to " himfelf." If by felf-determining power here be meant, what Dr. Weft fays he means *fimply*, That the Deity himfelf has a power to determine ; that he him- felf has a power to will or choofe ; we grant, that not only the Deity, but all intelligent beings have a felf- determining power. A felf-determining power accord- ing to this definition, is nothing but a power of will, which we all grant belongs to every intelligent and moral agent. Nor does this imply any thing inconfift- ent with the idea, that the Deity and all other intelli- gent beings are governed by motives, in the only fenfe in which we hold government by motives ; which is, that the Deity does every thing which he does, be- caufe there is a motive to do it, arifing from his own infinite wifdom and goodnefs.——But if by felf-deter- mining power, be meant a power by which God pro- duces volition in himfelf, by which " felf acts on felf " and produces volition," we join with Dr. Weft in reprobating fuch a power. He exprefsly fays, " The

C
" divine

" divine volitions are no effects produced by the Dei-
" ty." P. 28.——If any thing elfe be meant, whenever Dr. Weft will inform us what it is, (as we cannot
imagine any befide one or other of the forementioned
fenfes) we will inform him, whether we allow or deny
it, and will give our reafons.

As to the argument, that " The Deity being the firft
" caufe, his volitions cannot be determined by any
" caufe antecedent or extrinfic to himfelf ;" it may be
anfwered, Still he may will as he does, becaufe of motives and reafons arifing from his own infinite wifdom
and goodnefs. It may be further faid, that the fame
argument, which Dr. Weft here ufes to prove, that
God determines himfelf, will prove, that God created
himfelf : Thus, All who believe that there is a Deity,
muft grant, that he has a felf-creating power and did
create himfelf. For he being the firft caufe, his exiftence cannot be caufed by any thing antecedent or extrinfic to himfelf. But it no more follows from the
confideration, that God's *volitions* were not caufed by
any thing antecedent or extrinfic to God, that they
were caufed by God, than from the confideration, that
his *exiftence* was not caufed by any thing antecedent
or extrinfic to himfelf, it follows, that it was caufed by
himfelf. The truth is the divine volitions were no
more caufed, whether by God himfelf or by any other
caufe, than the divine exiftence was. The divine volitions are the divine holinefs uncreated and felf-exiftent. And one attribute of God is not more caufed or
created, than all his attributes, or than his exiftence.

An exemption from extrinfic caufality, in the acts
of the mind, is effential to Dr. Weft's idea of liberty.
Suppofe then, that a free volition is one that comes
into exiftence without any dependence on a caufe extrinfic to the mind, which is the fubject of that volition ; the confequence is, that either fuch a volition
is caufed by the mind itfelf, and " felf acts on felf and
" produces volition ;" or it is abfolutely without caufe,
and comes into exiftence by mere chance ; neither of
which

which will Dr. Weſt avow : Indeed he has already
exprefsly difavowed them both. And if he either exprefsly, or by neceſſary implication, avows them both,
that does not help the matter ; to be inconſiſtent re-
lieves no difficulty. 1974121

Liberty is by fome writers diſtinguiſhed into external and internal. Internal or the liberty of the
mind, is the principal fubjeĉt of the prefent inquiry ;
and this, as is implied in what has been faid already,
confiſts in the power or faculty of will. Every intelligent being who has this power, is free, or has internal liberty, and fo long as he retains this power, cannot be diveſted of liberty. I am fenfible, that our
opponents fuppofe, that fomething further, viz. a felf-
determining power is neceſſary to liberty : And to
this I ſhall particulaɪly attend in the next chapter.
As internal liberty confiſts in the very faculty of the
will, fo that which is external confiſts in opportunity
externally to execute our determinations and wiſhes.
To define internal moral liberty to be, " an opportu-
" nity and capacity of choofing and aĉting otherwife
" than the fubjeĉt in faĉt does," is nothing diſtinguiſh-
ing between the fyſtem of thofe who hold, that all
moral aĉtions are morally neceſſary, and that of thofe
who deny it. " Opportunity and capacity of choof-
" ing otherwife," may mean mere *natural* power, as before explained. When Pharaoh chofe to retain the
Ifraelites, he was under no natural inability of choofing to let them go. Still it was a matter of previous
abfolute certainty, that he would for a time refufe to
let them go, and had been divinely foretold.——If
" opportunity and capacity of choofing otherwife, than
" the fubjeĉt in faĉt does," mean any thing inconfiſtent
with the moſt abfolute moral neceſſity, it muſt mean
a previous uncertainty how he will choofe : And if
this be the meaning in the aforefaid definition of moral liberty ; I deny that any man has in this fenfe opportunity to choofe otherwife than he does. Every
event and confequently every aĉt of choice, is previ-

C 2   ouſly

oufly foreknown by God and therefore is previoufly certain : And to take it for granted, that any is previoufly to its exiflence, uncertain in the divine mind and in reality, is an intolerable begging of the queftion.

The following account has been given of liberty, as oppofed to moral neceffity : " I find I can abflain " from any particular good ; I can defer ufing it ; I " can prefer fomething elfe to it ; I can hefitate in " my choice ; in fhort, I am my own mafter to choofe, " or which is the fame thing, I am *free*." Perhaps this is as popular a reprefentation of liberty and as agreeable to the ideas of thofe who are the moft zealous advocates for liberty as oppofed to moral neceffity, as can be given.——But all this is talking in the dark and confounding the fubject by the ufe of ambiguous words ; particularly the word *can*. To fay, " I *can* abflain from any particular good," is the very fame as to fay, I have *power* to abflain, &c. But there are two fenfes to the words power and inability already noticed and explained. In one fenfe Pharaoh had power to let the Ifraelites go ; he was under no *natural* inability in the cafe. Still there was an abfolute previous certainty, that he would not for a time let them go. Therefore there was a moral neceffity, that he fhould not let them go, and he was morally unable to let them go ; and in this fenfe he was not free ; it was not a matter of uncertainty whether he would let them go or not.——This account of liberty reminds me of the argument, by which a certain man endeavoured to convince his neighbour, that there were no divine abfolute decrees. The argument was, that having a child newly born, he felt himfelf at liberty to call it by what name he pleafed, without regard to any divine decree. As if God had decreed, that he fhould call his child by a particular name, whether with or without his own confent.

Liberty or freedom muft mean freedom from fomething. If it be a freedom from coaction or natural neceffity, this is what we mean by freedom. The

mind

mind in volition is in its own nature free. But our opponents mean by freedom an exemption from all extrinfic caufal influence, and from all previous certainty. And when they hold, that the mind caufes its own volitions, they muft, to be confiftent, hold that it caufes them contingently and without any previous certainty that it would caufe them ; and they muft deny that the mind's caufation of them is determined, fixed or limited by any caufe whatever. For that the mind fhould caufe them according to a previous eftablifhment, would be as inconfiftent with liberty, as that it fhould not caufe them at all, as it implies an entire limitation of the mind in its operations.

The very inquiry, whether the mind in the exercife of the will, or as poffeffed of the power of will, be free, is apt to lead into error. It feems to imply, that freedom is fomething elfe than the *power* of the will. To inquire whether the mind as poffeffed of will be free, is to inquire whether the mind as poffeffed of freedom be free ; or whether freedom be freedom.

Men in general have no other idea of freedom, than a power of will, or an exemption from coaction or natural neceffity, as their language on the fubject implies no more than this. With them to act *freely,* and to act *voluntarily* is the fame thing, and they never once think of propagating one free act by an antecedent free act, or that in order to freedom it is requifite, that the acts of their wills fhould come to pafs without caufe and by mere chance : Nor do they once imagine, that in order to freedom, there muft be no previous certainty what their acts will be ; or that the divine foreknowledge or prediction is inconfiftent with liberty.

Liberty in the fenfe of our opponents, is not poffible or conceivable. By liberty they mean a power to caufe all our own volitions, and to caufe them freely. But that we fhould thus caufe them, is neither poffible nor conceivable. If we fhould thus caufe a volition, we fhould doubtlefs caufe it by a caufal act :

C 3   It

It is impoffible, that we caufe any thing without a caufal act. And as it is fuppofed, that we caufe it freely, the caufal act muft be a *free* act, *i. e.* an act of the will or a volition. And as the fuppofition is, that all our volitions are caufed by ourfelves, the caufal volition muft be caufed by another, and fo on infinitely : Which is both impoffible and inconceivable. It is no more poffible or conceivable, that we fhould caufe all our own volitions, than that all men fhould beget themfelves.

Some have faid, that volition or voluntary exercife is *liberty*. It is undoubtedly a *free act* and liberty is a property of that act ; but it is not more proper to call it *liberty* itfelf, than to call the apprehenfion of the equality between the three angles of a triangle and two rights, *intellect*, becaufe it is an act of intellect. The flying of a bird at large in the open air is a *free act*, but not *liberty* itfelf.

Our opponents fay, they plead for *that liberty, in men to do as they pleafe*. By this with refpect to the mind, they muft mean, either that the mind caufes its own volitions, or that it acts voluntarily. As to the firft, it has been in part confidered already, and fhall be further attended to in the next chapter. The laft is no more than we all allow ; and for our opponents to mean this only, is to give up the difpute.

It is generally if not univerfally granted by our opponents, that God is *neceffarily holy ;* and to be fure, the fcripture affures us, that " he cannot lie," and " cannot deny himfelf." And Dr. Weft grants, that he is *perfectly holy*, p. 38 ; and that he is *immutable*, ibid. Therefore he is *immutably* and *neceffarily* holy. Yet the Doctor fuppofes God to poffefs a felf-determining power. And although his *definition* of felf-determination, as obferved before, is not at all inconfiftent with the neceffity which we hold ; yet it is manifeft, that he fuppofes felf-determination to be inconfiftent with that neceffity. And did he mean, in afcribing felf-determination to the Deity, to afcribe
fomething

ſomething to him inconſiſtent with *immutable* and *nec-*
eſſary holineſs ? Does he believe, that it is not *abſo-*
lutely certain, that God will for ever continue to be
holy ? Yet abſolute *certainty*, as I have often ſaid, is
all the neceſſity for which we plead. The Doɕtor
therefore has fallen into a dilemma, or rather a trilem-
ma, and he may make his choice, whether to concede,
that there is no ſelf-determination in God, and that
therefore it is not neceſſary to liberty ; or that ſelf-
determination is not at all inconſiſtent with abſolute
moral neceſſity, and then he will give up the diſpute ;
or to hold that God is not neceſſarily holy, and that
he *can lie* and *can deny himſelf*. I wait for the Doctor's deciſion or explanation.

It is well known, that Dr. S. Clarke places liberty
in ſelf-determination or ſelf-motion ; and he holds,
that " liberty in the higheſt and completeſt degree is
" in God himſelf ;" and " that God is a moſt perfeɕt-
" ly free agent ;" yet he immediately adds, that " he
" *cannot but* do always what is beſt and wiſeſt in the
" whole. The reaſon is evident ; becauſe perfeɕt
" wiſdom and goodneſs are as *ſteady* and *certain* prin-
" ciples of aɕtion, as *neceſſity* itſelf." Perfeɕt wiſdom
and goodneſs therefore imply a *certainty* of aɕtion.
But *certainty* is the *neceſſity* in queſtion. How then
can any liberty or ſelf-determination inconſiſtent with
abſolute moral neceſſity, coexiſt in the Deity with that
neceſſity ?——Thus the moſt able advocates for ſelf-
determination, and Dr. Clarke as much as any of
them, are neceſſitated by their abſurd and contradictory ſyſtem, perpetually to contradiɕt themſelves.

Moſt of our opponents hold, that we are the efficient cauſes of our own volitions, and that in this our
liberty conſiſts. But Dr. Weſt expreſsly denies this
with regard to the Deity ; p. 28 ; " The divine vo-
" litions are no effeɕts, either produced by the Deity,
" or by any extrinſic cauſe." Indeed that volitions
are no effeɕts of any cauſe, is a favourite and principal doɕtrine of Dr. Weſt. Therefore the ſelf-deter-

mination

mination which he afcribes to both God and man, produces no volition in either. What then does it ? How does it contribute at all to liberty ? In the Deity it is confiftent with abfolute moral neceffity, as we have juft feen ; and what reafon can be given, why it is not as confiftent with the like neceffity in man ?

Or does liberty in God confift in a contingence or previous uncertainty of his volitions ? This, it is prefumed, will not be pretended ; as it overthrows the divine immutability, and is directly contradictory to what our opponents, particularly Dr. Clarke and Dr. Weft, hold, of the *neceffity* of God's moral perfections. And if liberty in God do not require fuch contingence and uncertainty, let a reafon be given why it fhould in man.——We deny, that caufing our own volitions and acting by chance are either realities or poffibilities ; but if they were both poffible and real ; fince they do not belong to the liberty of God, need we wifh for any more liberty or higher kind of liberty and power, than God has ? Or fhall we vainly imagine, that we poffefs it ?

Liberty is no *pofitive* exiftence. Exiftence or being is divided into *fubftance* and *mode*. But liberty is certainly no *fubftance*. Modes are divided into abfolute or pofitive, and relative. Liberty, as it is a power, falls into the latter clafs ; it is a relative mode. All powers are relations or relative modes. It is then, as I faid, no *pofitive* exiftence.

I have long fince thought, that this controverfy concerning *liberty* and neceffity, fo long agitated, might be eafily fettled to mutual general fatisfaction, if the difputants would but fully explain their own ideas of the fubjects of the difpute. But till this is done, what profpect or poffibility is there of fettling it ? Our opponents accufe us of denying the liberty of moral agents. Now the truth or falfehood of this charge depends on the ideas they affix to the word *liberty*. If by *liberty* be meant what Law in his notes on King, p. 248, defines it to be, " A certain phyfical
" indifference

" indifference or indeterminatenefs in its own exer-
" cife ;" then we do deny liberty. We deny that a
man is or can be indifferent in the exercife of his
liberty or his will.——Or if by liberty be meant, an
exemption from all previous certainty, fo that it is a
matter of uncertainty and mere chance, what our volitions are to be ; in this fenfe alfo we deny liberty.——Further, if by liberty be meant, an exemption
from all extrinfic caufality or influence, fo that our
volitions are efficiently caufed by ourfelves ; this alfo we deny.——But if by liberty be meant a power
of willing and choofing, an exemption from coaction
and natural neceffity, and power, opportunity and
advantage to execute our own choice ; in this fenfe
we hold liberty.

We wifh our opponents to tell us with the fame
precifion, what *they* mean by liberty and in what fenfe
they contend for it. Unlefs they do this, it fignifies
nothing for them to tell us, that we deny all liberty,
and that they are contending for liberty againft neceffity ; and as Dr. Weft has done, to give fuch general and vague definitions of liberty, of felf-determination, &c. as are perfectly confiftent with our ideas of
liberty and free action.

CHAPTER

C.HAPTER III.

Of Self-Determination.

LIBERTY and felf-determination are fo blended by our opponents in this controverfy, that it is impoffible to write a chapter on one of thefe fubjeƈts, with proper attention to the fentiments of our opponents, without running into the other. Therefore in the laft chapter I was neceffitated to fay many things concerning felf-determination. Yet I wifh to make fome further obfervations on the fame fubjeƈt.

All our opponents agree, that felf-determination is effential to liberty. Let us firft attend to what Dr. Weft fays on this fubjeƈt ; then we fhall make fome remarks on what Dr. Clarke and others have faid.

Dr. Weft tells us, that " determining, when we ap-" ply it to the aƈtive faculty, is the fame with volition." P. 16, 17. And " the fenfe in which we ufe *felf-de-* " *termination* is fimply this, that we ourfelves deter-" mine ; *i. e.* that we ourfelves will or choofe." Now I cannot believe, that Dr. Weft imagined, that Prefident Edwards, or any of his followers, would deny, that we ourfelves determine, will and choofe. We doubtlefs will and choofe as really as we think, fee, hear, feel, &c. But who or what is the efficient caufe in either cafe, remains to be confidered. To fay, that we are determiners in the aƈtive voice, and not the determined in the paffive voice, gives no fatisfaƈtion. We grant, that we are determiners in the aƈtive ; and yet affert, that we are determined, or are caufed to determine, by fome extrinfic caufe, at the fame time, and with refpeƈt to the fame aƈt : As when a man hears a found, he is the hearer in the aƈtive voice, and yet is caufed to hear the fame found, by fomething extrinfic to himfelf. It will not be pretended, that a man is the efficient caufe of his own hearing, in every inftance in which he hears in the aƈtive voice.

Though

Though Dr. West in general maintains, and has written an essay to prove, that volition is no effect and has no cause ; yet he sometimes forgets himself and falls in with the generality of the defenders of the self-determining power, who hold, that the mind is the efficient cause of its own volitions. He every where maintains, that volition is not the effect of an *extrinsic* cause ? Why does he express himself thus, if he do not suppose it to be the effect of an *intrinsic* cause ? The expression implies this. This is not all. In p. 24, he puts the question, " whether the mind in choof-
" ing or acting, do not modify itself ?" which he an-
swers in the affirmative, and says, that this " modifi-
" cation is the effect of the mind willing or choof-
" ing." The mind then in willing modifies itself, *i. e.* brings itself into the mode of willing. This mode then is volition ; and this volition is the effect of the mind willing, or the effect of volition. So that Dr. West here, in direct contradiction to his general doctrine, asserts, agreeably to Dr. Clarke and most writers of his class, that volition is an effect and has a cause ; is the effect of the mind whose volition it is, and is the effect of the mind willing or of a volition of that mind. Agreeably to this he says, p. 28, " No agent can bring
" any effects to pass, but what are *consequent* upon his
" acting ; *i. e.* that all effects are in consequence of
" the activeness or operativeness of some being :" And p. 22, " No being can become a cause, *i. e.* an effi-
" cient, or that which produces an effect, but by FIRST
" *operating*, *acting* or *energising* :" And in the same page, " Volition, when used intelligibly ——— is real-
" ly an efficient cause." Volition then is an efficient cause, and an efficient cause of a modification of the mind, which is another volition, and this by *first* operating, acting or energising : And doubtless this ope-
ration, act or energising is a volition. So that here we have three volitions in train, all necessary to the existence of one volition and of every volition. The *first* volition is an efficient cause of a *second*, called by Dr.
West

Weſt a modification of the mind; and it produces this effect by a *third* volition, which is the *operation, act,* or *energiſing of the firſt.*——What is this, but " ſelf act- " ing on ſelf and producing volition," and this by the inſtrumentality of an intermediate volition.   Dr. Weſt cannot conſiſtently deny any of theſe abſurdities of his ſcheme.   He cannot ſay, that one volition, as an efficient cauſe, does not produce a ſecond ; as he holds, that " the mind in willing modifies itſelf."   But according to him volition is the mind willing.   He al- ſo holds, that the ſaid " modification is the effect of " the mind willing ;" *i. e.* by his own definition, the effect of volition ; volition then is the *efficient cauſe* of the ſaid modification.   That this modification is voli- tion he will not deny.   Then we have one volition as an efficient cauſe, producing another volition as its effect.   But he grants that " no being can produce an " effect, but by *firſt, acting* or *energiſing.*"   This gives us the intermediate volition.

It has been long ſince charged on the advocates for ſelf-determination, that their doctrine involves the ab- ſurdity of one volition before every volition, and even before the firſt.   But Dr. Weſt has made improve- ment in the ſcheme : He has taught us, that ſelf deter- mination implies *two volitions* before every volition and before the *firſt.*

That volition is produced by the mind, as the effi- cient cauſe, is implied, however inconſiſtently with himſelf, in various other paſſages of Dr. Weſt's books ; as p. 25, " If volition or internal action be the effect " of an extrinſic cauſe, our reflections could never af- " ford us an example of an efficient cauſe."   " As we " are rational beings, it follows, that our volitions are " not the effects of an *extrinſic* cauſe, but that we are " *ſelf-determined.*"   " Conſcious, that we ourſelves " are the determiners and not the determined —— we " have the idea of our independence in willing and " chooſing."   Our volition muſt either be the effect of an extrinſic cauſe, or of an intrinſic one, or it muſt hap-

pen

pen without caufe. If it happen without caufe, our reflections could no more afford us an example of an efficient caufe, than they would on the fuppofition, that it is
the effect of an extrinfic caufe. So that the Doctor's argument neceffarily implies, that volition is produced by
the mind as the efficient caufe. In the fecond quotation
above, he fpeaks of our being felf-determined, as in direct oppofition to our volitions being effects of an extrinfic caufe. But there is no fuch oppofition unlefs by
our being felf-determined be meant, that our volitions
are the effects of an intrinfic caufe. If felf-determination here mean no more than that we are the *fubjects*
of a determination, or that we ourfelves determine, as
we ourfelves think, feel, &c. this may be, and yet that
determination may be the effect of an extrinfic caufe.
So that there appears to be no meaning in this paffage, unlefs, in direct contradiction to what Dr. Weft
elfewhere holds, it mean, that our volitions are *effects*
and have an *efficient caufe ;* that this caufe is our own
mind ; and this efficient caufe, as the Dr. declares all
efficient caufes do, produces its effect, " by *firft* ope-
" rating, acting or energifing ;" and thus felf would act
" on felf and produce volition," by an efficient operation.———Again ; if we were " confcious, that we
" ourfelves are the determiners, and not the determin-
" ed," we fhould thence derive no " idea of our inde-
" pendence in willing and choofing," if our willing and
choofing either were the effect of an extrinfic caufe,
or happened without caufe ; or unlefs we were the efficient caufes of our own willing and choofing.

Though all this is abundantly denied and renounced by Dr. Weft, as appears by quotations already
made ; yet it is the real ground work of his book,
and the only ground, on which he could confiftently
oppofe the doctrine of moral neceffity and extrinfic
caufality of volitions : And this is the common doctrine of the advocates for felf-determination. Thus
Dr. Clarke, in Papers between him and Leibnitz, p.
289, tells us, " The true and only queftion concern-
" ing

" ing liberty, is, whether the immediate phyfical caufe
" or principle of action be indeed in him, whom we
" call the agent ; or whether it be fome other reafon
" fufficient, which is the real caufe of the action, by
" operating upon the agent and making him to be,
" not the agent but a mere patient." I underftand
the Doctor by phyfical caufe, to mean efficient, producing caufe ; otherwife it is not to the purpofe.

Dr. Chauncy is ftill more explicit. " Self-deter-
" mination *gives rife* to our volitions ———— and is
" the caufe of them." *Benevolence of the Deity*, p. 128.
" A power in man, that fubjects *his volitions to his*
" *command*, is the only bottom, upon which agency
" can be founded." Ibid, p. 129. And in the next
page he fays, the fame power " conftitutes us agents,
" or beings that are *efficiently the caufes* of their own
" volitions."

Now this felf-determination, which " gives rife to
our volitions," and in which we are " the efficient
" caufes of our own volitions," is a determination or
act either of the will, or of fome other faculty. If it
be an act of the will, it is a volition. So that here
we have one volition caufed by another : And as the
doctrine is, that all our volitions are the effect of felf-
determination, they are all the effect of volition, the
caufing act the effect of a preceding act, and the firft
the effect of one before that. This abfurdity attending the fcheme of felf-determination, has been long
fince pointed out ; nor have the advocates of that
fcheme been able to fhow, that their fcheme does not
really labour under that abfurdity, if by that felf-determination, which is the caufe of volition, they mean
an act of the will.

But if this felf-determination be an act of the underftanding ; then it feems, that the will or mind willing, is influenced to volition by a dictate of the underftanding, or by a motive. Then we are at once
involved in what is fo hideous to Dr. Weft, and all
other believers in felf-determination, the government

by

by motives and the moral neceffity implied in it : Alfo our volitions are determined by extrinfic caufes and we are the paffive fubjects of the operation of thofe caufes.

Or if we fuppofe the determining act to proceed from any other faculty, if other there be, the difficulty will remain. Dr. Weft holds, " that there are three effen- " tial faculties of the mind, which ought always to be " confidered diftinctly ; and thefe are *perception, pro-* " *penfion* and *will* ;" and that " the laft only is prop- " erly the active faculty." Then doubtlefs that felf-determination, which is an *action*, and which gives rife to volition, is an act of this active faculty. In this cafe we have will putting forth felf-determin-ation, in order to give rife to volition ; as we had be-fore volition as an efficient caufe, firft operating, act-ing or energifing, in order to produce the effect vo-lition. As the will is, according to the Doctor, " the " only active faculty," he will not pretend, that voli-tion produced by felf-determination, is the effect of either of the other two faculties, as he reckons them, perception and propenfion. If he fhould fay, that it is the effect of *perception ;* this it feems is a paffive faculty ; and then felf-determination and all volition are the effects of a paffive faculty and of paffion, of which alone that faculty is by the terms capable ; and therefore, it feems, felf-determination and volition muft themfelves be paffions or mere impreffions, and we are paffive in them. Befides, perception confid-ered as a faculty, as Dr. Weft fingularly confiders it, appears to be nothing elfe, than intellect or the pow-er of underftanding. And if felf-determination pro-ceed from this, the confequence is, that the will is governed by the underftanding and by the dictates and motives which it fuggefts ; which brings us where we were before, into the midft of neceffity. The fame confequence will follow, if we fuppofe, that felf-deter-mination proceed from *perception* in the common fenfe of the word, meaning *an act* of the underftand-

ing

ing.———If Dr. Weft fay, that felf-determination proceeds from *propenfion*; then he entirely coincides
with Prefident Edwards, who afcribes a great part of
our volitions to difpofition, inclination, paffion and
habit, meaning certain biafes of the mind diftinct
from volition and prior to it.———Befides ; as propenfion is according to the Doctor a paffive faculty, if
volition and felf-determination proceed from this they
are paffions or impreffions, they proceed from an extrinfic caufe and we are paffive in them.

The caufing of one act of volition by another is
attended with this abfurdity alfo, it fuppofes the caufing act in this cafe to be diftinct from the act caufed;
when in reality they coalefce and are one and the
fame. For inftance, to choofe to have a choice of
virtue, is nothing but a choice of virtue ; to choofe
the choice of an apple, is to choofe an apple : So
that we have the volition before we have it, and in
order that we may have it.

Some fenfible of the abfurdity of fuppofing, that
the mind determines one volition by another, as
this runs into an infinite feries of volitions, and implies that there is volition before the firft volition,
have renounced this idea of felf-determination. A-
mong thefe we may reckon Dr. Weft. But at the
fame time he gives up felf-determination in every
fenfe in which we difpute it, and in every fenfe inconfiftent with the moft abfolute moral neceffity. This
has been already illuftrated.——— Others, to avoid the
fame difficulty exprefs themfelves differently : They
profefs to mean, that volition is caufed not by a preceding volition, but by *the man* or *the mind*, whofe
volition it is. But this gives no fatisfaction. Sup-
pofing it fhould be faid, that a certain carpenter himfelf was the efficient caufe or builder of fuch a fhip ;
and it fhould be thence inferred, that he built it by
working, labouring or exerting himfelf to the end of
building the fhip ; would not this be a natural and a
neceffary inference ? Would not the man, who fhould
affert,

affert, that the carpenter did indeed himfelf immediately build the fhip, but not by any labour or exertion,
whether of body or mind, be univerfally confidered
as talking abfurdly and contradictorily ? And does
not the man talk as abfurdly and contradictorily, who
afferts, that a man is the efficient caufe of his own
volition, yet puts forth no exertion, in order to caufe
it ? If any other way of efficiently caufing an effect,
than by act or exertion previous to the effect, be poffible or conceivable, let it be pointed out : Till this
be done, we who conceive fuch a way to be impoffible and inconceivable, have a right to fay fo, and to
prefume, that our opponents, who affert that there is
fuch a way, are unable to point it out, and have
no more idea of it, than we have.   If upon trial, they
fhall find, that they are unable to point out the way,
let them honeftly confefs, that all they mean by felf-
determination is what we and all allow, that they are
the *fubjects* of volition, and as Dr. Welt expreffes it,
that *they themfelves will and choofe.*

I perfectly agree with Dr. Weft when he fays, p.
22, " No being can become an efficient caufe, but
" by FIRST *operating, acting* or *energifing."* Operation,
act or energifing is as much prefuppofed in order to
an effect, as an efficient caufe is prefuppofed in order
to it.   To fuppofe an efficient caufe to produce an
effect without any act by which he produces it, is the
fame as to fuppofe the fame caufe produces the effect,
without any *efficiency :* It is as abfurd, as it would be
to fuppofe, that Dr. Weft wrote his effays without any
exertion in order to the production of them, or that
God created the world, without any creating act.   If
this be not true, let the falfehood of it be made to appear.
Let any man fhow, that an effect cannot as well come
to pafs without an efficient caufe, as without a caufing act ; and that the world could not as well have
come into exiftence without a Creator, as without a
creating act.

D   Some

Some of the advocates for self-determination hold, that the mind is the efficient cause of its own volitions, yet not by any *act* or *exertion* of the mind, but by the *power* or *faculty* of the will. And how can this power or faculty produce volition, unless it be exerted *first* in order to the effect ? The man, who is the subject of a certain volition, had the power of will long since ; yet it never produced that volition, we may suppose, till this moment. What is the cause or reason, that it produces it now and not before ? To say, it does, because it will, is to say either, that this volition is produced by another preceding, which runs into the infinite feries ; or that the power of will, or rather the man in the exercise of that power, is the subject of volition, because he is the subject of it, which is mere trifling.——On the whole the existence of a power of will in a man, will no more account for any particular volition, of which he is the subject, than the existence of the *man* will account for the same volition, or the existence of a ship-carpenter will account for the building of a certain ship ; or than Dr. West's having a power to write essays of Liberty and Necessity, will account for his actually writing them at the precise time, at which he did write them, or than his having an ear will account for his hearing a particular found at a certain time.

That we have a power of will or of determining is granted on all hands : But that we should efficiently cause our power of will, to put forth a volition, without exerting any efficiency to this effect ; only wants proof to make it credible, and explanation to make it intelligible or conceivable. Merely the circumstance, that we have a power to will and determine, no more proves, that without motive or any influence from without ; and without any causing act within, we cause that power to exert itself ; than the circumstance, that we have a power of hearing proves, that without any pulsation in the air, any causation

from

from without or from within, we caufe ourfelves to hear a particular found.

Some others, as well as Dr. Weft, have denied, that by felf-determination they mean the caufing of one act of the will by another. We have no objection to their denying this : But then we wifh them to inform us explicitly, what they do mean. If they have any meaning they doubtlefs can exprefs it intelligibly : And fo long as they do not exprefs a meaning different from what we mean by willing or choofing ; and fo long as their definitions of felf-determination exprefs, either bare volition, or the caufing of one volition by another, though they infift, that they mean fomething different from either of thefe ; I leave the reader to judge, whether they have any clear meaning to that word at all.

In converfation once with a gentleman of eminence among the advocates for felf-determination he told me, that Prefident Edwards had abufed thofe who write in favour of felf-determination, in reprefenting them as holding, that the mind caufes one act of volition by another. On my inquiring of the gentleman what then they did mean ; his anfwer was, " They mean, that in determining the mind determines." Whether this anfwer at all explained the matter ; or whether it convey any other idea, than that *the mind does determine, and has a volition*, without touching the queftion concerning the caufe, extrinfic or intrinfic ; I fubmit to the reader. If a man fhould fay, that in walking, he walks ; in writing he writes ; in hearing he hears ; it is prefumed, that no man could certainly hence conclude, that the fpeaker meant, that he was not influenced to walk or write, by motive or by fome extrinfic caufe ; or that his hearing was felf-determined.

If we caufe our own volitions at all, we caufe them either by a previous volition, or without fuch volition. If we caufe them by a previous volition, this is what I have been particularly confidering, and fhall fay no more upon it. If we caufe them without fuch voli-

tion,

tion, we caufe them involuntarily, without any defign, any motive or agency. Now I wifh it may be inquired, whether fuch a caufation of volition as this, if it be poffible or conceivable, as I contend it is not, be at all more favourable to liberty, than that volition fhould proceed from the influence of motive or fome other extrinfic caufe ; and whether it would be any advantage or privilege in any refpect ; and whether it would not be a great difadvantage and calamity to mankind, and an infupportable incumbrance on the influence of reafon, revelation, virtue, duty and happinefs both here and hereafter. For whatever any of thefe may dictate, and with whatever motives they enforce thofe dictates ; whatever virtue and our own happinefs may require, fince the felf-determining power is not influenced by thefe or any other motives ; and fince, as Dr. Clarke fays, " There is no connec-" tion at all between the perception of the underftand-" ing and the exertion of the active faculty ;" all thofe dictates and motives would be in vain ; the felf-determining power is a fovereign, ungovernable principle, perfectly deaf and unmoved by any motive, reafon, argument or reprefentation whether of duty or intereft. It therefore deftroys the very ufe not only of our reafon, of revelation and of the motives of both ; but of our affections, paffions, appetites and fenfes, in every part of our conduct as moral agents. For fo far as we are influenced by any of thefe, we are not felf-determined, and therefore, according to our opponents, we are incapable of moral action; and efpecially are we not felf-determined in the fenfe now particularly under confideration ; caufing our own volitions involuntarily and without a previous volition.

Self-determination uninfluenced by motive, is inconfiftent with all religion and morality and with all virtue and vice. To love God without motive, principle, aim or end, is no religion. To love and do good to mankind in like manner, is no virtue. To hate God or mankind in like manner, is no irrelig-

ion

ion or vice. Juſt ſo as to ſtealing, robbing, killing, &c.

The ſelf determining power is, as I ſaid, an ungovernable principle. It not only cannot be governed by reaſon, revelation, &c. But not by any laws human or divine ; for theſe are only motives. Nay, it cannot be governed by God, his providence or his grace. To be governed by either of theſe would be to be governed by an extrinſic cauſe, and under ſuch government men would be paſſive. If God in his providence govern and control them and their actions, they are limited, and act only by permiſſion, and have no power to act or not act, no liberty to either ſide, but are confined to one ſide. Where then is ſelf-determination ?——On the other hand, if men determine and control all their own actions, none of their actions are controlled by God.

Dr. Reid, a late ſtrenuous advocate for ſelf-determination ſays, " The name of a cauſe and of an agent, " is properly given to that being only, which by its " active power, produces ſome change in itſelf, or in " ſome other being. The change, whether it be of " thought, of will, or of motion, is the effect. Active " power therefore is a quality in the cauſe, which en- " ables it to produce the effect. And the *exertion of* " *that active power* in producing the effect, is called " action, agency, efficiency. In order to the produc- " tion of any effect, there muſt be in the cauſe, *not on-* " *ly power*, but the *exertion* of that power : For power " that is not exerted produces no effect." Eſſays on the Active Powers, p. 259. Therefore if we be the efficient cauſes of our own volitions, as Dr. Clarke, Dr. Chauncy, &c. held, we muſt not only have *a power* to produce them, but there muſt be an *exertion* of power in order to the production of volition. This exertion is doubtleſs an exertion of the will. Thus we run into the infinite ſeries ſeveral times mentioned. And however others attempt to evade the abſurdities

D 3   of

of this infinite feries, Dr. Ried and his followers muſt fall into them.

" All our power," ſays Dr. Reid, ibid, 299, " is direct-" ed by our will ; we can form no conception of power, " properly ſo called, that is not under the direction of " our will." Then we have no power to direct or determine our will, unleſs we go round in a circle. If our will direct *all* our power, as the Doctor aſſerts ; and our ſelf-determining power direct and determine our will, then we go round in a circle, our will directing all our power, and our ſelf-determining power directing our will. Glorious liberty this ! And this muſt be an age of glorious improvement and illumination, or we ſhould never have made ſuch diſcoveries as theſe ! Yet Dr. Reid had great reaſon to ſay, that all our power is directed by our will, otherwiſe ſome of our power might act involuntarily and our ſelf-determining power (if we have any) might direct and govern us without our conſent ; with which Dr. Reid's ſcheme would very ill agree. Still the Doctor in this gives up a point, which he had before poſitively aſſerted and had laboured hard to eſtabliſh, " that if the will be not, " nothing elſe is, in our power ;" p. 258. Now if the will be in our power, it is under our direction, or is directed by our power. So that we have the circle complete ; all " our power is directed by our will ;" and yet our will is directed by our power. Into what glaring inconſiſtences will not men run, rather than give up a favourite and indefenſible hypotheſis ! Yet they are ſo blinded by their attachment to that hypotheſis, that they ſee no inconſiſtency attending it.———The truth is, that both theſe principles, *that all our power is direct-ed by our will ;* and that *our will is directed by our ſelf-determining power,* are eſſential to the Doctor's ſcheme, and to the ſcheme of all who hold a ſelf-determining power. To reconcile theſe two principles deeply concerns them. But they have never yet been able to do it ; nor, it is preſumed, ever will be able.

Some

Some of the writers in favour of felf-determination feem to be fenfible of the *myftery* in it ; particularly Dr. Chauncy. " It is readily allowed," fays he, " lib-" erty in man, in oppofition to neceffity, is one of *the* " *great wonders of God.* The power in our nature, " that conftitutes us free agents, is an *amazing* contriv-" ance of infinite wifdom. The modus of its opera-" tion is *too great a deep* for us to fathom. It has *tri-*" *ed* and *puzzled* the greateft geniufes in all parts of " the world." *Benevolence of the Deity*, p. 13 . No wonder then, that nobody has ever been able to give a confiftent or intelligible account of this power. So long as thofe who believe in it, are puzzled with it, we may expect, that their accounts of it will be con-fufed, unintelligible and contradictory. But the ac-count of no one of them appears to be more contra-dictory than that of Dr. Weft. He gives up the idea of Dr. Clarke and Dr. Chauncy, that the mind is the efficient caufe of its own volitions ; yet he falls into the fame, in holding, that the mind in willing modifies itfelf, and that this modification is *the effect* of the mind willing, p. 24 ; and that we are independent in will-ing, p. 25. He holds that volition has no caufe ; yet holds, that the modification made of the mind by it-felf in willing, is *the effect* of the mind willing. He holds that volitions have no caufe ; yet denies, that he can be juftly charged with holding, that events take place without a caufe ; p. 27. Surely the Doctor can never expect, that his unbiafed readers will re-ceive his fyftem, until he fhall have removed thefe inconfiftences.

Archbifhop King is grofsly inconfiftent with him-felf, in holding, that the will determines itfelf to choofe certain objects, without the influence of motive or any caufe out of the will ; and yet holding, that the will is determined to choofe thofe objects, becaufe of the pleafure which will be in confequence of that choice. Law's *edition*, p. 276. In fuch a cafe the will is as much determined by motive, as if a man

D 4   were

were determined to go to a debauch, in the profpect of the fenfual pleafure, which he expected there.

Dr. Welt fays, p. 23, " Every effect is wholly paf- " five with regard to the caufe, which produces it." And this equally holds, whether the caufe be extrin- fic or intrinfic. " Confequently, if human volition " be an effect" even of an intrinfic caufe, " the man " muſt be paffive in willing. - But if man be paffive " in willing, he can be active in nothing elfe ; *i. e.* he " is no agent, but a mere paffive machine." What then is the great advantage, which the advocates for felf-determining power and the intrinfic caufation of volition, would gain, could they eftablifh their favour- ite doctrine ? According to their own fcheme, every volition would be an *effect*, a *paffive* effect, and " man " muſt be paffive in willing. But if man be paffive " in willing, he can be active in nothing elfe : *i. e.* he " is no agent, but a mere paffive machine." Ibid. More than this cannot be faid on this head, if we fup- pofe volition to be the effect of an *extrinfic* caufe. Therefore they are grofsly inconfiftent with themfelves in rejecting one of two hypothefes, on account of fup- pofed abfurdities, which equally attend the other, and yet retaining that other.

Although Dr. Clarke and others affert, that the true and only queftion concerning liberty, is, whether we be the efficient caufes of our own volitions ; yet they themfelves would not abide by this conceffion. For if it were previoufly fixed and eftablifhed, what par- ticular volitions we fhould efficiently caufe in our- felves, this would be as inconfiftent with their ideas of liberty, as the fuppofition, that they are produced by an extrinfic caufe. Gentlemen of that clafs uni- verfally hold, that abfolute decrees are inconfiftent with liberty, becaufe they eftablifh the actions decreed. Therefore if God have decreed that we ourfelves fhall efficiently caufe fuch and fuch volitions in our own minds ; this as effectually eftablifhes and fecures the exiftence of thofe volitions, as if he had decreed,

that

that they fhould be effeƀed by any other caufe.
Therefore not only does their idea of liberty require
felf-determination, but it equally requires perfeƀ previous uncertainty and chance, and an entire exemption from all rule, limitation or confinement, fo that
the mind not only produces its own volitions ; but
produces them at random and by mere chance, without the influence of motive and without any previous
certainty, what particular aƀs it fhall produce, and
whether any. Thus according to them felf-determination is aƀing by chance and becoming the fubjeƀ of
volitions without any proper caufe at all : For a caufe
that aƀs by chance and ftupidly, without motive or
defign, is no proper efficient caufe at all.

Dr. Weft fays, p. 17, " We have fet afide the no-
" tion, that the will determines all the prefent aƀs of
" the will : For we entirely join with Mr. Edwards
" in exploding that idea." What myftery there may be
couched under the *will*, I will not pretend to fay.
But as he " entirely agrees with Mr. Edwards in ex-
" ploding that idea," Dr. Weft muft hold not only,
that the will as a diftinƀ power of the mind does not
determine the prefent aƀs of the will ; but that the
mind in the exercife of the power of will, does not
determine thofe aƀs. For this is equally exploded
by Mr. Edwards, as the other. The Doƀor fays,
that " the will does not determine *all* the *prefent* aƀs
" of the will." But does it determine *any* of the aƀs
of the will, whether *prefent*, *paft* or *future* ? As he
agrees in this particular with Mr. Edwards, he muft
anfwer in the negative. All *paft* aƀs of the will were
once prefent ; and when they were prefent Dr. Weft
denies, that the will determined them : And he will not
fay, that the will determines them now that they are
paft. Alfo all future aƀs of the will erelong will be
prefent ; and when they fhall be prefent, they will
not, according to Dr. Weft's conceffion, be determined by the will. Therefore he will not fay, that they
are determined by the will now, before they come into

to exiſtence. Doubtleſs by whatever they are determined, they are determined by it at the very inſtant
of their coming into exiſtence. No cauſe produces
an effect, at a time before or after the exiſtence of
that effect : Therefore by this conceſſion of Dr. Weſt
it ſeems he holds, that no volition, paſt, preſent or
future is determined by the will, or by the mind in
the exerciſe of the will. Yet Dr. Weſt ſtrenuouſly
pleads for a ſelf-determining power : But what good
purpoſe does this power anſwer, ſince it determines
no act of will ? It ſeems it is a very innocent and
harmleſs thing, becauſe it is very inefficacious and
dormant, doing neither good nor hurt.

Dr. Clarke, in papers between Leibnitz and himſelf, p. 73, grants, that " nothing is, without a ſuffi-
" cient reaſon why it is, rather than not ; and why it
" is thus, rather than otherwiſe. But" ſays, that " in
" things in their own nature indifferent, mere will,
" without any thing external to influence it, is alone
" that ſufficient reaſon." By will the Doctor muſt
mean either an act of volition, or the power of the
will. If he mean that the former is the reaſon or
ground of our acts of the will, he runs into the infinite ſeries. If he mean the latter it is as abſurd as to
ſay, The ability of Dr. Clarke to write his replies to
Leibnitz, was alone the ſufficient reaſon why he wrote
them.

Dr. Price in his correſpondence with Dr. Prieſtly,
p. 136, ſays, " It cannot be juſtly ſaid, that ſelf-deter-
" mination implies an effect without a cauſe. Does it
" follow, that becauſe I am myſelf the cauſe, there is
" no cauſe ?" To this I anſwer, that though it does
indeed not follow, that becauſe I am myſelf the
cauſe of a volition, there is no cauſe ; as it is tak-
en for granted, that there is a cauſe, and that I am
that cauſe ; yet from the ſuppoſition, that volition is
not the effect of a cauſe extrinſic to the mind in which
it takes place, it will follow, that there is no cauſe of
it ; becauſe it is abſolutely impoſſible, that the mind
itſelf

itfelf fhould be the caufe of it. The impoffibility of this has been already ftated in the preceding difcourfe, and more largely illuftrated by other writers : And if any man will fhow the poffibility of the mind's cauf- ing its own volitions, and will remove the abfurdities attending that fuppofition ; *erit mihi Magnus Apollo :* It will then, and not till then, be incumbent on us to fpeak of felf-determination in a very different ftrain.

In fine ; thofe who plead for a felf-determining pow- er, either mean what Dr. Weft declares he means, that we ourfelves determine whenever we do deter- mine ; which is no part of the fubject of this contro- verfy, is difputed by none and is nothing oppofite to moral neceffity, extrinfic caufality of volition, &c. but amounts to this merely, that we are the fubjects of volition : Or they mean, that we are the efficient caufes of our own volitions. But thefe men feem never to have reflected fo far on the fubject, as to fee, that this idea of felf-determinatio runs into what has been fo often charged upon them, an infinite fe- ries of volitions caufing one another : And therefore when this difficulty is fuggefted to them, they are ei- ther filenced and have nothing to anfwer, or elfe an- fwer in fuch a manner as to fhow, that by efficiently caufing our own volitions they mean merely what Dr. Weft profeffes to mean, that we *will* or are the fub- jects of volition, which no more implies, that we caufe them, than that we caufe all our own perceptions and feelings follows from our being the fubjects of them.

" I take it to be an important truth," fays the Doc- tor, Part IJ, p. 19, " that wherever neceffity begins, " liberty ends ; and that a neceffary agent is a contra- " diction." What a pity, that the Doctor fhould under- take the defence of a propofition, which he is neceffi- tated perpetually to beg ! Or if he be not neceffitat- ed to beg it, what a pity that he fhould do it without neceffity ! He knows or ought to have known, that this which he here takes for granted, is not conceded ; that Prefident Edwards and all his followers hold, that
the

the moſt abſolute moral neceſſity is confiſtent with
perfect liberty, and that an agent acting under moral
neceſſity, is ſo far from a contradiction, that neither
God nor creature is or can be any other agent. If
Dr. Weſt ſhould ſay, that a neceſſary agent is a contradiction according to *his idea* of agent, *i. e.* a ſelf-
determinate agent or one acting by chance : Be it
ſo ; he ought to prove, and not aſſume, that his idea
is poſſible and according to truth.

" When a man conſiders," (ſays Dr. Weſt, p. 23,
Part II,) " that he is not moved by any extrinſic
" cauſe to do evil, but that his wickedneſs has *origin-*
" *ated wholly from himſelf*, he muſt feel himſelf ex-
" ceedingly vile and unworthy of any divine favour."
This is talking altogether in the clouds : What does
he mean by wickedneſs originated from a man's ſelf ?
He cannot conſiſtently mean, that " ſelf acts on ſelf
" and produces wickedneſs ;" for this he rejects as
abſurd. If he mean, that a man is himſelf the ſubject of wickedneſs, wicked volitions or actions ; this
is granted ; but it is not at all oppoſed to his being
moved by an extrinſic cauſe to that wickedneſs, any
more than a man's being the ſubject of pain is inconſiſtent with the pain's being effected by an extrinſic
cauſe. If there be any ſenſe beſide theſe two, in
which wickedneſs can be originated from a man's ſelf,
let it be pointed out.

" If men have an exiſtence diſtinct from Deity,"
ſays the Doctor, " endowed with a conſciouſneſs diſ-
" tinct from Deity, then they have a ſelf-active prin-
" ciple diſtinct from Deity ; *i. e.* they have a ſelf-de-
" termining power ;" ibid, p. 24. That men have an
exiſtence and conſciouſreſs diſtinct from Deity, is
granted ; but that it thence follows, that they have a
ſelf-determining power, if by that be meant any thing
diſtinct from a faculty of will influenced by extrinſic
motives and cauſes is not granted, and ought not to
have been taken for granted, nor aſſerted without
proof. From the ſame premiſes it would follow, that
brutes

brutes have a felf-determining power ; which is not generally allowed by the advocates for that power. For brutes have both an exiftence and a confcioufnefs diftinct from the Deity.

" He that cannot govern his own mind ; but is " conftantly determined by an extrinfic caufe, is cer-" tainly the fubject of mere chance and accident ;" ibid, p. 28. Indeed ! and is the planetary fyftem the fubject of mere chance and accident ? The mate-rial world cannot govern itfelf, yet not an hair of our head efcapes the notice or the difpofal of our heaven-ly Father.——Surely the Doctor afferted this without confideration.

" Our doctrine of felf-determination implying, that " when the mind acts, it always has an object in view, " and that there is always a reafon for acting, is as " fully confiftent with our being the fubjects of com-" mands and promifes, prohibitions and threatenings, " and eftablifhes as fure a connection between means " and ends, as he" [Prefident Edwards] " can fuppofe " to arife from the doctrine of Neceffity." Ibid, p. 29. Yet the Doctor's doctrine is, " that men are not " always governed by the ftrongeft motive," and that there is no fure connection between motives and ac-tion. Ibid, p. 6. Now the Doctor is fpeaking of the means and ends of moral agents and moral actions ; and particularly of commands and promifes, prohibi-tions and threatenings, confidered as motives and means of action. And does that doctrine which teaches that there is no fure connection between the ftrongeft motive, or even any motives, whether ftrong-er or weaker, and action, eftablifh as fure a connec-tion between fuch means and their ends, which are moral actions, as that doctrine which teaches, that there is a fure and infallible connection between fuch means and their ends ? Is it not furprifing, that the Doctor fhould affert fuch a thing ?

He tells us, ibid, p. 29, " That he holds no fuch " kind of felf-determination, as a power to act without " and

" and againſt every kind of reaſon or argument." But he does hold a power to act without and againſt the *ſtrongeſt* reaſons and arguments : Therefore he ought much more to hold a power to act without and againſt the weaker ; and conſequently a power to act without and againſt every kind of reaſon and argument. Nay, the Doctor does expreſsly hold a power to *reſiſt* all motives, reaſons and arguments, and a power to remain *inactive* notwithſtanding the ſolicitations of them all. And is it not ſtrange, that he who poſſeſſes a power to reſiſt and remain inactive, without and againſt every kind of reaſon and argument ; has not alſo a power to reſiſt them in acting againſt them ?

CHAPTER

CHAPTER IV.

Of Motives and their Influence.

DR. Welt has given his definition of a motive, p. 17 ; " It is the occafion, reafon, end or defign, " which an agent has in view, when he acts." And he grants, ibid, " that the mind acts upon motives ; " *i. e.* when the mind acts or choofes, it always has " fome end, defign or reafon, which is the occafion of " its acting or choofing. Therefore motives, in our " fenfe of the term, are the previous circumftances, " which are neceffary for action." And, Part II, p. 93 ; " Action *cannot* take place without fome object, rea- " fon or motive ; and the motive or reafon for acting *muft* " *be prior* to the action of the mind, and be *perceived* by " it, before it *can act.*" " Nothing *can* become an object " of choice, except it appears to be eligible ;" p. 95, Part II. Yet he maintains, " that there is no infallible connec- " tion between motive and action ;" and that " when mo- " tives have done all that they can do, the mind may " act or not act." The reafon which he affigns for this, is, " that though the mind never acts without " fome reafon or defign in acting ; yet there is no " need of affigning a. reafon for *not acting.*" P. 17, 18.——If by *acting or not acting* he mean a volunta- ry acting or not acting, or a choofing or refufing of the motives prefented ; it is to be obferved, as I have already obferved, that refufing is as real an action as choofing ; and a voluntary not acting is a *voluntary* refufal to act and to comply with the motives propof- ed, and is as real a volition as any other ; and there- fore by his own conceffion, " motive is neceffary to " it," equally neceffary as for any other volition or action.—— Or if by *not acting* Dr. Welt mean no act of either choofing or refufing, but a perfect inaction ; then what he fays, will come to this, That when mo-

tives

tives are propofed, the mind may choofe to comply with them, or it may refufe to comply with them, or it may do neither. But the impoffibility of this I endeavoured to illuftrate in the fecond chapter, and fhall fay no more on it at prefent.

But if it were poffible, that on the propofal of motives, the mind fhould *not act at all* ; how would it follow, as Dr. Weft fays, that there is no infallible connection between motive and *action ?* It is granted by Dr. Weft that motive is neceffary to every action, whether of choice or refufal ; and to fay as the Doctor does, that it is not neceffary for *not acting*, amounts to this merely, that it is not neceffary for involuntary, blockifh inaction or torpitude.——By infallible connection we mean no more than conftant invariable connection, fo that whenever the mind acts, whether in choice or refufal, it is under the perfuafive influence of fome motive, which, as Dr. Weft grants, " is the reafon " and occafion of its acting," and " a circumftance " neceffary for action." We pretend not but that the man, when motives are prefented, may poffibly fall into a fwoon or other ftate of involuntary ftupidity. If this fhould be the cafe, it would be nothing to the prefent purpofe. For the queftion before us is, whether volition be or be not in all cafes according to motive in the large fenfe of Prefident Edwards, including reafons, and external objects, with the tafte and bias of the mind. This is what is meant by a determination by motive. Let what will be the caufe of involuntary and torpid inaction ; fo long as it is granted, as Dr. Weft does grant, that motive is neceffary to volition, and that every volition, whether choice or refufal, is occafioned by motive, and never exifts without it, every thing is granted on this head, for which we contend.

Dr. Weft fays, " We cannot agree with Mr. Ed- " wards in his affertion, that motive is the *caufe* of voli- " tion;" p. 17. Mr. Edwards has very particularly informed us in what fenfe he ufes the word *caufe*. Thus,

p. 41 ;

p. 41 ; " I fometimes ufe the word caufe in this *In-*
" *quiry,* to fignify *any antecedent* either natural or mor-
" al, pofitive or negative, on which an event, either a
" thing or the manner and circumftance of a thing,
" fo depends, that it is the ground and reafon, either
" in whole or in part, why it is rather than not ; or
" why it is rather than otherwife. Or in other words,
" any antecedent with which a confequent event is
" fo connected, that it truly belongs to the reafon
" why the propofition, which affirms that event, is
" true ; whether it has any pofitive influence or not."
Now, does Dr. Weft deny, that motive is an antecedent, on which volition either in whole or part depends ? Or that it is a ground or reafon, either in
whole or part, either by pofitive influence or not,
why it is rather than not ? Surely he cannot with
confiftence deny this, fince he does fay, " By motive we " underftand the *occafion, reafon,* end or de-
" fign, which an agent has in view, when he acts ;"
and that motives are the *previous* " circumftances,
" which are *neceffary* for action ?" Surely a previous
circumftance, which is neceffary for action or volition, is an " antecedent on which volition depends ;"
and " a reafon which an agent has in view, when he
" acts," and " a reafon which is the occafion of his
" acting," " is a reafon either in whole or part, why
" the action is." So that however defirous Dr. Weft
may be, to be thought to differ, in this point, from
Prefident Edwards, it appears, that he moft exactly
agrees with him. Yet he fays, p. 11, " Mr. Edwards,
" by making motives the *caufe* of acts of the will, and
" by declaring, that the exiftence of the acts of the
" will is the effect of their motives, appears full as un-
" intelligible *to me,* as Chubb could poffibly appear
" to him." But as it appears, that Prefident Edwards
has explained himfelf to mean by *caufe* no other than
occafion, reafon or *previous circumftance neceffary for
volition ;* and that in this Dr. Weft entirely agrees
with him ; if Prefident Edwards appear abfurd to

E   Dr.

Dr. Weſt, Dr. Weſt muſt appear abſurd to himſelf, even as abſurd as Chubb could poſſibly appear to Preſident Edwards.

I do not pretend, that motives are the *efficient* cauſes of volition. If any expreſſion importing this, have dropped from any defender of the connection between motive and volition ; either it muſt have happened through inadvertence, or he muſt have meant, that motive is an *efficient cauſe* in no other ſenſe than rain and the rays of the ſun are the efficient cauſe of the growth of vegetables, or than medicine is the efficient cauſe of health.

When we aſſert, that volition is determined by motive, we mean not that motive is the efficient cauſe of it ; but we mean, that there is a ſtated connection between volition and motive, ſo that as Dr. Weſt ſays, " Whenever the mind acts or chooſes, it ALWAYS has " ſome reaſon" or motive, " which is the *occaſion* of " its acting or chooſing," and " is a previous circum- " ſtance neceſſary for action" or volition. This a- mounts to all we mean by an infallible connection be- tween motive and volition ; and therefore though Dr. Weſt denies ſuch a connection, he in fact holds it, as much as we do. By infallible connection be- tween motive and volition, we mean, that volition never takes place without ſome motive, reaſon or cauſe of its exiſtence, either in the views of the mind of him, who is the ſubject of the volition, in the diſ- poſition, bias or appetite of his mind or body, or from the influence of ſome extrinſic agent. In a ſenſe large enough to comprehend all theſe Preſident Edwards explains himſelf to uſe the word *motive*. His words are, " By motive I mean the whole of that which " moves, excites or invites the mind to volition, " whether that be one thing ſingly, or many things con- " junctly ;" p. 5. He then proceeds to enumerate ſev- eral things which operate as motives, viz. the *views* of the mind, the *ſtate, frame* and *temper*, &c. which the mind may have by nature, or which may have been

introduced

introduced by education, example, custom or *other means*.

Dr. Weſt grants an infallible connection between motive and volition ;——1. In that he grants, that motive is *neceſſary* to volition ;——2. In that he grants, that " there is *always* a *reaſon* for the mind's acting or chooſing, and that " when the mind acts, it " always has ſome end, deſign or *reaſon*, which is the " *occaſion* of its acting ; and in that he defines *motive* to " be the *occaſion, reaſon*, end or deſign, which an agent " has in view, when he acts." In theſe conceſſions not only does he expreſsly grant, that whenever there is a volition there is a motive ; but he implicitly grants alſo, that whenever there is a motive there is a volition. He expreſsly grants, that motive is the reaſon of the mind's acting. But the reaſon of the mind's acting is infallibly connected with its acting : Otherwiſe it is not the reaſon of its acting. If either the mind ſhould act without the ſuppoſed reaſon ; or if when the ſuppoſed reaſon exiſts, the action does not follow ; this fact in either caſe ſhows plainly, that the ſuppoſed reaſon is not the real reaſon of the action.——Again, motive is conceded to be the *occaſion* of the mind's acting. But if the motive exiſt and the action do not follow ; it is plain, that the motive is not the *occaſion* of the action.——As motive is allowed to be the *reaſon* of the action of the mind, it is as abſurd, that the motive ſhould exiſt without the action, as that the reaſon of an action ſhould exiſt without the action ; indeed it is the ſame thing. Let what will be ſuppoſed to be the reaſon of an action, if that ſuppoſed reaſon exiſt, and the action do not follow, this proves, the ſuppoſed reaſon is falſely ſuppoſed to be the reaſon ; and that either ſomething elſe is the true reaſon, or that the action came into exiſtence without reaſon.——If then motive be, as Dr. Weſt grants, the occaſion and reaſon of action, it is as abſurd and contradictory to ſay, that there is not an infallible connection between action and motive, as that there

is

is not such a connection between a thing and its cause.

Dr. West argues, that motives cannot be univerfally the caufes of volition, as this would imply, that they are the caufe of the divine volitions : But that " motives cannot be the caufe of the divine volitions ; " for this would be to affert, that motives were the " caufe of the first caufe." Now the fame reafoning will equally confute Dr. West's fcheme of motives ; thus, Motives cannot be neceffary occafions of volitions, as this would imply, that they are the neceffary occafions of the divine volitions. But to affert this, would be to affe , that motives are the neceffary occafions of the first caufe.

As volition always implies and fuppofes a motive ; fo does a motive as evidently imply and infer a volition. For by the very terms, that is no motive to a man, which does not perfuade, move or excite him to volition. This is the fenfe in which Prefident Edwards ufes the word motive. It is not pretended by the moft zealous advocate for the influence of motives, that the fame objects and reafons will always alike influence a man, and in like manner *move or be motives* to him ; unlefs it be fuppofed, that the ftate of the mind and every thing relating to it, be the fame. The mind of man is from various caufes exceedingly changeable, and by no means at all times fufceptible of the fame impreffions from the fame intellectual views and from the fame biafes. The intellectual views may be the fame, and the biafes may be different ; and the biafes may be the fame and the intellectual views may be different. It will not be denied, that there is an infallible connection between caufe and effect : Yet this does not imply, that the fame effect always follows from the fame caufe, unlefs by the fame caufe be meant, all the fame things and circumftances, which related to the effect, or may have had influence to produce it. And with the like explanation

tion of the word motive, it is true, that the fame motive is always attended with the fame volition.

Since then wherever there is a volition, there is a
motive, and wherever there is a motive, or, which is
Dr/ Weft's explanation of motive, wherever there is
the reafon and occafion of volition, there is volition,
and alfo fince wherever there is the fame motive in
the fenfe juft now· explained, there is the fame volition ; what is wanting to fupport the propofition, that
there is an infallible connection between motive and
volition ? A connection juft as infallible as that between
caufe and effect ?

Since our volitions are thus entirely limited, bounded and determined *according to* motives ; wherein
confifts the impropriety of faying, that our volitions
are determined *by motives ?* We mean no more by
the latter expreffion, than we do by the former.

If all our volitions be in this fenfe determined by
motives, in what fenfe can it be pretended, that they
are felf-determined ; or that we determine and caufe
our own volitions ? And what will become of the
whole doctrine of felf-determination ? It will not be
pretended, that we caufe all the objects, with which
we are furrounded, and which prefent themfelves to
us as objects of choice ; nor that we caufe all our natural biafes, taftes and appetites, which are the fources
of fo many volitions.——If it fhould be faid, that we
determine our own motives, determine which motives
we will comply with and which we will reject ; ftill as
this very determination is the act of the will, a motive
is neceffary to that. Thus we fhall go round in a
circle ; motive, determining, or (in the language of
Dr. Weft) *being previoufly neceffary* to volition, and
volition being neceffary to motive.

It feems, that allowing what Dr. Weft does allow,
no man can hold felf-determination, in any other fenfe
than one of thefe two ; (1) That we ourfelves determine, as we ourfelves think, perceive, hear, tafte, &c.
which is no more than we all allow ; and to explain

E 3   felf-determination

felf-determination thus, is to explain it away and give
it up; and, as has been fhown, it is thus given up by
Dr. Weft.——(2) That we efficiently caufe our own
volitions, but invariably according to motives, reafons
or preeftablifhed antecedents. This cannot be confiftently avowed by Dr. Weft, both becaufe he maintains, that volition is no effect and has no caufe, therefore we cannot be the caufe of it; and becaufe to be
the efficient caufes of our own volitions implies, that
" felf acts on felf and produces volition;" which is exprefsly renounced by him.

Dr. Weft, to prove, that there is no infallible connection between motive and volition fays, p. 17, 18;
" Though it is true, that the mind never acts without
" fome reafon or defign in acting; yet there is no
" need of affigning a reafon for *not acting*." By *not
acting*, Dr. Weft means, as obferved before, either *refufing* and *voluntary neglect*, or *entire inaction*. If he
mean the former, it is a real act of the mind and by
his own conceffion therefore is not " without a reafon
" and defign." If he mean the latter, his argument is
juft as conclufive to difprove an infallible connection
between motive and volition, as the fame argument is
to difprove the connection between caufe and effect:
Thus, though it be true, that an effect never comes to
pafs without a caufe; yet there is no need of affigning a caufe for *no effect*. It is undoubtedly true, that
perfect nihility requires no caufe: But no man in his
fenfes would hence infer, that an effect requires no
caufe, or that there is not an infallible connection between caufe and effect. In like manner " there is no
" need of affigning a reafon" or motive for perfect inaction, which is pure nihility. But it cannot be hence
inferred, that there is no need of a motive for action,
or that there is not an infallible connection between
motive and action. Dr. Weft denies an infallible
connection between motive and action, and he endeavours to prove it by making it out that there is no
connection between motive and *inaction*: And what

is

is this to the purpofe? How does it hence follow, that there is not an infallible connection between motive and *action ?*

Dr. Weft puts the fuppofition, that at a gentleman's table he has the offer of tea, coffee or chocolate ; that they can all be had with equal eafe, and all appear equally eligible to his mind, and that he determines to take coffee. He then adds, p. 18, " I believe, that it is " impoffible in this and a multitude of fimilar inftances " to affign any accident or circumftance, which deter- " mines the mind to its choice among things, which ap- " pear equally fit and eligible. Confequently here is " an undeniable proof of the liberty for which we " contend. And this inftance will explain my idea, " that there is always a reafon for acting or choofing : " But that there is not always a reafon for not acting ; " and that things may appear eligible to us, and yet " not be chofen ; *e. g.* I accepted the coffee, becaufe I " wanted fome refrefhment. Coffee appeared to me " properly fuited to anfwer my defire. This was a fuffi- " cient reafon for my receiving coffee. The other two " appeared equally eligible. About them I exerted no " acts : But this being a *mere negation*, could require " no pofitive reafon."——On this I remark,

1. If it were ever fo true, that in choofing between things perfectly indifferent, (if any fuch there be) the mind acts without motive, how would this prove, that it acts without motive in any other cafe ? And the inftances of its choofing things perfectly indifferent are fo rare, that with refpect to the main object of this difpute, they feem hardly worth mentioning. The great object of this difpute is, to inveftigate that liber- ty which is neceffary to virtue and vice, praife and blame. Dr. Weft, if I underftand him, contends, that an exemption from an infallible connection between motive and volition is effential to that liberty. Or if I do not underftand him aright in this inftance, he is at liberty to make his choice, whether or not to main- tain, that an exemption from fuch connection be ef-

fential

fential to that liberty, without which we cannot prac-
tife virtue or vice. If he maintain, that this exemption is effential to that liberty, I afk, Do we exercife
virtue or vice in thofe inftances only, in which we
choofe one of things perfectly indifferent ; or does it
follow from the fuppofition, that we act without motive in thofe inftances, in which we do choofe one of
things perfectly indifferent, that we alfo act without
motive in other inftances ; viz. in choofing one of
things perfectly different, as virtue and vice, wifdom
and folly, our eternal happinefs and eternal mifery ?
If it be not true, that we exercife virtue or vice in
thofe inftances only in which we choofe one of things
perfectly indifferent ; nor that from the fuppofition,
that there are things perfectly indifferent, and that we
act without motive when we choofe one of fuch things,
it follows that we act without motive in other cafes
too ; what is the great advantage of a power of choofing without motive in fuch a rare cafe ? And is it
worth while to difpute about it ? If we exercife moral
agency in thofe inftances only, in which we choofe
one of things perfectly indifferent ; our moral agency
is confined to very narrow limits indeed, not extend-
ing to one of ten thoufand of our rational voluntary
actions, as, I prefume, our opponents themfelves will
grant. If we exercife moral agency in thofe inftances,
in which we choofe one of things entirely different,
either we are perfuaded and influenced by the difference and fo are governed by motive, and then the influence of motives is not inconfiftent with moral agency or with liberty ; or we choofe and act without any
regard to the difference of the propofed objects : But
this muft be proved, to obtain credit. If our opponents fuppofe that it follow from our acting without
motive, when (as they fay) we choofe one of things
indifferent, that alfo we act without motive, when
we choofe one of things not indifferent ; let them
fhow that it does follow. They have not as yet
done it.

2. In

2. In the paſſage quoted above, Dr. Weſt conſid‑
ers his choice of coffee, as a real act of his mind a‑
riſing from a reaſon or motive; but his neglect or re‑
fuſal of tea and chocolate as a mere *negation*, which
requires no reaſon or motive. But I appeal to every
candid reader, whether a voluntary refuſal of any ob‑
ject, be not as real an act of the mind, as a choice.
If ſo, in truth and according to Dr. Weſt's conceſſion,
it requires a reaſon and motive, as much as any other
act. I do not mean, that his refuſal of tea and cho‑
colate in the caſe put, is neceſſarily a diſtinct act from
his choice of coffee : It may be no more a diſtinct
act, than ſuppoſing coffee alone had been offered him,
and he had accepted it rather than nothing, his ac‑
ceptance of it and his refuſal of nothing had been two
entirely diſtinct acts. The truth is, that his choice
of coffee is one complex comparative act, implying a
preference of coffee to tea and chocolate. I am ſen‑
ſible, that Dr. Weſt holds, " that choice, when uſed
" about the determination of the mind reſpecting the
" things that appear to us equally eligible, does not
" include in it the idea of *preference* ;" p. 16. But what
elſe is meant by *preference*, than the chooſing of one
thing rather than another or in the neglect of that
other, when both are offered ? If Dr. Weſt mean by
preference any thing different from this, he ought in
all reaſon to inform us what it is. The reaſon which
the Doctor gives, to ſhow that a choice of one of two
equally eligible things, is not a preference is, that
" they are both conſidered as equally eligible :" P.
16 : *i. e.* they are, (if I may ſo ſay) equally *chooſable*
or equally worthy of choice. And if one cannot be
preferred, becauſe they are equally worthy of choice ;
let it be ſhown, that it is not equally impoſſible that
one of them ſhould be *choſen* when they are equally
worthy of choice. If the conſideration that they are
equally worthy of choice, preclude the poſſibility of
preference, why does it not equally preclude the poſ‑
bility of *election* or *choice* ?

Dr.

Dr. Weſt ſays, that his acceptance of coffee, as it was an act, required a reaſon; but about tea and chocolate he exerted no act; and this being a mere negation, could require no poſitive reaſon. Now if coffee or nothing had been offered him, and he had accepted the coffee, he might as well have ſaid, that his acceptance of coffee, as it was an act, required a reaſon; but about nothing he exerted no act; and this being a mere negation, could require no poſitive reaſon. The truth is, every act of choice is a comparative act, whether one or more things be offered to our choice. When only one thing is offered, the compariſon is between that and nothing. When one of ſeveral things is offered, the compariſon is between thoſe ſeveral things. And if we accept the one thing, which alone is offered, we no more refuſe or decline the alternative *nothing* or the abſence of that one thing, than when we accept one of ſeveral things we refuſe the reſt.

3. If when ſeveral things, which Dr. Weſt calls equally eligible, are offered, and a man chooſe one of them, it be true, that he exerts no act about the reſt; the ſame would hold, though the things were not equally eligible and the things refuſed were manifeſtly moſt eligible: And thus it would be moſt eaſy to account for an act of preference of a moſt inferiour object, to a moſt ſuperiour one. It is but ſaying, that about the laſt " I exerted no act: And this be-" ing a mere negation would require no poſitive reaſon." Thus ſuppoſe a guinea and a ſhilling be offered to a beggar: He takes the ſhilling, but leaves the guinea. May not the beggar account for his conduct in the ſame way that Dr. Weſt accounts for his, in taking the coffee in the neglect of the tea and the chocolate? He might ſay, " I accepted the ſhilling, becauſe I " wanted a little money: The ſhilling appeared prop-" erly ſuited to anſwer my deſire. The guinea ap-" peared equally" and much more " eligible: About " that I exerted no act. But this being a mere ne-
" gation,

gation, could require no pofitive reafon." But the queftion would ftill remain unanfwered, Why did not the beggar exert an act about the guinea, as well as about the fhilling, or even in preference to it ? Or, which comes to the fame, why did he exert an act about the fhilling in the neglect of the guinea ? Juft fo, why did Dr. Weft exert an act about coffee, in the neglect of tea and chocolate ? Whatever be the proper anfwer to the laft queftion, will doubtlefs as properly anfwer the former. Nor need Dr. Weft puzzle himfelf and his readers about things *equally eligible.* His principles are juft as applicable to any other things, and equally prove that there is no connection at all between motive and volition, as that there is not an infallible and univerfal connection.

4. Dr. Weft grants, that " when the mind choofes, " it always has fome *reafon,* which is the occafion of " its choofing." Therefore when he chofe coffee in the neglect of tea or chocolate, there was fome reafon for it. But I appeal to the reader, whether according to the Doctor's own ftatement of the cafe, there was any reafon why he fhould choofe coffee in the neglect of tea and chocolate, and whether there was not the very fame reafon why he fhould have chofen tea or chocolate in the neglect of coffee. He fays, they all appeared equally eligible to him. Therefore there was no reafon, according to him, why he fhould choofe one, to the neglect of the others.

In his fecond part as well as in his firft the Doctor grants, that " the mind never acts without fome rea- " fon for acting." P. 14, and 29. Yet he holds, that of things equally agreeable, it fometimes choofes one and leaves the reft. Now what is the reafon of its acting in this cafe ? It is not enough to affign a reafon why the mind fhould take *fome one* of feveral things propofed. As all thofe things are fuppofed to be equally eligible, a reafon ought to be given why it finally takes one particular one in the neglect of the reft. Unlefs this be done, no reafon is given
why

why it acts in this manner, in this cafe ; and therefore for ought that appears, it acts without reason, which is contrary to the Doctor's conceffion. Therefore let the Doctor either retract his conceffion, and hold that the mind fometimes acts without any reason ; or renounce the idea, that it fometimes chooses one of feveral things equally eligible, in the neglect of the reft.

The Doctor fays, p. 28, Part II, " When two ob-" jects are equally fit, if one is taken and the other " left ; the mind had a purpofe to anfwer." We fhould have been greatly gratified, if the Doctor had pointed out, what purpofe the mind had to anfwer in taking that one which it did take, and in leaving the reft by fuppofition equally fit to anfwer the fame purpofe, for which the one is taken. Until he does point out the purpofe, he muft excufe us in withholding our affent and denying his propofition.——The Doctor in this repeats what he had faid in his firft part, that " about that which is not taken the mind exercifes no act at all." To this I have already anfwered, that the mind does exercife an act about it, that the act of the mind is complex and comparative, having a refpect to more objects than one, becaufe more are fuppofed to be offered and brought into the view of the mind ; that the mind does as really exercife an act about the object left, as if it were ever fo inferiour or fuperiour to the one taken ; and that the Doctor's reafoning, if it prove any thing, proves too much, viz. that if things ever fo unequal be offered and the mind choofe the bafeft and that which is in the loweft degree fuited to anfwer its purpofe, it may be ftill faid to have a reafon for the action. " But about the other, which is " not taken, the mind exercifes no act at all —— no " reafon can be affigned for the nonexiftence of that " which is not."

However, perhaps the Doctor will avow this laft obfervation, though he has not exprefsly done it as yet : For he " denies, that men are always governed " by the ftrongeft motive." P. 6, Part II. To

avoid

avoid all difpute about words, let it be remembered, that by being *governed* by the ftrongeft motive, is meant no more than that the mind always *follows*, or *coincides with* the ftrongeft motive : And by *ftrongeft* motive Prefident Edwards has explained himfelf to mean, " that which has the greateft degree of previous " tendency to excite choice ;" p. 6. Or it is the moft *perfuafive* motive. Now will Dr. Weft fay, that when feveral motives are propofed to a man, he fometimes paffes by the moft perfuafive, and follows the leaft perfuafive ? If fo, what is the reafon and what is the motive of its action in this cafe ? He allows, that there is a reafon and a motive for every action : Let him point out the reafon and the motive in this action.

The Doctor, p. 31, Part II, fays, " If the mind " never acts without fome motive or reafon for acting, " then it follows, that the motives or reafons for a vir- " tuous conduct, and the reafons and arguments againft " the practice of iniquity, ought to be fet before us in " the *ftrongeft* light, to *enable* us to choofe virtue and " to avoid vice."———1. Are we then unable to choofe virtue and to avoid vice, unlefs the motives to the former and againft the latter, " be fet before us in the *ftrongeft* light ?" It feems then, that unlefs thofe mo- tives be *thus* fet before us, we are under no obliga- tion to choofe virtue and to avoid vice, becaufe we are not *able* to do it : For it is no part of Dr. Weft's fyftem, that our duty extends beyond our *ability*. He denies the diftinction between natural and moral ne- ceffity and inability, and holds, that where neceffity or inability begins, liberty and moral agency end. Part II, p. 19.———2. Of what advantage can it be " to fet the motives to virtue and againft vice in the " *ftrongeft* light," if there be no connection between the *ftrongeft motives*, and volition ? Surely none at all. It is therefore implied in the paffage juft quoted, as in many other paffages in Dr. Weft's book, that there is a connection between fuch motives and volition, and that fuch connection is not inconfiftent with liberty.

ty. Yet as the Doctor " denies, that we are always
" governed by the *strongest motives*," he must hold,
that there is no *sure* connection between the strongest
motive and volition. Then the question arises, What
degree of connection between the strongest motive
and volition does he grant to exist and to be consistent with liberty ? If the highest degree of probability,
reaching to the step next to certainty, be allowed in
the case, what should render the only remaining step
so baleful to liberty, as to be inconsistent with it ? Or
if it be allowed, that the probability, according to
the degree of it, does indeed diminish liberty ; then
it diminishes moral agency too ; and therefore such a
representation of the motives to virtue, as " sets them
" in the strongest light," and makes it more or less
probable, that they will influence to a certain conduct,
has in reality no tendency to persuade to a *virtuous*
conduct ; because just so far as it has a tendency to lead
to any particular conduct, it destroys moral agency and
precludes the possibility of *virtue*. And such a representation is so far from " enabling us to choose vir-
" tue," that so far as it has any effect on us, it renders it impossible that we should choose it *morally ;*
and any other than a *moral* choice of virtue, if other
there be, is no subject of exhortation.

The Doctor asserts, " that there is not an infallible
" connection between motives and volition ;" p. 80,
Part II. And in the same page, " That the infalli-
" ble connection between motives and volition can-
" not take place, till the mind has determined to ex-
" amine the several motives or reasons for acting in
" any particular manner, in order that it may adopt
" the best. In that case the mind will *certainly* choose
" *that which appears the best.*" Indeed ! This is coming down wonderfully : This is acknowledging an infallible connection between motive and volition in all
cases, in which the mind *examines the several motives
or reasons for acting :* It is also acknowledging, that
in every such case the mind is governed by the *strong-*

est

eſt motive, as " it *will certainly* chooſe that which *ap-*
" *pears to be the beſt.*" Of courſe there is an infallible connection between motives and volition in all
caſes, except thoſe in which the mind acts abruptly
and without due conſideration. And is it indeed
true, that when the mind acts abruptly, it does not
chooſe that which *appears* to be beſt, but that which
at the time appears to be worſt, or at leaſt leſs good
and eligible, than ſomething elſe, at the ſame time in
view of the mind ? When men act abruptly and without due conſideration, no wonder if they be miſled
by mere appearance, which is not always well founded. But do they in ſuch a caſe, act without regard
to any appearance well or ill founded, and even contrary to the greateſt appearance of good ? That this is
generally fact, needs to be confirmed by ſomething
ſtronger, than mere aſſertion or implication.

Dr. Weſt, throughout his books in general oppoſes
the infallible connection between motive and volition,
as inconſiſtent with liberty and moral agency : But in
the paſſage on which I am now remarking, grants
ſuch a connection whenever " the mind" acts with
proper deliberation, and " examines the ſeveral mo-
" tives and reaſons for acting in a particular manner."
It ſeems then, that on Dr. Weſt's plan, whenever the
mind acts with proper deliberation, it is under ſuch
an infallible neceſſity of ſo acting, as is inconſiſtent
with liberty and moral agency, and conſequently muſt
be deſtitute of liberty and moral agency ; and that it
poſſeſſes liberty and moral agency then only, when it
acts abruptly and without proper deliberation. Will
the Doctor avow this conſequence ? Or if he ſhould
ſay, that although when " the mind has examined the
" motives and reaſons, it will *certainly* chooſe that
" which appears to be the beſt," and there is an infallible connection in the caſe ; yet that connection is not
inconſiſtent with liberty and moral agency ; why does
he diſpute againſt that connection at all ? If it do not
infringe

infringe liberty and moral agency, why is it fo violently oppofed ?

The Doctor, in p. 85, Part II, quotes thefe lines
from Prefident Edwards ; " I fuppofe none will de-
" ny, that it is poffible for motives to be fet before the
" mind fo powerful ———— as to be invincible ;" and
then he remarks on them, " If he means, that *argu-*
" *ments* may be placed before the underftanding in fo
" ftrong a light, as to become invincible, and fuch as
" the mind cannot but yield to, it is readily granted,
" and is nothing to the purpofe : For the underftand-
" ing is not the active, but the perceptive faculty of
" the mind ; and liberty is placed in the will, which
" is the only active faculty of the mind. But if the
" meaning is, that motives may be fo ftrong, as *necef-*
" *farily to determine the will*, this is denied to be pof-
" fible, while the mind has the free exercife of *reafon*.
" But when the mind is fo violently agitated, as to
" lofe the free exercife of reafon, as in the cafe of
" running in a fright ———— liberty is deftroyed.————
" Things that are not eligible in themfelves nor in
" their confequences, cannot become objects of choice ;
" which is to fay, there can be no motive to choofe
" them, though we may find it difficult, and in fome
" cafes impracticable to bring our propenfities to fub-
" mit to our choice. When one is convinced, that
" he has contracted a wrong habit, he finds no diffi-
" culty in *choofing* to overcome that habit ; but
" he will have a vaft deal of difficulty in his en-
" deavours to overcome it, becaufe in every unguard-
" ed hour, he will be liable to be led aftray by his evil
" habit. And therefore fuch a perfon may fay with
" the Apoftle, *To will is prefent with me, but how to*
" *perform that which is good, I find not ; for the good*
" *that I would, I do not ; but the evil that I would not,*
" *that I do.* Here we fee, that we may have a power
" to choofe, when we find it extremely difficult and
" in fome cafes impoffible to do the things which we
                                                " have

" have chofen. This fhows the *abfolute neceffity* of
" divine grace to *ftrengthen* us to do our duty."

On this remarkable paffage, I beg leave to obferve,

1. That Dr. Weft, according to his own principles,
cannot confiftently maintain, that " when the mind
" lofes the free exercife of *reafon* its *liberty* is deftroy-
" ed." For *reafon* belongs to " the underftanding,
" the perceptive faculty," and not " to the will, the
" only active faculty ;" but " liberty is placed in the
" will." Therefore according to him liberty is not
affected by what takes place in the underftanding, as
the free exercife of *reafon* does. On this ground it is,
that he pleads, that thofe arguments which are invincible to the underftanding, are nothing to the purpofe
as to the queftion concerning liberty, which is placed
in the will. The ground of the argument manifeftly
is, that there is no certain connection between the underftanding and the will ; and therefore that which
overbears the underftanding, does not at all, on that
account, affect the will. Therefore that fear, which
overbears reafon, does not on that account affect the
will or liberty. Otherwife if that fear which overbears
reafon and the right exercife of the underftanding, do
on that account affect and deftroy liberty ; why do
not thofe arguments, which are invincible to the underftanding and overbear it, alfo affect and deftroy
liberty ; which is denied by Dr. Weft.

2. In this paffage, Dr. Weft, however inconfiftently
with himfelf, holds, that motives neceffarily determine
the will. In the firft place he declares, that it is impoffible, that motives fhould be fo ftrong as neceffarily to determine the will, while reafon remains. Yet
in the fame paffage he afferts, that " when once we
" are convinced, that things are for our greateft good,
" we can eafily choofe them," and " things that are
" not eligible in themfelves nor in their confequences,"
and of courfe things that we do not " *perceive*" to be
in either of thefe refpects eligible, " cannot become
" objects of choice." In p. 93, Part II, the Doctor

F   fays,

fays, " The object, *motive* or *reafon* for acting muft be
" prior to the action of the mind and *perceived* by it,
" before it can act." " Nothing *can* become an ob-
" ject, except it appears to be eligible." Ibid, p. 95.
" There *muft appear* fome fitnefs or pleafingnefs to the
" mind, antecedent to its choice." Ibid. Nothing then
can be an object of choice or be chofen, which is not
and does not *appear* to be *eligible, fit* and *pleafing*. Now
all objects of choice are of two kinds, pofitive or negative, the poffeffion or abfence of the things propofed
for choice. And things which do not on the whole
appear to be eligible, cannot be chofen ; then the abfence of them being propofed for choice, is of courfe
chofen, and muft be chofen, becaufe it muft appear
eligible. The poffeffion and the want, the prefence
and the abfence, of the fame things cannot, upon the
whole, be at the fame time eligible : This would imply a contradiction.——To refufe an object is to
choofe the abfence or want of it. Therefore to refufe
thofe things which appear to be eligible is impoffible :
Of courfe fuch things muft be chofen ; there is a neceffity of it, otherwife that would be chofen, which
does not appear to be eligible, which Dr. Weft declares to be impoffible.

The fame thing may be more briefly and perhaps
more clearly expreffed thus ; Dr. Weft grants that
nothing can be chofen which does not appear to be
eligible. Therefore the abfence of that which appears
eligible cannot be chofen, becaufe that cannot on the
whole appear eligible while the prefence and poffeffion of the object appears eligible : And as the abfence of the object cannot be chofen, or, which is the
fame thing, the object cannot be refufed ; of confequence it muft be chofen ; and fo there is an infallible connection between motive and volition, and motives neceffarily determine the will.

If to this it fhould be anfwered, that though thofe
things, which are not feen to be eligible, cannot become objects of choice, and therefore we cannot refufe

or choose the absence of those things which we perceive
to be eligible ; yet we may not act at all with respect to
them ; and may neither choose nor refuse them ; I
reply, as I have said before, that is an impossibility ;
there is no medium with respect to any thing offered
as an object of choice, between choosing and refusing ;
neither to choose nor refuse in such a case is to be block-
ishly insensible. Or if it be said, that we only consider
and deliberate on the offer ; still we *choose* to deliberate.

3. According to this passage, a man can never
choose vice or sin. For surely they are neither eligible in themselves, nor in their consequences, and
therefore according to this passage, " cannot become
" objects of choice," *i. e.* cannot be chosen. But will
Dr. West abide by this ? Or if to avoid this consequence, the Dr. should say, that his meaning is, that a
thing which is not *seen* or *veiwed*, as eligible in either
of those respects, cannot be chosen ; I answer, this
implies, that the will in all its acts complies with the
dictates of the understanding, and is necessarily determined by motive, as I have just now endeavoured to
illustrate ; nor, as I can conceive, is there any way to
avoid this consequence, but by recurring to what is
denied to be possible, a supposed power of the mind,
to act or not act at all, and to be perfectly torpid, in
view of whatever motives. To take this for granted
is a prostrate begging of the question.

5. As this passage holds forth, that the human mind
always acts upon motive and cannot act without it,
and therefore as is illustrated in a preceding paragraph,
is always determined by motive ; so it follows, that it
is always determined by the *strongest* motive, that
which appears the most eligible, or has the greatest
previous tendency to induce volition. Surely there
can be no motive or reason to act on a weaker motive in preference to a stronger : This can never appear
eligible ; and Dr. West holds, that the mind never
acts without some reason or motive ; without the appearance of something as eligible.

F 2   6. As

6. As the will is the only active faculty, and the feat of liberty and moral agency, fo there is no morality in any other faculty, actions or impreffions, than thofe of the will ; and Dr. Weft fuppofes in this very paffage, as well as elfewhere, that our propenfities and habits do not belong to will. Therefore, provided we *choofe* things, which are for our greateft good, it is of no confequence, as to morality, whether or not " we find it difficult and impracticable to bring our " propenfities to fubmit to our choice ;" of no more confequence, than whether we can bring our underftandings to be as acute and comprehenfive, as we may choofe. And though we have contracted a wrong habit, if we " choofe to overcome it," it is of no more confequence in a moral view, that we find " a vaft " deal of difficulty in our endeavours to overcome " it ;" or that we are " liable to be feduced and led " aftray by it;" than that we find a vaft deal of difficulty in our endeavours to overcome our ignorance of aftronomy, and then that we are liable to be led aftray by falfe guides and falfe witneffes. For fo long as our will and choice are right, all in which there is liberty and moral agency, is right, and fo long we cannot poffibly be led aftray from our duty. And if our wrong propenfities and habits, under thefe circumftances be not fubdued, it will imply no fault in us, provided, as is fuppofed by Dr. Weft, thofe propenfities and habits confift not in the active or moral faculty or depend not on it : For on this fuppofition they are not of a moral nature and imply nothing morally wrong.

7. Nor is it true, as Dr. Weft here afferts, that though we eafily choofe that which is good, we ftand " in *abfolute neceffity* of divine grace, to ftrengthen us " to our duty." So far as we choofe that which is good, our wills are right, and our moral part is right. So far therefore we actually do our duty, and have no neceffity of divine grace to ftrengthen us, to do that which we have done already. Does the Doctor fuppofe,

pofe, that our duty calls us beyond our ſtrength ? And
that it obliges us to act againſt *abſolute neceſſity*. ?

8. Nor if we were to be aſſiſted by divine power to
perform any thing beyond the reach of our moral faculties, would there be any *grace* in ſuch aſſiſtance.   It
is *grace* to enable a man to perform his duty ; but
it is no grace, to enable him to perform that which is
not his duty ; *e. g.* to fly to the moon.

The Doctor ſuppoſes, that Preſident Edwards held,
that there is always *a reaſon for not acting*.   No doubt
there is always a reaſon for the mind's refuſing an object offered.   But Preſident Edwards never held, that
the mind ever ſinks itſelf into perfect inaction and
torpor ; and of courſe he did not hold, that there is a
reaſon for this.

The Doctor inſiſts, that " The mind determines *up-*
" *on* motives, and is not properly determined *by* mo-
" tives ;" p. 87. This ſeems to be a mere diſpute about
words.   The Doctor might as well have ſaid, that vegetables grow *upon*, or *in conſequence* of the rain, and
not *by* the rain.   And would it be worth while to diſpute that matter with him ?

" Strange ſo much difference there ſhould be
" 'Twixt *tweedle-dum* and *tweedle-dee*."

It is conſidered by the compilers of the *Encyclopæ-
dia* lately printed at Philadelphia, as an invincible argument againſt the infallible connection between motive and volition, that if equal motives were ſet before
a man to travel an eaſtern road and to travel a ſouth-
ern road, he would, on the ſuppoſition of ſuch a connection, travel in a diagonal line, to the ſoutheaſt.
But this is contrary to fact and experience.   Therefore they conclude, there is no ſure connection between motive and action.   They might juſt as conclu-
ſively have proved, that there is no infallible connection between evidence and the opinions of men.
Thus, on the ſuppoſition that the arguments, that the
world was created in the ſpring and that it was created in autumn, balance each other, the concluſion

F 3   muſt

muſt be, that it was created in neither of thoſe ſeaſons, but midway between them. If the arguments, that Dr. Weſt wrote the Eſſays on liberty and neceſſity, and that ſome other perſon wrote them, ſhould be equal ; we ought to believe that neither of them wrote them ; but a middle man between them.

Dr. Weſt, in his ſecond part, inſiſts more largely on the ſubjeɛt of chooſing between things equally eligible, than in his firſt part ; and puts the caſe of four equal lines, one of which is to be touched ; and he ſuppoſes that he determines to touch one of them, and this determination he ſuppoſes to be without motive and without extrinſic cauſe. Now in any ſuch caſe there appears to be no more difficulty in accounting for my determination to take or chooſe one in particular, than there is in accounting for my ſeeing or thinking of one in particular. Though our thoughts roam freely and apparently without control, yet Dr. Weſt will not pretend, that they happen by mere chance and without a cauſe. Juſt ſo as to our volitions ; they no more happen in any caſe without a cauſe, than any other events. Nor can the mind itſelf, in which they take place, be the efficient cauſe of them, without running into an infinite ſeries of volitions, and implying volition before the firſt volition.——— Therefore let the Doɛtor bring as many inſtances as he pleaſes, of things apparently indifferent, ſo long as choice among them has a cauſe, and a cauſe extrinſic to the mind too ; they make nothing to his purpoſe. I aſk Dr. Weſt, Is his determination to touch one of his equal lines, which he calls C, an uncauſed event ? He will not pretend it. Is it efficiently cauſed by the mind itſelf, in any other ſenſe, than as the mind is the ſubjeɛt of it, or as it is the cauſe of all its own thoughts and feelings ? To anſwer in the affirmative, and not to clear the anſwer of the abſurdities and impoſſibility charged upon it, is mere dogmatizing.———To all inſtances, in which creatures are ſuppoſed to chooſe one of ſeveral indifferent things, my my anfwer is, that though we cannot point out the particular motive or accident, which is the occafion of the choice of that particular one ; ftill this choice has a caufe, and a caufe extrinfic to the mind too, and it is as eafy to account for our choofing one of feveral indifferent things, as to account for our thinking of one of them in particular.

But perhaps the Doctor meant to evade this, by faying, that in the very act of determining to touch one of his equal lines, viz. C, he " voluntarily called it to mind." What does the Doctor mean by this ? That he firft wifhed to think of C, and that in confequence of this wifh, it came to his mind ? If he did mean this, it is to be prefumed, that he will not undertake to defend it. And as I can imagine no other meaning of " voluntarily calling C to mind," I muft be excufed from further anfwer until I am better informed. If the Doctor mean, that he wifhed to think of one of his lines, and then C came to his mind ; the queftion returns, What made C come to his mind ?

But the Doctor argues, that the *Creator* has a felf-determining power, and that he does or may exert that power in creating two or more perfectly fimilar bodies and in placing them in different fituations, or in caufing one of them to move, while the other is at reft, &c. As to all fuch cafes I obferve,

1. That every determination of God is as eternal, as unchangeable and neceffary, as his exiftence is, and therefore none of his acts are any more felf-determined, than his exiftence. To fuppofe otherwife is to fuppofe that the Deity is mutable. If therefore he have determined to create ever fo many bodies perfectly alike, and to difpofe of them in different circumftances, this is no proof of felf-determination in the Deity, if by that term be meant any thing oppofite to the moft abfolute and irreverfible moral neceffity : I fay *moral* neceffity, becaufe all neceffity of moral acts, is moral neceffity.

F 4

2. If

2. If God have created two bodies perfectly alike, and placed them in different fituations ; it will not follow, that he has done it without wife defign and motive.

3. But why did he not place them in a reverfe of fituations, that which is on the right hand, on the left, and that which is on the left hand, on the right ? And fo with refpect to reft and motion.——The anfwer has been long fince given by Prefident Edwards ; Thefe bodies, though faid to be numerically different, are no more different than the fame found repeated at different times. Thefe founds are as numerically different as the bodies, and with the fame reafon it may be afked, why was not the firft found made laft and the laft firft ? Or why were not thefe numerically different founds interchanged ? The abfurdity of putting this queftion mutt appear to every one, becaufe it implies, contrary to the very fuppofition, that the founds are different in fome other refpect than time. So the queftion, why the two perfectly alike bodies were not interchanged in their fituation, implies, contrary to the fuppofition, that thofe bodies differ in fome other refpect befide their fituation.

The Doctor fuggefts feveral confiderations to fhow, that thefe bodies do differ in fome other refpect befide their fituation ; as that one of 'them may be in motion, the other at reit. And what is motion but a change of fituation ? So the fame found may move from one place to another ; yet no body would conclude from that merely, that it was a different found from a perfectly fimilar found, i. e. different from a repetition of the fame found in a different place or at a different time.——Alfo the Doctor infifts, that thofe fimilar bodies are *numerically* different ; that is, they differ in number, fo that you may number them, and if you pleafe, may call that on the right hand No. 1 cr A, and that on the left hand No. 2 or B. And in the fame manner you may number the founds ; and you may as well afk why found No. 2, was not

made

made firſt, as why No. 2 of the bodies was not placed on the left hand. If two bodies be different numerically only, they differ in no other refpeẞ, than in fituation ; for if they did not differ in fituation, they would become one body.

The Doẞor proceeds, p. 15, " That they [the " bodies] are numerically different from each other, " appears from this confideration, that if the globe A, " on the right hand, fhould he removed to a far dif- " tant place, the Deity could create another juſt like " it, and put it in the fame place from which A was " removed." So if found A fhould be removed from the place in which it was firſt made to a far dif- tant place, the Deity could caufe another found juſt like it, in the fame place, from which A had been re- moved.――P. 16. " It is evident, that thefe two " globes are really two, as though they were ever " fo diffimilar." This is no more evident, than that the two founds are as really two, as though they had been ever fo diffimilar.――Ibid. " And they were " made to anfwer different purpofes ; and yet being " perfeẞly fimilar, A could have anfwered the pur- " pofes of B and B of A." So the found A may have been made to relieve Saul troubled by an evil fpirit ; and the found B may have been made to anfwer the purpofe of the temple worfhip. Yet being perfeẞly fimilar and indeed no more than the repetition of the fame found, A could have anfwer- ed the purpofe of B, and B of A.

Dr. Weſt fays, that Prefident Edwards, in fuppof- ing that two globes perfeẞly alike, are the fame in every refpeẞ except their fituation, has confounded fimilar- ity with identity ; p. 16, Part II. Prefident Edwards does indeed fuppofe, that two globes perfeẞly alike in all refpeẞs except their fituation, are the fame in all refpeẞs except their fituation ; and if they could be alike in their fituation too, as they then would be in the fame place, no doubt Dr. Weſt will grant, that in that cafe they would become one and the fame globe :

globe : If not let him point out in what refpeæ they would not be the fame.

The Doætor dwells long on the cafe of the two globes, and yet every thing that he fays to make out, that they are two in any refpeæ befide place, may be faid to make out, that perfeæly fimilar founds given in different times or places, are not the fame found repeated. What he fays, p. 16, may be applied to the cafe of the founds thus ; " What fuperiour fitnefs has" the found A, to the found B, " that makes it neceffa- " ry, that it fhould be" given firft and be continued in one place ? " Or what fuperiour fitnefs has" the found B to the found A, " that makes it neceffary, " that it fhould be" given in the fecond place in point of time, and fhould be moved to another place in point of fituation ? " It is certain no reafon can be " affigned : For they being perfeæly fimilar, one " cannot in the nature of things be more fit than the " other. So then, here are two very different effeæs " of the divine power, without any poffible reafon" why found A fhould not be given in the fecond place and be moved, and found B, in the firft place and not be moved.

The Doætor conceives, p. 17, that the ideas advanced imply, " that one and the fame body may be " in two different places at the fame time." No doubt they do imply, that a body which is in all refpeæs one and the fame with another body, except fituation, may be in a different place from that other body at the fame time ; and may be the fubjeæ of effeæs different and contrary to thofe, of which that other body may at the fame time be the fubjeæ.

All that the Doætor fays on this fubjeæ, implies, that a body different from another numerically only, differs from it in fome other refpeæ befide fituation. But he will doubtlefs perceive, that this is an error, if he refleæ, that provided the diverfity of fituation were removed and they were at the fame time in the fame place, they would no longer be numerically different.

ent.——Yet Dr. Weſt ſays, p. 17, " If they differed
" only in place, then put A in the place of B, and it
" would become B ; and B, by changing with A,
" would become A ; which is not the caſe : For
" ſhould we ſee A and B change places, ſtill we ſhould
" call each by the ſame name we did before." If
you put A in the place of B, it would become B, in
the ſame and no other ſenſe, than if you make the
found A, in the place and time of the found B, it will
become B. If we ſhould ſee thoſe two bodies change
their places with each other, ſtill they would be all
the while in different places, as much ſo as two founds
would be, if we ſhould hear the found, which is now
in this apartment, gradually move to another place,
and the perfeɛtly ſimilar found, which is now made in
the adjoining apartment, gradually move into this
apartment. Thoſe founds being all the while thus
different in place, do not become in all reſpeɛts one
found ; the difference of place ſtill remains : And is
all the difference of the bodies ſuppoſed to be ſeen
to interchange places.——And if the globes ſhould
be annihilated and then be created anew, and that
which is now on the right hand ſhould be created on
the left, and *vice verſa ;* this would be as abſurd a
ſuppoſition, as to ſuppoſe, that if the two perfeɛtly
ſimilar founds now exiſting in this apartment and in
the adjoining apartment, ſhould ceaſe ; that which is
now in the adjoining apartment could be renewed in
this apartment, and that which now exiſts in this a-
partment could be renewed in the adjoining, in the
ſtead of the one which is now there. Every one
muſt ſee, that this implies, that the founds are different from each other, in ſome other reſpeɛt, than their
place ; which is contrary to the ſuppoſition.

The Doɛtor proceeds, ibid, " If one of the globes
" ſhould be daſhed in pieces, it would not in the leaſt
" affeɛt the other, but it would be as whole as it was
" before." So if one of the perfeɛtly ſimilar founds
made in different places, though at firſt entirely me-
lodious,

lodious, fhould become harfh and grate on the ear, it would not in the leaft affe&t the other. Yet Dr. Weft grants, that thefe before the alteration of one, are only the repetition of the fame found.

The Do&tor continues, " If the two globes were " one and the fame in every refpe&t, except their oc- " cupying two places at the fame time, then whatever " accident fhould take place with refpe&t to one, " would equally take place with refpe&t to the other : " That is, if A be dafhed in pieces, B muft fhare the " fame fate ; which we fee is not the cafe." This is faid without proof or reafon given for its fupport, and therefore a bare denial is a fufficient anfwer. If two founds in every other refpe&t one and the fame, fhould be made in two places, whatever accident fhould take place with refpe&t to one, might not in the leaft affe&t the other.

The fum of my anfwer concerning the two globes, is, That they are no more two, than two perfe&tly fim- ilar founds made in different places or times ; that the fuppofition of their being interchanged, is as ab- furd as the fuppofition, that the two founds fhould be interchanged ; that it implies, contrary to what is fup- pofed, that they are different from each other, in fome other refpe&t befide fituation ; and finally, that it is no more in the power of the Deity to interchange them, than to interchange the two founds.——If Dr. Weft fhould reply to this, as he often has done in other cafes, that " this is paft his power to conceive :" Be it fo ; what follows ? That therefore it cannot be true ? And is Dr. Weft's fkill to conceive the ftand- ard of truth ?

" To fay, that no two things can have equal de- " grees of eligibility and fitnefs in the divine mind, is " to confound the reafon of a&ting, with a&tion itfelf ; " and to make the Deity a mere paffive being, or a " mechanical medium of fate." Part II, p. 19.——
The Do&tor has not told how this confounds the rea- fon of a&ting with a&tion, and he muft not expe&t,

that

that all his readers will receive it upon his mere affertion. It is to be prefumed, that many of them will
ftill believe, that the divine mind always acts according to the dictates of wifdom, and on account of fuperiour fitnefs choofes whatever it does choofe, and
that this is not to confound the reafon of acting with
action, but to preferve them diftinct.——If for the
Deity to act always voluntarily according to the dictates of perfect wifdom, be what the Doctor means by
his being " a mere paffive being," we grant it ; but
we appeal to the reader, whether the Doctor be not
in this cafe guilty of a perverfion of language ; or at
leaft whether he be not guilty of begging the queftion, in fuppofing, that there is no action but that
which is felf-determinate ; as that is manifeftly fuppofed in the propofition now under confideration.——
As to " the mechanical medium of fate," the reader
will fay, whether it be not *mere rant,* unworthy of a
grave philofopher and divine.

Dr. Weft frequently fays, and every where takes
it for granted, that in the divine mind there may be
innumerable things, which differ in many refpects,
which yet may have equal degrees of eligibility and
fitnefs to anfwer God's particular purpofes ; and among
thefe innumerable things the Deity can choofe one
and not another, and, with refpect to any of them can
act or not act.——That things thus different may be
equally fit to anfwer the purpofes of God is not granted and ought not to have been afferted without proof
or inftance. It appears to be a mere conjecture ;
and if mere conjectures be admitted as truth, truth is
the moft uncertain thing in the world. Befides, it is
very improbable, that things differing in feveral refpects, fhould be equally adapted to the fame purpofe. As to the idea that God can in any cafe act or
not act, this appears to be an impoffibility, for the reafons already mentioned.

" If a man is led *by any means* or *motives* or *reafons,*
" to choofe that which he formerly abhorred," fays the
Doctor,

Doctor, " and to abhor that which he formerly loved,
" *he is still as free as ever he was ;* for nothing being
" an object of choice, but what appears eligible, it is
" impoſſible that the mind ſhould chooſe that which
" is neither eligible in itſelf, nor in its conſequences; *i. e.*
" nothing is an object of choice but eligible things.
" When then things appear to us eligible, which former-
" ly we abhorred, and we abhor things, that formerly
" were eligible, we have only changed the objects of
" our choice, but not our freedom : We are as free
" now, as we were before." Part II, p. 30. The
truth ſo naturally obtrudes itſelf on every man, that it
is difficult. for him conſiſtently to contradict it.* The
Doctor here grants, that when a man chooſes an object, by " whatever means, motives or reaſons he is
" led to the choice," " he is ſtill free." Therefore to
be led by motives in any caſe is not inconſiſtent with
freedom ; therefore to be led by them *always,* in an
eſtabliſhed and *infallible connection* between motives
and choice, is not inconſiſtent with freedom. Why
then does he diſpute Preſident Edwards for holding
ſuch a connection?-------Beſides, Dr. Weſt here grants,
that if a man be led *by any means* to chooſe an object,
ſtill he is *free.* Then he is free, when he is led to
chooſe an object, by *an extrinſic cauſe.* Nay, he is
free, when he is led by *a divine influence,* to chooſe
an object. It is further to be obſerved, that in this
paſſage, Dr. Weſt declares, that it is *impoſſible,* that
the mind ſhould chooſe any thing, which does *not appear to it eligible.* What then becomes of ſelf-determination ? Has the mind a power to make things appear agreeable or diſagreeable at pleaſure ; to control
all its own views, and to create its own happineſs in
any circumſtances whatever ? This indeed is the thor-
ough ſcheme of ſelf-determination advocated by Archbiſhop King, but which has been ſince given up,
though inconſiſtently, by Dr. Clarke, and ſo far as I
know, by all other believers in ſelf-determination ; and

to

* *Naturam expellas furca, tamen uſque recurret;* Hor. Ep. I, 10.

to be fure cannot be confiftently adopted by Dr. Weft for many reafons ; particularly this, that Dr. Weft holds that the will always follows motive ; but this fcheme is, that the will always goes before motive.

" Mr. Edwards and his followers," fays Dr. Weft, " fuppofe, that there muft be a particular reafon why " every determination of mind ———— is in this partic- " ular manner, rather than any other ———— which " will imply, that there can be no two objects in the " mind ———— equally eligible.———The contrary we " know to be true by our own experience." Part II, p. 14. How does Dr. Weft know what our own experience is ? He may indeed claim a right to know his own experience ; but I defy him to tell what my experience, or the experience of any other man, is, unlefs he have had information. Who then gave him a right to fpeak in the *plural* number in this cafe ? And whom does he mean, when he fpeaks of our ex- perience ? If he mean mankind in general, I call on him for proof, and wifh he had been a little more re- ferved in this inftance. Strong affertions are equally open to all ; and if they be good arguments, it is ea- fy to prove, that the experience of mankind is direct- ly the reverfe of what Dr. Weft afferts it to be.

As to the queftion, whether any two objects are, at the inftant of the choice of one of them, equally eligible in the view of the mind ; I anfwer it in the negative ; and in my own experience never found them to appear any more equally eligible, than any two objects, to be equally the objects of my fight or of the attention of my mind. And as to the various inftances of feveral eggs, guineas and fpots on a chefs board, one of which is propofed to be taken or touch- ed ; there is no more difficulty, as I have faid already, in affigning a reafon, why one of them rather than any other, is taken or touched, than why one rather than any other, is more particularly feen or attended to, by the eye or the mind. The circumftance, that one of them is more directly and particularly feen or

attended

attended to, is a fufficient reafon, why that rather than any of the reft fhould be taken or touched : And when this circumftance takes place with regard to any one of feveral guineas for inftance, they are not all, or do not appear, equally eligible. That which is the immediate object of fight or attention is, for that reafon, moft eligible : And how that came to be more particularly the object of fight or attention, I am under no more obligation to account, than Dr. Weft or any other man.

It is a fentiment entertained by fome, that we ef-ficiently caufe our own volitions, but invariably ac-cording to motives, reafons or preeftablifhed antece-dents. Dr. Clarke expreffes this in various parts of his metaphyfical works ; as in the following, " The " true, proper, immediate, phyfical caufe of action, is " the power of felf-motion in men, which exerts itfelf " *freely* in confequence of the laft judgment of the un-" derftanding. But the laft judgment of the underftand-" ing is not itfelf a phyfical efficient, but merely a *moral* " *motive upon which* the phyfical efficient, or motive pow-" er begins to act." *Being and Attributes*, p. 93. " The " experience of a man's ever doing what he judges rea-" fonable to do, is not at all an experience of his being " under any *neceffity* fo to do. For *concomitancy* in " this cafe is no evidence at all of phyfical connec-" tion. Upon fuppofition of *perfect liberty*, a reafon-" able being would *ftill conftantly* do what *appeared* " *reafonable* it fhould do : And its *conftantly* doing fo, " is no proof at all of its wanting liberty or a phyfical " power of doing otherwife." *Remarks on Collins*, p. 25.——Dr. Price entirely agrees in this fentiment with Dr. Clarke. " A felf-determining power, which " is *under no influence of motives* —— has never " been contended for or meant by any advocates for " liberty.——Every being who acts at all, muft act " for fome *end* and with fome *view*." *Correfpondence with Prieftly*, p. 156. " The *influence of motives* is " perfectly

" perfectly confiftent with liberty and indeed fuppofes
" it." *Reid on the Active Powers,* p. 275.

On thefe paffages I remark,

1. Dr. Clarke, as well as the other advocates for
felf-determination, abundantly contradicts thefe fentiments. Thus in his fecond letter to the gentleman at
Cambridge, fpeaking of the final perception of the
underflanding and firft operation of the active faculty,
he fays, " I think there is no connection at all be-
" tween them ; and that in their not being connected
" lies the difference between action and paffion, which
" difference is effential to liberty."——But if a man
" on the fuppofition of perfect liberty," " conftantly
" do what appears reafonable ;" then a man may in a
confiftence with perfect liberty conftantly act agreeably to the final perception of his underflanding ; *i. e.*
the final perception of the underflanding and action,
or " the operation of the active faculty," may be conftantly connected confiftently with liberty. And is
conftant connection, no connection at all ? And if in
their not being connected lies the effence of liberty,
the effence of liberty cannot be confiftent with their
conftant connection.

2. That Dr. Clarke places liberty in a *phyfical
power* to do an action. His words are, " A being's
" conftantly doing what appears reafonable it fhould
" do, is no proof of its wanting liberty or a phyfical
" power of doing otherwife." He evidently ufes *liberty* and *phyfical power,* as fynonymous expreffions. Many other paffages might be quoted from Dr. Clarke,
Dr. Price, and other principal authors of that clafs, in
which they exprefsly affert or evidently fuppofe, that
whoever has a *phyfical* power to do an action, is free :
and that the reafon why motives are not inconfiftent
with liberty, is, that they infer not a phyfical neceffity or inability. But this is no more than we all grant.
Peter had the fame phyfical or natural power to confefs his Lord, which he had to deny him ; and Judas,
the fame phyfical power to be faithful to him, as to

G   betray

betray him. Nor do the moſt abſolute decrees and predictions deſtroy this phyſical power. So that abſolute decrees and predictions are, on this plan, perfectly conſiſtent with liberty.

3. Theſe paſſages imply, that though the mind is the efficient cauſe of its own volitions ; yet this efficiency is limited to exert itſelf or to be exerted, according to motives and the dictates of the underſtanding. But this, on the plan of thoſe who deny that volition can be free and yet be the effect of an extrinſic cauſe, is no more liberty than the ſlave exerciſes, who moves and acts at the control of his maſter ; or than the man has, who walks in a priſon and whoſe liberty is bounded and determined by the walls and gates of the priſon, and by the conſent of the gaoler. We might as well ſay, that a ſlave is in poſſeſſion of his liberty and is not controlled by the will of his maſter, but controls himſelf according to the will of his maſter ; as that we are free with the liberty of ſelf-determination and contingence, and yet be always limited to determine ourſelves according to the influence of motives. If there be a real connection between motive and volition, that connection is as inconſiſtent with liberty as if motives were the efficient cauſes of volition ; provided liberty mean contingence or previous uncertainty of action : And if liberty mean ſelf-cauſation of volition, and this ſelf-cauſation be under the control of motives or any extrinſic cauſe, ſtill where is liberty in the ſenſe contended for by our opponents ? Volition in this caſe is equally limited and controlled, as if it were efficiently produced by motive.

Such ſelf-determination as this, is not at all inconſiſtent with efficacious grace, abſolute decrees, and the moſt firm preeſtabliſhment of all events and volitions. If ſelf-determination exert itſelf according to motives only, let God in his providence bring the proper motives into view, and we are efficaciouſly determined, or if you pleaſe, it is efficaciouſly brought to pafs, that we fhall determine ourfelves in a particular limited manner ; and let God decree abfolutely that thofe motives fhall come into view, and he abfolutely decrees and foreordains what our conduct fhall be. So that this kind of felf-determination does not at all anfwer the purpofe of avoiding the dreadful doctrine of abfolute decrees, the fatality implied in that doctrine, or other doctrines connected with it.

4. If a man caufe his own volitions according to motives only, and this be a univerfal rule ; doubtlefs this rule was eftablifhed by fome caufe. This rule is an eftablifhment ; this eftablifhment is an effect, and requires a caufe as much as any other effect. Who or what is that caufe ? It is doubtlefs either the Firft Caufe, or fome fubordinate caufe appointed by him. In either cafe the original caufe of this eftablifhment, by which intelligent creatures caufe their own volitions according to motives, is God. Alfo he in the courfe of his providence brings all thofe motives into our view, on which we act. And doubtlefs both this eftablifhment and the coming of the motives into our view were caufed by him, in confequence of a previous determination to caufe them. Therefore this fcheme of felf-determination not only is confiftent with abfolute decrees and the efficacious providence of God; but it neceffarily implies both thefe. It neceffarily implies, that God has decreed all our volitions and is either mediately or immediately the caufe of them all. Therefore it is inconfiftent, that thofe who efpoufe this fcheme of liberty and felf-determination according to motives, fhould oppofe the doctrines of God's abfolute decrees and efficacious grace.

5. Befide this, the common abfurdity of felf-determination equally attends this fcheme of determining ourfelves according to motives ; I mean the abfurdity of an infinite feries of volitions caufing one another. If all free volitions be caufed by the fubject, that volition in which a man complies with a motive, muft have been caufed by himfelf and by a preceding volition ;

lition ; and this laſt volition, for the ſame reaſon, muſt have been cauſed by one preceding that, and ſo on infinitely.

6. Nor is this all. The doctrine now under con-fideration is, that every volition is according to a mo-tive, and is under the perſuaſive influence of it. Therefore every one of that infinite ſeries of volitions muſt have been put forth in the view of ſome motive. So that here we have not only an infinite ſeries of vo-litions producing one another ; but an infinite ſeries of motives, according to which they do produce one another.

Dr. Reid holds, that " there are innumerable ac-" tions done by a cool and calm determination of the " mind, with fore-thought and will, but *without motive.*" *Active Powers*, p. 275. This is directly contrary to Dr. Weſt. He holds, as before quoted, " That the " infallible connection between motives and volition " cannot take place, till the mind has determined to " examine the ſeveral motives or reaſons for act-" ing——In that caſe the mind will certainly chooſe " that which appears the beſt ;" Part II, p. 80 ; *i. e.* will certainly act *with* motive.——It is equally con-trary to Dr. Reid himſelf. In the next page he grants, " that an action done without any motive can neither " have merit nor demerit ;" and ſays, that this is a ſelf-evident propoſition, and that he knows of no au-thor that ever denied it. Now an action in which there is neither merit nor demerit, is not a moral ac-tion. But is not every action done by a cool and calm determination of the mind, with fore-thought and will, a moral action ? If it be, ſince according to Dr. Reid, ſuch an action may be done without a motive, it follows, that, directly contrary to what Dr. Reid him-ſelf aſſerts, an action done without a motive, can have merit or demerit : Or a moral action may have no merit or demerit in it. Or if an action done by a cool and calm determination of mind, be not a moral action, then in this controverſy we have no more to do with it, than we have with the beating of the pulſe

or

or winking of the eyes : For this controverfy refpects moral actions only.——Again, in the page laft referred to, Dr. Reid tells us, " If a man could not act with-" out motive, he would have no power at all." But if we have a power to act without motive, this power, according to Dr. Reid, does not enable us to do thofe actions, which have either merit or demerit ; *i. e.* moral actions. Therefore for the purpofes of morality, of virtue and vice, reward and punifhment, fuch a power would do us no good. So that according to Dr. Reid, we have no power to perform any moral action. For according to him, power to act with motive only, is no power at all. Therefore whatever power we have, is a power to act without motive. But a power to act without motive, is a power to perform thofe actions only, which have neither merit nor demerit ; *i. e.* which are no moral actions.——Yet in p. 277, he fays, " The actions, which are done with-" out a motive, are of moment in the queftion con-" cerning *moral liberty*." By *moral* liberty I conclude, he means that liberty, in the exercife of which we act morally, or with merit or demerit. Therefore queftions concerning this liberty are queftions concerning *moral* actions. But how can thofe actions, which have no morality in them, be of moment in queftions concerning *moral* actions ? Can the periftaltic motion or the action of the folids on the fluids in the human conftitution, be of moment in a queftion concerning malice or envy ?

In the page laft quoted, Dr. Reid fays, " If we " have a power of acting without motive, that power " joined to a weaker motive, may counterbalance a " ftronger." What if it may ? The action or actions, which fhould be the refult in fuch a cafe, would not be of a moral nature. For if an action done entirely without motive be not of a moral nature, as Dr. Reid grants, that which is done againft the ftronger motive, being on the whole done without motive, muft alfo be not of a moral nature. As the weaker motive is

G 3

withftood

withstood and balanced by a part of the strength of the stronger, so far as a man acts against the excess of the strength of the stronger, he must act without motive. Therefore if a man be influenced by a regard to his duty, as with the force of 1, to preserve his temperance ; and be influenced by his appetite, as with the force of 2, to intemperance, and then by a self-determining power determine himself to temperance against the stronger motive ; there is according to Dr. Reid's own concession, no virtue and no morality in the determination. Who then would wish for such a power as this ? And why did Dr. Reid think it worth his while, to dispute for it ? Surely in disputing for it, he spent his time and strength in a very useless manner.

Though Dr. Reid holds, as just quoted, that " if a " man could not act without motive, he would have " no power at all ;" yet he holds, as has been quoted also, that " the influence of motives is perfectly con- " sistent with liberty and indeed supposes it." And he defines liberty, p. 251, to be " a power over the " determinations of the will." Therefore as " the in- " fluence of motives is perfectly consistent with *liber-* " *ty* and supposes it ;" and as " a power over the de- " terminations of the will" is liberty ; the influence of motives is perfectly consistent with " a power over the " determinations of the will :" And if a man could not act without motive, but always acted under the influence of it, he in the first place, " would have no power at all ;" in the second place, he would have some power ; viz. " a power over the determinations " of his own will," which according to him, is *liberty,* and not only is consistent, with the influence of motive, but is supposed in it.——But the defenders of the self-determining power are fated to inconsistency, and self-contradiction, and not one of them more so than this Dr. Reid.

He also holds, that in order to have any power at all, we must have a power to act without motive, and
therefore

therefore without the influence of motive. But the influence of motive is, according to his own confeffion, fuppofed in liberty. Therefore to have any power at all, we muft have a power to act without that which is fuppofed in liberty and therefore without liberty itfelf: And if we have that which is fuppofed in liberty, and of courfe have liberty itfelf, we have no power at all ; *i. e.* if we have a power over the determinations of our own will, which is liberty ; we have no power at all and have no liberty ; or if we have power and liberty, we have no power nor liberty.———— But it is endlefs to trace the abfurdities of the felf-determining power and of the moft acute writer that ever undertook the defence of it. It is indeed a burdenfome ftone, which like that of *Sifyphus*, will forever roll down on the heads of thofe who give it a place in their building.

If we have a power to act without motive, we have a power to act without end or defign ; and fuch an action is as totally without morality, as the blowing of the wind, or the motion of a cannon-ball : And a power to perform fuch an action, is not a power to perform any moral action, nor can fuch a power be called *moral* liberty ; but it is a power to diveft ourfelves, in that action at leaft, of all moral agency.

To choofe any thing without motive, is really a contradiction ; it is to choofe it and not choofe it, at the fame time. Whatever is chofen, is chofen as being agreeable in fome refpect or other ; and whatever is agreeable, is agreeable either in itfelf immediately or on account of its connection with fomething elfe and its fubferviency to it, which fomething is immediately agreeable in itfelf. Now whatever is agreeable on account of its connection with fomething elfe, is chofen on account of that fomething elfe, as the motive. Whatever is in itfelf agreeable to a man, is chofen from the motive of his appetite, tafte or bias, which is included in Prefident Edwards's fenfe of motive. And whatever is not agreeable to a man on one or

other

other of thefe accounts, is not agreeable at all, and therefore is not chofen.

To choofe an object without motive, is to choofe it without any end or defign, either of immediate or remote gratification of any principle in him, who makes the choice : And whether this be poffible or conceivable, I wifh every candid perfon to judge.

An act of choice without a motive, in the large fenfe of motive as defined by Prefident Edwards, is an event without a caufe : For every caufe of volition is included in Prefident Edwards's definition of motive. " By motive," fays he, " I mean the whole " of that which *moves*, excites or invites the mind to " volition, whether it be one thing fingly, or many " things conjunctly ;" p. 5. Accordingly in his further explanation of his idea of motive, he mentions all agreeable objects and views, all *reafons* and arguments, and all internal biafes and tempers, which have a tendency to volition ; *i. e.* every *caufe* or occafion of volition. And if an immediate divine influence or any other extrinfic influence, be the caufe of volition, it may be called a *motive* in the fame fenfe that a bias is. Now, if an act of choice be without motive in this fenfe, it is abfolutely without a caufe. The evafion of Doctor Clarke and others, that the mind itfelf is the caufe of its own volitions, has been already confidered ; befide other abfurdities, it has been found to lead to an infinite feries of volitions caufing one another : which is as great an abfurdity, as an infinite feries of men begetting one another.——Or if it were allowed, that a man does efficiently caufe his own volitions without motive : ftill he muft caufe them without defign or end, and therefore muft caufe them in the dark and by mere chance.

Archbifhop King in Law's edition, p. 394, fays, " The will cannot be determined to good by objects." Then all the good and evil in the univerfe cannot determine one act of the will. In p. 354, he fays, " The more free any one is and the lefs liable to ex-

" ternal

" ternal motions, the more perfect he is." Therefore
the lefs liable a man is to be influenced by the divine law and its precepts, by the beauty of virtue, by
right and wrong, by the divine glory, or by the rewards and punifhments of virtue and vice here or
hereafter ; the more perfect he is ! ! !

If motives have not influence on men they are not
capable of moral government. The whole of moral
government depends on influencing the fubject by
the motives of laws, precepts, penalties, rewards and
punifhments, &c.

However, the Archbifhop is perhaps the moft confiftent advocate for felf-determination, that has ever
written. Clarke, *paulum* Price and Reid grant too
much. They grant, though they do not hold to it
throughout, that the will always acts according to motives, and allow the influence of motives ; yet they
hold, that the will determines itfelf and caufes its own
acts ; which is juft like the idea of fome concerning
the power of the civil magiftrate, a power to govern
the people, who have the entire government of the
magiftrate. But Archbifhop King ftrikes a bold ftroke.
He holds, that there is " a faculty" in human nature
" naturally inclined to exercife, and that one exercife
" is more agreeable than another, not from any nat-
" ural fitnefs in one rather than another ; but from the
" application of the faculty itfelf : For another would
" often be no lefs agreeable, if it had *happened* to be
" determined to that." Ibid, p. 269. " It is the very
" nature of an *active* power, to make an object agree-
" able to itfelf, *i. e.* good, by its own proper act.
" For here the goodnefs of the object does not pre-
" cede the act of election, fo as to excite it, but elec-
" tion makes the goodnefs in the object ; that is, the
" thing is agreeable becaufe chofen, and not chofen
" becaufe agreeable. We cannot therefore juftly in-
" quire after any other caufe of election, than the
" power itfelf." Ibid, p. 279, 280. It feems then,
that it is the nature of a felf-determining power to
exercife

exercife itfelf, not in any particular manner, but in any manner and every poffible manner. It preffes like water in a ciftern on every fide alike, endeavouring to flow out in exercife. And whenever it does in faĉt flow out in any particular exercife, there was no caufe or reafon for this exercife, more than for any other poffible exercife : The only caufe or reafon is the natural inclination of this power to flow out in any and all poffible exercifes. This is juſt as good accounting for any particular exercife of this power as it would be, to account for the Archbiſhop's writing his book, by faying, that he had a general power and inclination to write fomething or other.

In this fcheme of Dr. King we. fee the genuine idea of *liberty of indifference :* It is an equal inclination, previoufly to eleĉtion, to all poffible eleĉtions and volitions, and a perfeĉt indifference to all conceivable objeĉts ; fo that no particular objeĉt or fituation is more fuited to give pleafure or mifery to a man, than another ; and pleafure and pain are the confequence and depend entirely on a man's own choice and will ; fo that it is entirely in a man's power and depends entirely on his own will, to render Nebuchadnezzar's furnace more pleafant, than a bed of down perfumed with rofes.

It is further obfervable, that according to this account of the felf-determining power, whenever it does exercife itfelf, it does it by *mere chance,* or as Dr. King himfelf expreffes it, it *happens* to be determined to that exercife. Thus we have the famous liberty of contingence or perfeĉt uncertainty, a liberty of blind fate or chance !

Our opponents hold, that the governing influence of motive is inconfiftent with liberty and moral agency ; then if a man be influenced by any motive to a compliance with the gofpel and its precepts, or by any temptation to the commiffion of any aĉtion commonly reputed ever fo criminal ; in reality there is no virtue in the former nor vice in the latter : Becaufe cauſe the influence of the motive deſtroys liberty and moral agency, the man is wrought upon by an extrinſic cauſe and therefore is a mere patient and not an agent. Therefore no man needs to be at all afraid of any temptation, nor according to this ſcheme ought *the Lord's Prayer* to remain any longer without correction : The light of this improved age requires a new edition of it *corrected* and *improved.*

If it be objected that motives do indeed have an influence to perſuade men, but not a *certain infallible* influence ; I anſwer, juſt ſo far as they have influence, their influence *is* certain and infallible, becauſe it is an influence that really exiſts. That which does exiſt, *certainly* exiſts, and it is an infallible truth, that it does exiſt.

Or if it be pleaded, that the mind is ſtill free, becauſe motives are not the efficient cauſes of volition ; I anſwer, that the ſame plea would prove, that a Weſt-India ſlave is free, becauſe his actions are not efficiently cauſed by his maſter or driver, and they only exhibit ſuch motives as influence the ſlave himſelf to perform thoſe actions : And the ſame plea will prove, that moral neceſſity is perfectly conſiſtent with liberty. For moral neceſſity is a mere previous certainty of a moral action ; and this is no more the efficient cauſe of the action, than the perſuaſive motive, which is the occaſion of an action.

I am entirely willing, that the advocates for the ſelf-determining power ſhould take their choice of either Dr. Clarke's ſcheme of *conſtant concomitancy* of motives and volitions ; or Archbiſhop King's ſcheme, that motives have no influence, and that previouſly to election all things are perfectly indifferent to the man who makes the election. If they chooſe to adopt the ſcheme of *conſtant concomitancy,* they at once allow an infallible connection between motives and volition ; they muſt give up the power to act or not act, the liberty to either ſide, and their favourite argument from chooſing one of ſeveral indifferent things ;
they

they muſt renounce the independence and ſovereign-
ty of the will, and allow that it is as really bounded,
limited and controlled by motives, as the ſlave is by
his driver, or as the will is by moral neceſſity; and
there is nothing of their boaſted liberty left worth
contending for, nothing but the pitiful power of man-
ufacturing volitions according to the mandates of motives; juſt as a Weſt-India negro manufactures ſug-
ar under the laſh of his driver.

Or if they chooſe Archbiſhop King's ſcheme; abſurdities no leſs glaring will follow. If all things before election be indifferent, then every election-is
made without motive, reaſon, end, deſign or any conſideration right or wrong; every act of choice is an
act of as perfect ſtupidity, as the motion of a canon
ball or the falling of a ſtone; every man by choice
or rejection makes any. object either agreeable or diſagreeable, good or bad, to himſelf; every man, in
every ſituation has the perfect control of his own happineſs and miſery; and it is but for him to chooſe to
lie on a gridiron, which he can as eaſily do, as chooſe
any thing elſe, and he converts it into a bed of
roſes.———This is ſelf-determination *to ſome purpoſe.*

Such exclamations as the following have been
made, in relation to this ſubject; " If man be gov-
" erned by motives, how is he free? Where is free-
" dom? What liberty has man more than a beaſt?
" All his actions are ſubject to a fatal chain of cauſes
" and effects?" But ſuch exclamations may juſtly be
retorted, on either of the forementioned hypotheſes of
determining our own volitions agreeably to motives,
or without motives. If we determine them agreeably to motives only; then we are limited to motives, we can go in one track only, we can act no otherwiſe than according to the dictates of ſovereign and
all controlling motives. Then " how is man free?
" Where is freedom? What liberty has man more
" than a beaſt? All his actions are ſubject to a fatal
" chain of motives."———Or if it be ſaid, that we determine

termine our own volitions without motives, end, defign or any confideration good or bad ; as in this cafe
we aɛ̃t with perfeɛ̃t ftupidity, it may with the greateſt
propriety be demanded, " How are we free ? Where is
" freedom ? What liberty has man more than a beaſt ?"

If there be, as Dr. Clarke, Dr. Price, &c. allow, a
conſtant concomitancy or conneɛ̃tion between motives
and volitions ; this conneɛ̃tion is an eſtablifhed law ;
as really fuch, as the conneɛ̃tion between a certain
temperature of the feafons and the growth of vegetables. Now of this eſtablifhment there is fome author :
It is an effeɛ̃t and has an efficient caufe. Nor will it
be pretended, that the mind, which is the fubjeɛ̃t of
the volitions, is the efficient caufe of this eſtablifhment. This befide other difficulties attending it,
would imply a direɛ̃t contradiɛ̃tion ; as it is now
granted, that the mind aɛ̃ts invariably according to
motives ; and yet in eſtablifhing the influence of motives, it muſt aɛ̃t without that influence, i. e. without
motive. For a motive can have no influence, before influence is given to it ; and nothing can be a
motive, which has no perfuafive influence or tendency. Therefore the influence of motives and the con-
neɛ̃tion between them and volitions, are the effeɛ̃ts of
fome caufe extrinfic to the mind. And this caufation of the influence and confequences of motives, or of
the conneɛ̃tion between motive and volition, is really
a caufation of volitions themfelves, and that by an extrinfic caufe.——Thus the authors juſt mentioned
and thofe who with them acknowledge a conſtant concomitancy of motives and volitions, are brought into
a dilemma. If they hold that this concomitancy and
conſtant conneɛ̃tion is caufed by the mind itſelf, they
muſt grant, that it is caufed without motive, and fo
contradiɛ̃t the very principle they grant, of conſtant
concomitancy. If they allow, that this conneɛ̃tion is
caufed by fome other caufe, than the mind itſelf ;
they muſt of courfe grant, that volitions are the ef-
feɛ̃ts of an extrinfic caufe.

" If

" If volition and agreeable perception," fays Dr.
Weſt, p. 12, " be one and the fame thing, then mo-
" tive and volition are one and the fame thing : For
" nothing can be a motive, but an agreeable percep-
" tion ; or ———— motive is the perceiving of the
" fitneſs of an object to anfwer a particular purpoſe."
Hence he argues, that " if motive be agreeable per-
" ception, and agreeable perception be a volition, and
" motive be the cauſe of an act of the will, then an
" act of the will is the cauſe of an act of the will."
And that " motive and volition are one and the fame
" thing."———No doubt Dr. Weſt has a right to tell his
own fenfe of the word *motive*. But when Prefident
Edwards has particularly given his fenfe of that
word, and it appears to be entirely different from that
of Dr. Weſt, the Doctor has no right to argue from
his fenfe, to confute the Prefident. He by motive
meant not only a perception of the fitneſs of an object
to a particular purpoſe, but, as has been already obferved, " the whole of that which moves, excites or
" invites the mind to volition ;" and not only " the
" views of the mind," but " the ſtate, frame, temper
" and habit of the mind," however cauſed. Therefore
many volitions may be cauſed or occaſioned by motive
in this fenfe, which are not cauſed by any perception
at all, but by appetite, bias, taſte, &c. And if a man
perceive ever ſo clearly the fitneſs of an object to anfwer a particular purpoſe, and in this reſpect its agree-
ablenefs, this is not the fame as actual choice of that
object, all things confidered. A man may perceive,
that hard and conſtant labour is well fitted to the increafe of his property ; yet he may not chooſe it.

Though it ſhould be faid, that every agreeable perception is a volition ; it would not follow, that a volition is a motive to itſelf, which is what Dr. Weſt
means, if he mean to fix any abſurdity, in faying, that
motive and volition are one and the fame. There is
no abſurdity in the ſuppoſition, that one volition
ſhould be a motive to another volition ; that a ſtrong

wiſh for honour ſhould be a motive to determine a
man to generoſity, hoſpitality, a general good treat-
ment of his neighbours, and many ſervices uſeful to
the public ; and charity requires us to believe, that a
deſire to do good, was the motive, which made Dr.
Weſt willing to write and publiſh his *Eſſays on Liberty and Neceſſity.*——The principle from which Dr.
Weſt endeavours to faſten an abſurdity on Preſident
Edwards, is that nothing can be a motive but an agreeable perception ; which is both contrary to truth and
contrary to Preſident Edwards.

Archbiſhop King ſpeaks abundantly of " depraved
elections." What does he mean by *depraved elections ?* Elections not according to truth, reaſon or divine revelation ? But if a man were to chooſe according to theſe, he muſt not be perſuaded to ſuch election by *any regard* to truth, reaſon or divine revelation ; this would imply, that all things were not perfectly indifferent to him before election, and that ſome
things are choſen, becauſe they are previouſly adapted to excite choice, and not agreeable merely becauſe
they are choſen, as he holds in places before quoted.
Beſides ; if a man chooſe what is agreeable to truth,
reaſon or revelation, *from a regard to* truth, reaſon or
revelation, or which is the ſame thing, from the motive of truth, reaſon or revelation, he is *perſuaded, influenced* and *wrought upon* by thoſe motives ; conſequently he is *paſſive* in being the ſubject of this influence of the motives, and not free in the ſenſe of freedom, which the Archbiſhop holds——Again, if a man
chooſe what is dictated by truth, reaſon or revelation,
from regard to any thing elſe than truth, reaſon or revelation ; as he is influenced by motive, which is the
thing which he regards, he is in the ſame ſenſe not
free. Therefore to be free in that ſenſe he muſt
chooſe it from no regard to any thing, but without
motive, end or deſign. And in ſuch a choice what
there is of depravity or virtue, more than there
is

is in the fhining of the fun or in the blowing of thé wind, let any man point out.

Whether there be an infallible conneǎion between motives and volitions or not; ftill fo far as they influ- ence and have effeǎ ; fo far the fubjeǎ is wrought upon by an extrinfic caufe and is paffive ; and there- fore according to our opponents, fo far his liberty and moral agency are deftroyed. Why then fhould mo- tives ever be ufed with any man ? We ought not to ufe them, wifhing that they may have no effeǎ or in- fluence at all. Nor ought we to ufe them, to deftroy moral agency, and to turn men into machines. For what purpofe then fhould we ufe them ? We common- ly ufe them to perfuade. But to perfuade is to influ- ence a man by motive, which is an extrinfic caufe ; and under the influence of motive, he is paffive ; and in fuch a cafe our opponents fay his liberty and mor- al agency is deftroyed. But if they be not in this way deftroyed ; an infallible conneǎion between motive and volition is not inconfiftent with liberty ; and there- fore why fhould Dr. Weft or any other man difpute againft it ?

Moft, if not all writers in favour of felf-determina- tion allow, that men *generally* aǎ on motive ; and I pre- fume they would not deny, that whenever they do aǎ on motive, they are *perfuaded* to aǎ *by the motive*. Therefore on their principles, men are generally de- prived of liberty and moral agency, generally aǎ as mere machines and paffive inftruments ; and all their objeǎions againft an infallible conneǎion between mo- tives and volition, may be retorted, with refpeǎ to the general conduǎ of mankind : And as to the liberty and moral agency exercifed in fome rare inftances, when men aǎ without motive, as when they are fup- pofed to choofe between things perfeǎly indifferent ; it is a mere trifle not worth difputing about.

Dr. Price declares (Correfpondence with Prieftly, p. 347,) " That by determining as we pleafe," he means, " our poffeffing a power to make either of two
" motives

" motives the ftrongeft ; *i. e.* to make either of them
" the motive that fhall prevail, and the motive on
" which we fhall pleafe to determine." But this act,
by which we make one motive the ftrongeft, muft be
without motive. If it be not without, but be under
the influence of motive, not we, but that prior motive
makes that motive ftrongeft, on which we pleafe to
determine. And as the compliance with that prior
motive is an act in which we determine as we pleafe,
a ftill prior motive is neceffary to that act, and we
muft give ftrength to that motive too, and fo on to
infinity.——On the other hand, if without motive we
make one motive ftronger than another, we in this
cafe at leaft act without motive ; which is contrary
to what Dr. Price abundantly profeffes : He fays,
" A felf-determining power which is under *no influ-*
" *ence from motives*, has never been meant by any
" advocates for liberty."——But if we may and do
act without motive in making one motive to prevail;
why may we not immediately act without motive, as
well as firft without motive make one motive the
ftrongeft, that we may comply with it ? Befides ; to
give ftrength to a motive, that we may comply with
it, is really, in the act of giving that ftrength, to comply with the motive, and to choofe the object which
it recommends. It is like giving money to a friend,
that he may procure for us a certain commodity.
This certainly implies, that we choofe and wifh for
that commodity.

In the fame page Dr. Price puts the queftion ;
" Has a man urged by contrary inclinations, no con-
" trolling power over his inclinations, to make one of
" them preferably to the other, the inclination which
" he will follow ?" I anfwer, no ; there is a contradiction in it. The fuppofition implies, that before
he " makes one of them the inclination that he will
" follow," it is not the inclination which he choofes
to follow. But this is not true : In that he voluntarily makes it the inclination that he will follow, it is

H   implied

implied that he is inclined to follow it. He is willing
and choofes to follow it, and therefore he voluntarily makes it the inclination, which he will follow.
Thus it is previoufly what he makes it to be ; and
he is willing before he is willing. In making it the
inclination, which he will follow, he does follow it.
He follows it before he follows it.

Dr. Price in the fame book, p. 348, fays, " I am
" fenfible, that it is nonfenfe, to deny the influence
" of motives, or to maintain that there are no fixt
" principles and ends, by which the will is guided."
Then is it not nonfenfe, to affert, that we give ftrength
to motives ? And that we make an inclination, the
inclination that we will follow ? This feems to be the
inevitable confequence, unlefs we give ftrength to one
motive, under the influence of another, and fo run into the infinite feries.

Dr. Clarke in his Remarks on Collins, p. 12, 13,
fuppofes, that motives have *fome* influence, but not a
prevailing, governing one ; and that over and above
the perfuafive influence of motives, the felf-determining power muft by its own force exert itfelf to produce volition. Thus, p. 12, he reprobates the fuppofition, that if a man be not determined by motives
neceffarily, *i. e.* certainly and really ; he can in no
degree be influenced by them. But to be influenced
by motives, is to be really and effectually influenced,
juft fo far as the fubject is influenced by them at all :
And fo far as he is influenced or perfuaded by them,
fo far is he governed and determined by them : For
that is what we mean by a determination by motives.
On the other hand, fo far as a man is not influenced
or determined by motive, he acts without motive and
without regard to it. So that there is no medium
between no real or perfuafive influence of motive,
and a *determining governing* influence.

Again, p. 14, he reprobates the idea, " that mo-
" tives and reafons can be of no weight and no ufe
" at all to men, unlefs they *neceffitate* them ; and that
" if

" if a perfon be not determined *irrefiftibly*, then he
" muft be totally indifferent to all actions alike, and
" can have no regard to motives and reafons of ac-
" tion at all." By *neceffitating* and *determining irre-*
fiftibly, if he mean any thing to the purpofe, he muft
mean really and actually to influence by perfuafion,
fo as to give fome bias or inclination to the will.
And it is plain, that if motives do not at all bias or
incline the will, the man remains in a ftate of total
indifference, and " has no regard to motives or rea-
" fons of action at all." Nor is there any medium
between an inclination of the will and total indifference ; for this is the fame as to fay, that there is no
medium between an inclination of the will and no inclination of it. And if " motives and reafons" do
not incline men's wills and have no previous tendency to incline them, " they are of no weight or ufe at all
" to men ;" and if a perfon be not really inclined by
them, he is totally indifferent to them.

In the fame page, the Doctor confiders it as need-
ing proof, " that a felf-moving power is inconfiftent
" with having any regard to reafons of acting." So
far as a perfon is perfuaded to act, by reafons and
motives ; fo far he is *influenced* by motives, in the
fenfe, in which we hold, that any perfon is influenced by them ; therefore fo far is not felf-determined or
felf-moved. Or if by felf-determination be meant,
that under the effectual perfuafion of motives, we
caufe our own volitions ; (though we deny the poffibility of caufing our own volitions) yet as to liberty
in the fenfe in which I oppofe it, it would come to
the fame. The flave, who always acts by motives
exhibited by his mafter, is as abfolutely controlled
by his mafter, as the whip in the mafter's hand. Befides, to be effectually perfuaded by motive to volition, and to caufe our own volition independently of
extrinfic influence, is a direct contradiction.

" The doing of any thing *upon* or *after* or *in confe-*
quence of, that perception" (the perception of motive)

H 2

tive) " this is the power of felf-motion or action,
" which ————— in moral agents we call *liberty*."———
If the doing be merely in confequence of motive,
without any *influence* of the motive perfuading to the
doing ; that which in this cafe is called a motive, is
very improperly fo called. So a motive would be
no reafon at all for the doing. If it be a reafon and
properly a *motive*, it *moves* the agent to the doing ;
confequently the doing is not *felf*-motion, unlefs felf-
motion and motion excited by an extrinfic caufe are
one and the fame. Nor is this motion a *free action*
in a fenfe oppofed to moral neceffity. It is not free
from extrinfic caufality, nor of courfe free from a dependence on an extrinfic caufe. Every effect is dependent on its caufe. Nor is it free with a liberty of
contingence. This implies, that fomething happens
without a caufe.

If it fhould be faid, that motive in this cafe is not
the *efficient* of the action or doing : This is granted ;
but at the fame time, for reafons already given, it is
denied, that the man himfelf is the efficient caufe of
it. He who eftablifhed the laws of nature, fo called,
is the primary caufe of all things. What is meant by
efficient caufe in any cafe, in which an effect is produced according to eftablifhed laws ? For inftance,
what is the efficient caufe of the fenfation of heat from
fire ? If it be anfwered, fire is the efficient caufe ; I
alfo anfwer, that the motive is the efficient caufe of
the volition and doing aforefaid. If it be faid, that the
Great Firft Caufe is the efficient of the fenfation of
heat ; the fame Great Agent is the efficient caufe of
volition, in the fame way, by a general law eftablifhing a connection between motives and volitions ; as
there is a connection between fire in certain fituations
and the fenfation of heat.

To allow, that we are free, though we always act in
confequence of motives, unlefs by acting be meant an
action not excited or influenced by motive, and of
which the motive is no reafon, is to plead for no oth-

er

er liberty, than is perfectly confiftent with the moft abfolute moral neceffity and with abfolute decrees.

Doctors Clarke and Price confider the man free, who efficiently caufes his own volitions according to motives, becaufe he himfelf and not the motives, is the efficient caufe. Yet as by the fuppofition he caufes them according to motives, he is limited by them. And is a flave free, who manufactures a commodity under the control and lafh of his mafter ? Or is the convict free, who himfelf walks around the ftake, to which he is chained ? Yet according to the fyftem of the faid gentlemen, the flave and not the mafter is the efficient caufe of his own volition to labour. The convict and not the ftake, is the efficient caufe of his own volition to walk around the ftake. Nor is the mafter the efficient caufe of the limitation of the volitions of his flave ; he merely exhibits the motives to their limitation : And it will not be pretended, that the ftake is the efficient caufe of the limitation of the volition of the convict.

Dr. Price, in Correfpondence with Prieftly, p. 341, fays, " that no influence of motives, which is fhort of " making them phyfical efficients or agents, can clafh " with liberty." Now the walls, gates and bars of a prifon are not *phyfical efficients or agents ;* yet they are as inconfiftent with the liberty of the prifoner, as if they were fuch efficients and agents, and ftood around him with gun and bayonet, to confine him to the fpot ; or as if they had built and made themfelves for the purpofe of his confinement. So if man be limited to act agreeably to motives only, they are as inconfiftent with his liberty, as they would be, if they were intelligent agents, had created themfelves and had eftablifhed the connection between themfelves and volition. It is as to liberty, immaterial who or what has eftablifhed the connection between motives and volitions, provided the connection be infallibly eftablifhed : As it is immaterial as to the liberty of a prifoner, who or what made the walls, gates and bars of the prifon,

H 3   whether

whether the walls, gates and bars themfelves, any extrinfic caufe, or even the prifoner himfelf. If he had
built and made them all, had locked himfelf in and
had flung the key through the grates, he would be as
effectually deprived of his liberty, as if the fame things
had been done by any other agent.——Thefe obfervations lead to a further anfwer to the plea, that we
give ftrength to the motive which determines us.
What if a man fhould give ftrength to a motive ? After it is thus become ftrong, it as effectually governs
the man, and as really deprives him of his liberty, as
if it had derived its ftrength from any other fource.
Suppofe a man were poffeffed of creating power, and
fhould create another man ftronger than himfelf, and
this other man fhould bind the former hand and
foot : Would he not be as effectually deprived of his
liberty, as if he had been in the fame manner bound
by any other man ?

CHAPTER

CHAPTER V.

In which it is inquired, whether Volition be an Effect and have a Cause.

THE title of Dr. West's second *essay* is, " That vo-
" lition is not properly an effect, which has a
" cause." Whether his meaning be, that it is an effect which has no cause, or that it is not an effect at
all, the words do not determine ; but from the sequel
I conclude, the latter is his meaning. This, as has
been already noticed, is indeed contradicted by the
Doctor, as in this passage, p. 24, " The modification in
" question" (*i. e.* the modification which the mind gives
itself in willing or acting, which the Doctor explains
to be volition) " is the consequence or EFFECT of the
" mind willing or choosing." Then volition is an *effect ;* and an effect of a preceding volition.

I presume the Doctor has the merit of originality
in this part of his system. Many things in the common
scheme of self-determination do indeed imply, that volition has no cause ; viz. Liberty as opposed to all
necessity or certainty ; the sovereignty and independence of the will ; its exemption from all influence of
motive or extrinsic cause, &c. Still I have not met
with one writer before Dr. West, who had boldness
enough expressly to avow the sentiment. Dr. Clarke
and all the rest hold, that volition is the effect of the
mind itself in the exercise of its self-moving or self-determining power. And Doctor Price, when charged by
Dr. Priestly with holding, that volitions come to pass
without a cause, rejects the imputation and takes it
hardly, that ever it should have been made to him or
his system. Correspondence with Priestly, p. 349.

But let us examine the reasons, by which Dr. West
endeavours to support this doctrine. They are the
following ;

H 4

1. That

1. That volition is an abſtract term and ſignifies ſomething, which cannot exiſt without a ſubject ; or volition is nothing but the mind willing or acting ; and therefore is not an effect ; p. 21.——But ſuppoſe volition be nothing but *the mind willing* or *acting ;* is that ſtate of the mind or the mind in that ſtate, not an effect ? Dr. Weſt will not deny, that the mind abſolutely conſidered is an effect. If then the mind *willing* or in the exerciſe of volition, is not an effect ; it ſeems, that the mind while without volition is an effect or a creature ; but in the exerciſe of volition ceaſes to be an effect, and therefore ceaſes to be a creature. Will Dr. Weſt avow this ?——Motion is an abſtract term and ſignifies ſomething, which cannot exiſt without a ſubject ; or motion is nothing but a body moving. But will it hence follow, that motion or a body moving is not an effect ? No more does it follow from the argument of Dr. Weſt now under conſideration, that volition is not an effect ? The Doctor grants, that volition is the modification or mode of the mind ; and is not that mode an effect ? If it be not an effect, becauſe it is a mode of the mind, then doubtleſs no other mode of the mind is an effect. And ſtrip the mind of all its modes, and you will take away the mind itſelf ; becauſe ſome of thoſe modes are *eſſential* modes. If all the modes of the mind, eſſential and accidental, taken ſingly and collectively, be not effects ; the mind itſelf is not an effect.——On the principle of Doctor Weſt's argument, no mode whatever is an effect. The principle is this, That whatever cannot ſubſiſt of itſelf out of any ſubject. is not an effect. But no mode, ſolidity, extenſion, figure, colour or motion, can ſubſiſt without a ſubject. Therefore not one of them nor any other mode is an effect. And if not one of thoſe modes by itſelf, is an effect, all of them taken together are not an effect ; and therefore body or matter is not an effect : Yea neither matter nor ſpirit is an effect. And as matter and ſpirit with their modes, comprehend the whole creation ; it will follow,

that

that no *creature* is an effect ; *i. e.* no creature is a creature.

2. That volition or the mind willing, is not an effect, because it is an efficient cause.———Dr. West believes, that a carpenter is the efficient cause of a ship : And does he therefore believe, that the carpenter in building the ship is not a creature ? This would follow on the principles of this argument. The principle is, that whatever is an efficient cause, cannot be an effect. Therefore as a carpenter is the efficient cause of a ship, he is not an effect, or not a creature. Dr. West and others take it for granted, that if volition be an effect, it cannot be a cause. This is just as absurd as to hold, that unless a carpenter be uncaused, he cannot build a ship ; and that a creature can be the cause of nothing.

3. That if the operation or action, which is essential to the idea of a cause, be itself an effect ; then its cause must operate to produce the said effect ; and consequently the last mentioned operation being an effect, must have another cause to produce it, and so on *in infinitum ;* and this infinite series of causes and effects entirely excludes the first cause and any efficient cause ; p. 22.———But it is denied, that in the case here supposed, an infinite series of causes and effects is involved. Suppose it be true, that the action which is necessary to constitute a man an efficient cause, be the effect of an extrinsic cause ; how does it follow, that there must be, in this case, an infinite series of causes ? We maintain that action may be the effect of a divine influence ; or that it may be the effect of one or more second causes, the first of which is immediately produced by the Deity. Here then is not an infinite series of causes, but a very short series, which terminates in the Deity or first cause.——— I know that it is often *supposed* and *asserted* by Dr. West, that volition cannot be an effect at all ; and that it is *supposed* by all others, who maintain Dr. West's general scheme, that it cannot be an effect of an extrinsic

trinfic caufe. But their fuppofing it is a mere affump tion of the thing in difpute, in this part of the argu- ment. Let them *prove* it and they will do fomething to the purpofe.———Again ; the caufe or feries of caufes, which is implied in the idea, that volition is an effect, is fo far from excluding the firft caufe and any efficient caufe, as Dr. Weft fays, that it inevitably leads to the firft caufe, and implies, that there is an efficient caufe of all volition in creatures, as well as of every thing elfe fhort of the firft caufe.

4. That volition in the Deity is no effect, but is on- ly the Deity confidered as willing or caufing ; and therefore to affert, that volition is no effect, is not in itfelf an abfurdity. Why then may we not affert, that volition in the creature is no effect ? P. 23.——On this I obferve, It is granted, that volition in the Dei- ty is not an effect ; but it no more hence follows, that volition in the creature is not an effect, than that ex- iftence and knowledge in the creature, are not effects, becaufe they are not effects in the Creator.

5. That if human volition be an effect, then man muft be paffive in willing, but if he be paffive in willing, he can be active in nothing elfe ; *i. e.* he is no agent, but a mere paffive machine. But if man be active in willing, then volition cannot be the effect of an extrinfic caufe, and will be nothing but the mind acting or operating ; p. 23. ——No doubt if human volition be an effect, man is fo far paffive in willing, as to be the fubject of the influence of that caufe which produces volition ; ftill he is active too in volition, is ftill an agent and not a *mere* paffive machine. In volition man is both paffive and active ; paffive as he is the fubject of the influence of the caufe which excites volition, and active in the exercife of it. As the day-labourer is paffive in that he is influ- enced by the profpect of wages, to confent to labour, and active in exerting and in confenting to exert him- felf in labour. Nor does it follow from a man's being active in volition, that volition cannot be the effect of an extrinfic caufe. The idea, that it does follow, takes

for

for granted the very thing in queftion, viz. that an action cannot be an effect, efpecially of an extrinfic
caufe. Dr. Weft ought to have proved this.

Befides ; why does the Doctor fay, " If man be
" active in willing, then volition cannot be the effect
" of any *extrinfic* caufe ?" Ibid. His doctrine equally
implies, that it is not the effect of an *intrinfic* caufe.
His doctrine is, that volition is, in general terms, not
an effect and has no caufe. But now, it feems the
Doctor recedes from this, and holds only, that volition is not the effect of an *extrinfic* caufe, implicitly
granting, that it is *an effect,* and an effect of an *intrinfic* caufe.

The Doctor tells us, that " if man be paffive in
" willing ——— he is ——— a *mere paffive machine ;*"
p. 23.———How does this appear ? A man is paffive
in his intellectual views ; but is he in thofe views a
mere paffive *machine ?* The human intellect is very
different from what we commonly call a *machine.*
Or if by *machine* the Doctor mean any thing that is
influenced by an extrinfic caufe ; I grant, that in
this fenfe, both the human intellect and human will
are *machines ;* and in granting this, I grant no more
than is implied in the moral neceffity for which I
plead. Yet fuch an application of the word *machine,*
would be a grofs perverfion of it.

6. That the Deity has not only acted from all eternity ; but is continually acting upon the whole creation, for the prefervation and government of it. Yet
thefe operations and energies of the Deity are not effects, though they take place in time. Therefore the
energies or volitions of the human mind are not effects, though they alfo take place in time ; p. 24.———
But I deny, that the operations or energies of the
Deity *begin* in time, though the effects of thofe operations do. They no more begin in time, than the divine exiftence does ; but human volitions all begin
in time. There is no fucceffion in the divine mind ;
therefore no new operations take place there. All
the

the divine acts are equally from eternity, nor is there any *time* with God. " One day is with the Lord as " a thousand years and a thousand years as one day." The *effects* of those divine acts do indeed all take place in time and in a succession.——If it should be said, that on this supposition the effects take place not till long after the acts, by which they are produced ; I answer, they do so in our view, but not in the view of God. With him there is no time, no before nor after with respect to time ; nor has time any existence either in the divine mind or in the nature of things, independently of the minds and perceptions of creatures ; but it depends on the succession of those perceptions. So that from the consideration, that the divine energies and operations are no effects, it no more follows, that human volitions are no effects, than from the consideration that the divine existence and knowledge are no effects it follows, that *our* existence and knowledge are no effects.

7. That if volition were an effect, we could not be the *causes* of any effects : At the most we should be *mere passive instruments ;* p. 25.——This wholly depends on the meaning of *words,* as most of Dr. West's arguments do. If by *cause* the Dr. mean a *self-determinate* cause, he, *as usual,* begs what he has no right to expect will be given him. But if by *cause* he mean a rational, voluntary agent, acting under the persuasive influence of light and motives ; we may be such causes, though volition is an effect ; and acting as such causes we may produce effects. Thus Noah built the ark ; Moses hewed two tables of stone, &c.——And if under the name of a *passive instrument* the Doctor mean to include such a rational, voluntary agent, as I have just described ; I grant, that in this sense we are passive instruments, and it is impossible, that a rational creature should be any other than such a passive instrument. But I reprobate the calling of such an agent a mere passive instrument, as a great abuse of language.

But

But suppose volition were not an effect ; should
we then be caufes of effects ? or should we then be
lefs paffive inftruments ? If volition were no effect,
we ourfelves should no more be the caufes of it, than
any extrinfic caufe. It would happen in us by mere
chance. And should we in the exercife of that volition, which is without caufe and is merely accidental,
be any more caufes of an effect, than we should be
in the exercife of a volition excited by a proper motive ? If any reafon can be given to show, that we
should, let it be given. Though it may be pleaded,
that when we become the subjects of volition by mere
chance, we are not the subjects of the operation of a
caufe in the production of volition, and in that fenfe
are not paffive ; yet in this cafe volition takes place
in our minds equally without our caufation, our previous agency or confent, as if the fame volition were
caufed by fomething extrinfic. So that if we be not
equally *wrought upon* in thefe two cafes, we are e-
qually *inactive*, and therefore can no more be *caufes*
in the one cafe, than in the other : And there is
nothing more favourable to liberty or felf-determination in the one cafe than in the other.

8. That if volition were an effect, we could have
no more ideas of caufe and effect, than a blind man
has of colours. For we being paffive in our ideas of
fenfations, they could never fuggeft to us the ideas of
caufe and effect ; and if volition or internal action
be the effect of an extrinfic caufe, our reflections
could never afford an example of an efficient caufe,
and fo we muft for ever be deftitute of the ideas of
caufe and effect ; p. 25.——On this I obferve,

(1.) It wholly depends on the meaning of the word
caufe. If as I before obferved, it mean a felf-determinate caufe, which " acts on itfelf and produces volition ;" I grant, that we have no idea of fuch a caufe,
more than a blind man has of colours. Nor has Dr.
Weft any idea of fuch a caufe, as he reprobates it
and does not believe in its exiftence. Neither God
nor

nor creature can be such a cause as this ; it is an impoffibility ; it is perfectly like the animal, which President Edwards fuppofed the traveller profeffed to have feen in *Terra del fuego.* But if caufe mean a rational, voluntary agent producing effects under the influence of motives ; fuch caufes we ourfelves are or may be ; and the idea of fuch a caufe we derive from every artificer, whom we fee employed at his trade, from every hufbandman, who in our view tills the ground, and from every external action which we perform.

(2.) Though we are paffive in our ideas of fenfation, yet every idea of that kind, for the very reafon that we are paffive in it, fuggefts to us the ideas of both caufe and effect. In that we are paffive in thofe ideas both caufe and effect are implied. If no caufe operated upon us to produce the effect, fenfation, we fhould not be paffive in fenfation. It is true, the becoming paffively the fubjects of fenfation, does not fuggeft to us the idea of a felf-determinate or felf-actuating caufe ; for fuch a caufe does not exift, is an impoffibility, and therefore no idea of it can be conceived ; as I have already endeavoured to fhow.

(3.) This argument fuppofes, that we get the idea of an efficient caufe by the experience, that we ourfelves are the efficient caufes of volition. But in the firft place we deny, that we ever do experience ourfelves to be the efficient caufes of volition : And in the fecond place, if we did, it would be entirely inconfiftent with Dr. Weft's propofition now under confideration ; it would prove, that volition is an effect, and that we ourfelves are the efficient caufes of it.

(4.) Be it fo that " our reflections can never afford " us an example of an efficient caufe ;" what abfurdity follows ? We avow that our reflections cannot afford us an example of fuch a caufe. We neither efficiently caufe our own volitions nor our own perceptions. Yet we are not deftitute of ideas of

caufe

caufe and effect, as I have already fhown.———But certainly according to Dr. Weft our reflections do not afford us an example of an efficient caufe of volition ; for volition is, according to him, no effect and has no caufe.

9. That if our volitions were the effects of an extrinfic caufe, we could never have the idea of dependence and independence, and therefore could not connect our ideas together, *i. e.* could not be rational beings. And as we are rational beings, it follows, that our volitions are not the effects of an extrinfic caufe, but that we are felf-determinate, and that we get the ideas of dependence and independence, by experiencing in ourfelves, that in willing and choofing we act independently of any extrinfic caufe ; p. 25.

This implies, that in volition we act independently, and that from fuch independent actions we derive the idea of independence. But this again is a fheer begging of the queftion. How does it appear, that we act independently ? The Doctor might as well have taken it for granted, that we act felf-determinately. We no more grant, that we acquire the idea of independence, by experiencing it in volition, than that we acquire the idea of an efficient caufe by experiencing ourfelves to be the efficient caufes of our own volitions. And if any man have the idea, that any creature is in volition independent of all extrinfic caufes, this idea is not allowed to be according to truth. As to the divine independence, which is indeed entire and abfolute, Dr. Weft will not pretend, that we get the idea of this by experiencing the like independence in ourfelves. We no more get that idea in this way, than we get the idea of the divine omnipotence, by experiencing omnipotence in ourfelves. So that though we have the ideas of dependence and independence, can connect our ideas together and are rational beings, it by no means follows, as Dr. Weft infers, " that our volitions are not the effects of an ex- " *trinfic* caufe, and that we are felf-determinate."

And

And why does the Doctor continually deny volition to be the effect of an *extrinsic* cause ? The propofition which he has undertaken to fupport, equally implies, that it is not the effect of an *intrinfic* caufe.

10. That volition is only the relation of the energy of a caufe in producing an effect, and therefore is not an effect, and has no proper exiftence of its own ; p. 26.———If volition be only the *relation* of the energy of a caufe, it is not the *energy* itfelf or *action* of a caufe ; and how then is it a part of the fubject of the prefent inquiry ? The prefent inquiry and difcuffion relate to the voluntary *actions* of a rational being. As to the relations and external denominations of thofe actions, they may be and commonly are different in every action, yet the actions themfelves may be the fame.———Befides ; the Doctor will not pretend to deny, that volition is an action of the mind, or as he choofes to exprefs it, *the mind acting*. And is the mind acting only the relation of the energy or action of that mind ? And has the mind acting " no proper " exiftence of its own ?" If it have, it is an effect doubtlefs, becaufe it is a creature. An action of the human mind is an event, and an event coming to pafs in time, and therefore has a caufe : And Dr. Weft fays, he " cannot be charged with holding, that events " take place without a caufe ;" p. 27.

11. That no agent can bring any effect to pafs, but what is confequent on his acting. Therefore it is very abfurd to call the acting or activenefs of a being, an effect ; becaufe it introduces the utmoft abfurdity into language, by confounding and blending things together, which are very different ; p. 28.———It is an undoubted truth, that no agent can bring any effect to pafs, but what is confequent on his acting. But how does it hence follow, that it is very abfurd to call the action of a being an effect ? And how does this confound and blend things together, which are very different ? It will not be denied, that the prophefying of a prophet may be the act of that prophet ; yet acting

by

by infpiration he is excited to that act by a divine agency. No doubt the Divine Being brings to pafs this effect by a previous act or exertion of himfelf. But where is the abfurdity of calling this prophefying an effect of the divine influence ? How does the calling of it fo, confound and blend the divine influence and the act of the prophet, which are acknowledged to be very different from each other ?

12. That caufe and effect are not fynonymous terms ; and therefore " in whatever fenfe any thing is " a caufe, in that fenfe it is not proper to call it an " effect ; for this reafon, that caufes confidered as " caufes, are not effects." Part II, p. 90. This is juft as conclufive reafoning as if the Doctor had faid, the words *tree* and *effect* are not fynonymous terms. Therefore in whatever fenfe any thing is a *tree*, in that fenfe it is not proper to call it an *effect ;* for this reafon, that *trees* confidered as *trees* are not *effects*. Rain confidered as the caufe of the growing of grafs, is an effect ; a medicine confidered as the caufe of a cure, is ftill an effect ; and Dr. Weft confidered as the author of feveral effays on liberty and neceffity, is as really a creature of God, as he is when he is confidered to be in the exercife of his favourite liberty or power of *not acting* and is in perfect *torpor.*—— The Doctor proceeds, " The mind acting is the mind " caufing ; for I conceive, whenever the mind acts, " it produces fome effect." Ibid. If the Doctor mean that whenever the mind is the fubject of an *internal* act or volition, it produces fome *external* effect ; this is manifeftly a miftake, and the Doctor himfelf will not avow it. If he mean, that whenever it is the fubject of volition, it produces that volition as an *effect ;* this in the firft place is giving up what he himfelf had written an effay to prove, viz. that volition is not an effect ; and fecondly it is a begging of the main point. In fhort, Dr. Weft is a moft fturdy metaphyfical beggar. But as charity demands no gratuities to fuch beggars, he is to expect none.——He adds to the

I   laft

laſt quotation, it " will introduce the greateſt confu-
" ſion in language, to ſpeak of the mind, conſidered
" as cauſing, as being an effect." But what confuſion
of language is it, to ſpeak of Dr. Weſt conſidered as
the author of eſſays on liberty and neceſſity, as being
a creature ? I hope, when the Doctor ſhall write again,
he will *ſhow* that it confounds language, and not merely *aſſert* it.

The Doctor, in the page laſt quoted, ſays, " The
" queſtion is, whether every act of the will is a new
" effect produced by the Deity or by ſome other
" extrinſic cauſe." I do not allow this to be the queſtion. The Doctor aſſerts in general terms, that volition is not properly an effect. The queſtion is entirely general, whether volition be an effect of any cauſe,
extrinſic or *intrinſic.* When this queſtion ſhall have
been ſettled, a ſubſequent one may ariſe, whether it
be an effect of *extrinſic* cauſe.

Thus I have conſidered Dr. Weſt's arguments to
prove, that volition is not an effect and has no cauſe.
Whether they do really prove it, the reader will judge.

Dr. Price in his Correſpondence with Prieſtly, p.
341, ſays, " An agent that does not put himſelf in mo-
" tion, is an agent that is always acted upon, and an
" agent that never acts." On this I remark, that it
is not true, that every agent, who does not put himſelf in motion, is always acted upon, by an extrinſic
agent The Deity did not at firſt put himſelf in motion, meaning by *motion* volition.——If he did, he
was before without motion or volition. And Dr.
Price would not pretend, that God exiſted from eternity without any volition, and that when he came down
within the limits of time, he put himſelf into volition, *i. e.*
he created volition in his own mind. Or if by being
acted upon, Dr. Price meant, the Deity's acting according
to the moſt wiſe and holy reaſons, which his infinite underſtanding can ſuggeſt ; no doubt in this ſenſe the Deity himſelf is acted upon ; and if this be inconſiſtent
with agency, inſtead of but one, as Dr. Price ſays,
there

there is *not one* agent in the univerfe. God no more put himfelf in motion or volition at firft, than he put himfelf into exiftence. Nor has he at any time put himfelf into any particular volition. This would imply a new thing and a change in God.

To fay, that an agent that is acted upon cannot act, is as groundlefs, as to fay that a body acted upon, cannot move ; unlefs the main queftion is begged, by fuppofing, that action means felf-determinate action.

The advocates for felf-determination are in like manner guilty of begging the queftion, by ufing *active power* to mean a felf-determining or felf-moving power ; a power which puts itfelf into exercife, without the agency or influence of any extrinfic caufe. We deny the exiftence and poffibility of fuch a power : We hold, that it is as impoffible, as that an animal fhould beget itfelf, or take one ftep before the firft ftep. If this be meant by *active power*, we deny that any being poffeffes it ; and our opponents ought to be afhamed to beg it.

Dr. Weft holds, that volition is no effect and has no caufe : He alfo holds, that volition is a modification of the mind. Indeed it is manifeft, that the mind willing, is the mind in a different mode or differently modified, from what it was, when not willing. Now is the event of this modification taking place in the mind, not an effect ? And is it uncaufed ? Then not only does an event come to pafs without caufe, which Dr. Weft denies ; but it happens by mere blind, ftupid, undefigning chance.——It might as well be faid, that the event of a canon ball moving is not an effect, as that the event of the mind willing is not an effect.

It is pleaded, that if volition be the effect of an *extrinfic* caufe, it is wholly paffive : Dr. Weft joins with others in this plea, p. 23. But if volition be the effect of an *intrinfic* caufe, it is equally paffive. For as Dr. Weft himfelf fays very rightly, p. 23, " Every " effect is wholly paffive with regard to the caufe " which produces it."

I 2

Dr.

Dr. Weſt ſays, volition is " a property of a mind."
P. 21, 22. Therefore when volition exiſts in the
mind, it is the ſubjeƈt of a property of which before
it was deſtitute. Now is not this an effeƈt ? Does
not ſome efficient cauſe, either the mind itſelf or ſome
other cauſe, endue it with that property, as really as
if it were endued with any other property ? Or as if
a body were endued with a particular colour ?

He further holds, page 6 and 7, that " virtue and
" vice are mere modes or attributes of a rational agent."
But virtue and vice are voluntary aƈts of the mind,
or volitions. Therefore volitions are modes or attributes of a rational agent. But according to him theſe
modes have no cauſe and are no effeƈts. And if ſome
modes be not effeƈts, how ſhall we know, that other
modes or any modes are effeƈts ? If no modes be effeƈts, ſince we know nothing of ſubſtances but by
their ſenſible modes and qualities ; how ſhall we know,
that ſubſtances themſelves are effeƈts ?

Volitions are aƈts and events : And if ſome e-
vents be uncauſed, why may not all ?

Dr. Weſt contradiƈts and gives up his doƈtrine,
that volition has no cauſe, in all thoſe places, in which
he allows, that volition is not without motive : As
when he grants, " that the mind aƈts upon motives" ———— " that when the mind aƈts or chooſes,
" it always has ſome end, deſign or reaſon, which is
" the occaſion of its aƈting or chooſing." ———— that
" motives are the previous circumſtances which are
" neceſſary for aƈtion," &c. &c. Motives then are
the reaſons, the occaſions, the neceſſary previous circumſtances or antecedents of volition. And what are
theſe but *ſecond cauſes ?* Cauſes in the ſenſe, in which
Preſident Edwards explains himſelf to uſe the word
cauſe with relation to this very ſubjeƈt, p. 41, 42.——
We ſay, that fire is the cauſe of the ſenſation of heat ;
that rain and ſun-ſhine are the cauſes of vegetation,
&c. Yet they are no more than the ſtated antece-
dents. In the ſame ſenſe motives, according to Dr.
Weſt,

Weft, are caufes of volitions. Befides, all fecond caufes are the effects of the firft caufe. Therefore ultimately volitions are effects of the Great Firft Caufe.

If volition be no effect, it is not the effect of the mind in which it exifts. That mind has no control over it : It comes to pafs without its wifh or confent, as fully as if it were the effect of fome extrinfic caufe. How then is the mind any more, or in any more defirable fenfe, free, than if volition were produced by an extrinfic caufe? Which would a wife man choofe ? to have all volitions take place by pure accident, by blind chance and fate ? or to have them ordered by a wife and good caufe, in the application of proper motives ? And are we agents in the former of thefe cafes, more than in the latter ? On this hypothefis volitions are his, in whofe mind they exift, in this fenfe only, that he is the fubject of them. And this is true on the fuppofition, that they are caufed by an extrinfic caufe. And how on this plan, are we more accountable for our volitions and actions, than on the fuppofition, that they are produced in us by an extrinfic caufe ?

If volition be no effect and have no caufe, it proceeds from no power or faculty in human nature as its caufe ; not from the power of will, nor even from any *felf-determining power*, whether it confift in the will or in any other part of human nature. What then is the advantage of the felf-determining power fo ftrenuoufly advocated ? It cannot produce one volition nor one free act. How then does liberty confift in it ? or depend on it ? Or how does it contribute any aid toward liberty ? And what becomes of the boafted independence and fovereignty of the will ?

That a volition is produced in me by fome extrinfic caufe, is not at all oppofed to liberty, unlefs by *liberty* be intended *contingence* or an exemption from all caufality. If I could caufe a volition in myfelf, it would be as neceffary, as if it were produced by fome other caufe. Dr. Weft rightly obferves, that " every " effect is wholly paffive with regard to the caufe,

I 3 " which

" which produces it." As the volition then produced
by myfelf is wholly paffive, it could not be more paffive, if it were produced by fome extrinfic caufe.

Dr. Weft, in p. 25, fays, " Our confcioufnefs, that
" we are felf-active, fuggefts to us the ideas of caufe
" and effect, of dependence and independence :" i. e.
Our confcioufnefs that we are the bare fubjects of volitions, which are no effects at all, whether of ourfelves
or of any other caufe, and therefore are not dependent
on any caufe, fuggefts to us the ideas of caufe and effect, dependence and independence. Whether this
be rational, let the reader judge.

In p. 26, Dr. Weft explains himfelf to mean by volition, " the relation of energy exerted by a caufe in
" producing an effect ;" and fays, " It cannot be con-
" fidered as being an effect of any caufe whatever, or as
" having any proper exiftence of its own." In fupport of this idea he quotes Prefident Edwards, where
he fays, that action and paffion are fometimes ufed to
fignify the mere relations of activenefs of fomething
on another, and of paffivenefs or of being acted upon by another thing ; and that in this cafe they do
not fignify any pofitive effect or caufe or any real ex-
iftences. Hence Dr. Weft infers, that according to
Prefident Edwards, he cannot be charged with holding that events take place without a caufe.——On this
it may be obferved,

1. Prefident Edwards tells us, that whenever the
word action is ufed to fignify a mere relation, it does
not fignify an action or fome motion or exercife of
body or mind. But Dr. Weft generally ufes volition
to fignify an action or exercife of the mind : And yet
in the paffage now under confideration, he gives an
explanation of volition, in which he fays it fignifies
" the relation of the energy of a caufe," and therefore
not the energy itfelf, the exercife, exertion or act of
that caufe. Prefident Edwards did not fuppofe, that
the word action generally and properly fignifies a mere
relation ; but that it generally and properly fignifies a
positive

pofitive exiſtence,* or an event which has as real an exiſtence, as any faƈt or event. As to the word *volition,* Preſident Edwards never conſiders that as ſignifying a mere relation. Whereas Dr. Weſt conſiders this to be the proper meaning of volition.

2. As to the paſſage, which Dr. Weſt quotes from Preſident Edwards, the latter had good reaſon to ſay, that when the *aƈtion* is uſed to exprefs not any exertion, faƈt or event, but the *mere relation* of aƈtivity with reſpeƈt to ſomething as the ſubjeƈt ; it ſignifies no effeƈt or cauſe and no real exiſtence. This may be illuſtrated by ſome other relation ; as fonſhip, the relation between father and ſon. A father is a real exiſtence, and every created father is an effeƈt. So is a ſon. But *fonſhip* is no real exiſtence ; nor is it a proper effeƈt or cauſe, more than the relation between the three angles of a triangle and two right ones. Now volition is not ſuch a mere relation : It is a real poſitive aƈt, motion or exerciſe of a mind, and Dr. Weſt abundantly grants this.

3. If volition be a mere relation of energy, it is not " an exertion of an aƈtive principle," " an aƈt of " the will," " an exerciſe of the mind," &c. as Dr. Weſt aſſerts it to be. Beſides, if it be a mere " *rela-* " *tion* of the energy exerted by a cauſe" or mind, what is the energy, aƈt, exerciſe or exertion of which volition is the relation ? Surely an aƈt or exertion, and the relation of that aƈt ; a thing and the relations of that thing, are not one and the ſame. The ſame thing may have different and oppoſite relations. The ſame man may ſuſtain the oppoſite relations of a father and a ſon. And if ſuch a man be the ſame thing with his relations, he is the ſame thing with his fonſhip, and the ſame thing with his fatherhood. Thus, as two things which agree with a common meaſure, agree between themſelves, it will follow, that fonſhip and fatherhood are the ſame thing.

I 4   4. By

* It will be remembered, that logicians and metaphyſicians divide beings into ſubſtance and mode, and conſider modes as having as real and poſitive an exiſtence, as ſubſtance.

4. By volition Dr. Weſt means either an act of the mind, or not. If he do mean an act of the mind, volition with him is not a mere relation, but a proper poſitive event or fact ; and therefore muſt be an effect and have a cauſe ; or an event takes place without a cauſe. If he do not by volition mean an act of the mind, it is ſurely not a *free* act; and if we do not act freely in volition, we do not act freely at all, *i. e.* we are not free agents. It is generally granted, and to be ſure Dr. Weſt's whole book implies, that all the moral liberty which we have is exerciſed in volition. But if volition be a *mere relation*, and not an act and a free act ; we have no liberty ; and by holding, that volition is a mere relation and not an act, Dr. Weſt gives up all that liberty for which he diſputes.

The Doctor, in his ſecond part, p. 1 2, grants that "acts " of the will, volition, choice and determination of the " mind may with *propriety* be called effects, when they " ſignify thoſe determinations or concluſions, which " the mind makes in conſequence of its comparing " two or more things together." Therefore ſome acts of the will are effects. How is this conſiſtent with what the Doctor holds both in his former book and in this, that volition cannot be properly called an effect ? Beſides ; what the Doctor here ſays, is applicable to all volitions, and therefore all volitions are according to his own account, effects. For all volitions are " de- " terminations or concluſions, which the mind makes " in conſequence of its comparing two or more things " together." If two or more things be expreſsly propoſed, and one of them be choſen, it is the very caſe here ſtated by Dr. Weſt. Or if one thing only be expreſsly and poſitively propoſed as the object of our choice, ſtill there is a real competition between this thing and the abſence or neglect of it ; and the mind comes to a determination in conſequence of its comparing theſe two together. Therefore according to Dr. Weſt's own account every volition " may with " propriety be called an effect ;" and yet according to

the

the fame Dr. Weft, " volition cannot be properly called an effect." " How can thefe things be ?"

But Dr. Weft endeavours to evade this confequence,
by faying, " I have ufed the term *volition* to fignify
" *the mind confidered as acting.* In this fenfe and in
" this only, I fay volition is not *an effect.*" But the
mind confidered as acting, acts in confequence of
comparing two or more things together, and fuch an
act Dr. Weft allows to be an effect. Alfo he grants,
" that the human mind and all its powers and facul-
" ties are effects ;" p. 13. But will he fay, that the
human mind with all its powers and faculties *dormant*
and *inactive*, is an effect, but the fame mind with its
powers and faculties *acting*, is not an effect ? And
does it ceafe to be an effect or a creature, as foon as
it begins to act ?

" If volition be only the mind acting ; and if the
" mind acting is properly a caufe, then it is not prop-
" er to call it an effect." Ibid, p. 13. But what or
where is the impropriety of calling it an effect ? In
fuch a difpute as this, to affert fuch a novel propofition without proof or illuftration, is unreafonable. By
the fame reafoning it may be proved, that any man
who makes any thing is himfelf not an effect or creature. Thus, If a carpenter at work be properly a
caufe of a fhip, then it is not proper to call him an effect or creature ; and if Dr. Weft writing be properly the caufe of feveral effays on liberty and neceffity ;
then it is not proper to call him a creature.

" When volition is ufed to fignify the mind act-
" ing, in that view it is properly a caufe and not an
" effect ;" ibid, p. 28. What if it be properly a caufe ?
This does not prevent its being properly an effect too,
any more than the Doctor's being properly the caufe
of feveral effays prevents his being, or proves that he
is not, properly a creature of God.——" Caufes as
" caufes, are not effects ;" ibid, p. 13. Then authors
as authors, are not the creatures of God.

" The

The Dr. argues, ibid, p. 94, That an action cannot be the effect of the Deity, becaufe " an effect is
" moft certainly paffive in coming into being ————
" but this will imply *paffive action* or *inactive action*,
" which is abfurd." I grant, that an effect is in this fenfe
paffive, that it is produced by the agency of the efficient caufe ; and in that fenfe a volition caufed by
the Deity or other efficient caufe is paffive. If Dr.
Weft mean by paffive action, an action which in its
production is caufed by an extrinfic caufe, I grant it;
and however Dr. Weft pronounces it *abfurd*, he
knows, that it is as eafy for another to pronounce it
not abfurd ; and the one pronunciation is juft as good
proof as the other. Volition is action, and if the
Doctor will prove to the conviction of candid inquir-
ers, that fuch an action cannot be the effect of a divine agency or other extrinfic caufe ; he will do
fomething more than affirm the contrary to be abfurd. As to the expreffion *inactive action*, if by this
he mean, that the action is the effect of an extrinfic
caufe, I grant it, and demand proof that the idea of
fuch an action is abfurd. If he mean an action,
which is not voluntary ; I know of no perfon who
pleads for fuch an action.

What the Doctor fays here, as well as almoft his
whole book, may be eafily retorted. Suppofe volition is not from an extrinfic caufe, but from the fubject as the caufe ; ftill it is as really and fully paffive
with refpect to its caufe and in coming into exiftence,
as if it were the effect of an extrinfic caufe. It would
as much be the fubject of the operation of this
intrinfic caufe, in order to its exiftence. Therefore
in this cafe too we have *paffive action* and *inactive
action.*

The Doctor in p. 23, Part I, fays, " How can
he" [man] " be an agent, if volition be the effect of
" an extrinfic caufe ?" To which I anfwer by afking
another queftion or two ; How can he in volition be
                                                        an

an agent, if it be the effect of an intrinfic caufe ? The volition is ftill as paffive in this cafe and equally pro- duced by the efficiency of its caufe, as it is when pro- duced by an extrinfic caufe. And how can man be an agent, if as the Doctor holds, volition be the effect of no caufe, extrinfic or intrinfic ? In that cafe, it is merely cafual or accidental, like the motion of one of Epicurus's atoms in the infinite void.

CHAPTER

CHAPTER VI.

*Of Foreknowledge and the Certainty or Neceſſity impli-
ed in it.*

DR. Weſt begins his third eſſay thus ; " We ſhall " endeavour to ſhow, in this eſſay, that infalli-
" ble foreknowledge in the Deity does not prove, that
" events take place in conſequence of an antecedent
" or previous neceſſity ;" p. 29. Let foreknowledge
prove or not prove what it will, unleſs events take
place abſolutely without a cauſe, they do take place
in conſequence of an antecedent or previous neceſſity. Unleſs they take place abſolutely without a cauſe,
they are effects ; and every effect neceſſarily follows
its cauſe. Dr. Weſt grants, p. 23, " that every ef-
" fect is wholly paſſive with regard to the cauſe which
" produces it." And as it is paſſive, it is brought into
exiſtence by the cauſing or neceſſitating influence of
its cauſe. Its exiſtence therefore " takes place in
" conſequence of an antecedent or previous neceſſity ;"
and this is true of all events, which do not happen without
cauſe. But Dr. Weſt denies, that any events take
place without a cauſe. Therefore he muſt concede,
that all events " take place in conſequence of an
" antecedent neceſſity."

If to this it ſhould be ſaid, that though all events are
effects, and are neceſſitated by their reſpective cauſes,
and in that reſpect take place in conſequence of an
antecedent neceſſity : Yet as volitions are the effects
of the mind, in which they exiſt, this cauſe does not
produce them or exert its producing act, in conſequence
of an antecedent neceſſity ; I anſwer, The mind, if it
do efficiently cauſe volitions, cauſes them either in
conſequence of an antecedent certainty, or without
that certainty. If it cauſe them in conſequence of
antecedent certainty, it cauſes them under the influence

ence of moral neceffity; for antecedent certainty of moral actions is all we mean by moral neceffity. If it caufe them without that certainty, it caufes them contingently and by mere chance or blind fate.

Befides, if the mind caufe its own volitions, it neceffitates them into exiftence, and therefore they come into exiftence under the influence of antecedent neceffity; and the caufing act is an event and therefore muft have a caufe, and *this* caufe muft neceffitate *this* event into exiftence; and fo it runs into an infinite feries of acts caufing one another, every one of which comes into exiftence in confequence of an antecedent neceffity.

That the infallible divine foreknowledge of any event does imply all that antecedent neceffity of the future exiftence of that event, for which we contend, may appear thus :——The infallible or certain foreknowledge of any event is a knowledge of the certainty or certain truth, that the event will come into exiftence; and that certainty which is the object of this knowledge, is all the neceffity, for which we contend. This is what Prefident Edwards calls philofophical neceffity, which with regard to moral actions is moral neceffity; and it muft exift at the time the knowledge of it exifts, and indeed in order to be the object of knowledge : And as the knowledge is by the fuppofition *foreknowledge*, therefore it muft exift before the event foreknown, and therefore the certainty or neceffity of that event muft exift before the event itfelf; of courfe it is *antecedent* neceffity. To fuppofe otherwife is to fuppofe, that a certainty or certain truth may be feen and known before it exifts, and that what is not, may be feen and known to be.

Dr. Weft argues, p. 32, that becaufe " the Deity is " poffeffed of an underived felf-exifting knowledge, " which is independent of any caufe or medium what- " ever, and his knowledge can extend to all futuri- " ties, independent of the imperfect mode of inferring " conclufions from their premifes ; confequently in-
" fallible

" fallible prefcience in the Deity cannot imply any
" antecedent neceffity of the event foreknown." By
antecedent neceffity we mean antecedent certainty or
antecedent certain truth. Now does Dr. Weft mean,
that fince the Deity poffeffes an underived and felf-
exiftent knowledge, therefore he fees and knows, that
there is a certainty of the future exiftence of an event,
when there really is no fuch certainty ? Or that God
knows that to exift, which does not exift ? He does
mean this, if he mean any thing to the purpofe. For
if he mean, that God fees a certainty which exifts, it
does exift in order to be feen ; and therefore antecedent certainty or moral neceffity is implied in the divine prefcience. But let the knowledge of God be
ever fo underived, felf-exiftent and independent, it
will not enable him to difcern that which is not, to fee
truth or certainty, before it exifts, or to fee truth to
be falfehood and falfehood to be truth.——If by *independent* knowledge he mean a knowledge which is not
dependent on the truth and has not truth for its foundation and object ; he muft ftill mean, that God can
know a propofition to be true which is not true.

It is manifeftly implied in what Dr. Weft fays on
this fubject, that if divine foreknowledge were derived through any *medium*, or if it be founded on decrees,
it would be utterly inconfiftent with human liberty.
But fince it is, as he fuppofes, immediate and not dependent on decrees, it is perfectly confiftent with human liberty.——That there will be a general rejection
of antichrift and antichriftian errours, we know by the
medium of divine prediction : And does the Doctor
believe that this our knowledge is more inconfiftent
with the liberty of thofe, who fhall reject antichrift,
than the abfolute and underived knowledge of God ?
Or than our own knowledge of the fame fact, if it
were intuitive and underived ?

The Doctor adds, " If this definition of the divine
knowledge," viz. that it is underived, felf-exiftent and
independent, " be juft ; then it will follow that there

" is

" is no previous or antecedent *certainty in the things*
" *themselves*, upon which divine prescience is founded.
This manifestly implies, that God foreknows things
before they are future, and sees a certainty before it
is. " By certainty," says the Doctor, " in the things
" themselves, previous to the divine knowledge, *must*
" *be meant* some medium distinct from the things them-
" selves, by which they render themselves evident
" to the divine knowledge." He here asserts, but
brings nothing to prove what he asserts. And what
signify such bare assertions ? Does the Doctor expect
his readers will receive them as proofs ? May they
not justly demand evidence, that this *medium* which he
here mentions, must be meant by certainty in things
themselves ? By that certainty I mean no such thing :
But positively I do mean what President Edwards declares that he meant, " The firm and infallible con-
" nection between the subject and predicate of the
" proposition," which affirms them to be connected ;
or the *real truth* of the proposition. For instance it
is a real truth, that I am now writing, and the certainty or reality of this truth or fact, is the ground of the
divine knowledge of it ; and this certainty consists in
the firm and indissoluble connection of the subject and
predicate of the proposition which affirms, that I am
writing. This certainty or truth of the thing is no
" medium distinct from the thing" or fact " itself, by
" which it renders itself evident to the divine knowl-
" edge ;" but it is the real existence of the very thing or
fact.——Again, it is to all Christians a real and certain futurity and truth, that Jesus Christ will judge in
righteousness. But the truth and certainty of this future event is not a *medium* distinct from the futurity of the event itself, by which it renders itself evident to the divine mind ; but it is the real and infallible futurity of the event itself and consists in the firm
and infallible connection between the subject and
predicate of the proposition which affirms the futurity
of the event. Now will Dr. West pretend, that there
is

is no truth or no firm and infallible connection between the subject and predicate of the proposition,
that *I am now writing*, which is the foundation of the
divine knowledge of that event ? If this were so, real
truth and fact would not be the foundation, rule or
object of the divine knowledge ; but God might in-
differently know truth to be falsehood and falsehood
truth.

Or if by " the medium by which things render
" themselves evident," the Doctor mean *the truth and
reality of things ;* I grant that what ever is known
whether to God or creatures, is known by this medium ;
and this is true of the most self-evident propositions
and of the most independent and underived knowledge. But to call this *a medium* of knowledge is a
perverfion of language. Surely truth is not the medium by which itself is known.

Dr. West himself notwithstanding his abundant labour " to show, that infallible foreknowledge in the
" Deity does not prove, that events take place in con-
" sequence of an antecedent necessity ;" fully and frequently grants all that we maintain. Thus, p. 37.
" That the Deity does perfectly discern all connec-
" tions between subjects and predicates ———— is
" readily granted." Now this implies, that the said
subjects and predicates are really and in themselves connected, and in order of nature before that connection
is discerned. This real and certain connection is the
certainty or certain truth of things themselves, of
which we have been speaking ; and which with regard
to moral events and actions is moral necessity. P. 41.
" The future volitions of moral agents are so infalli-
" bly and indissolubly connected with the divine fore-
" knowledge, which has had existence from all eterni-
" ty, that it is impossible, that the Deity should be de-
" ceived ; and therefore all these volitions will most
" *certainly* take place." P. 46. " There may be a
" *certainty* ———— that such a thing will take place,"
speaking of an human action. But certainty with regard

gard to moral actions is moral neceſſity, and if all volitions foreknown by God will *certainly* take place,
they will take place by moral neceſſity.——P. 52.
" All things from eternity to eternity being preſent to
" the divine mind, *he ſees all things as they are.*"
Therefore if he ſee ſome events as certainly future,
they are certainly future ; for he ſees them as they
are. And this certain futurity is the object of the
divine knowledge, and in the order of nature is antecedent to it, as really as the exiſtence of this paper,
on which I am writing, is in the order of nature
antecedent to my ſight of it. But this antecedent
certain futurity of any moral action, is antecedent
moral neceſſity. Therefore as all moral actions are
foreknown by God in conſequence of an antecedent
moral neceſſity, much more do they *come into exiſtence* in conſequence of ſuch an antecedent neceſſity.——P. 53. " Deity would from all eternity have
" infallibly foreknown this propoſition, *as a certain
" truth,*" viz. the propoſition concerning Peter and
Judas denying and betraying their Lord. It ſeems
then that whatever propoſition concerning a future
event is infallibly foreknown by God, is foreknown
as a certain and infallible truth ; or which is the ſame
thing, it is known, as an infallible truth, that the event
will come to paſs ; and therefore it is a certain and
infallible truth antecedently in the order of nature to
the knowledge of it ; and therefore the event being a
moral act, was morally neceſſary antecedently to the
foreknowledge, and much more antecedently to the
event itſelf.——P. 52. " This neceſſity being only
" a conſequence founded upon *the certainty of the
" thing* foreknown." Thus notwithſtanding all Dr.
Weſt's clamour againſt Preſident Edwards, becauſe
he had ſpoken of a *certainty in things themſelves,* he
himſelf here expreſsly holds the very ſame. And
will Dr. Weſt deny, that this "certainty of the thing
foreknown" is the ground of the divine foreknowledge of that thing, in the ſame ſenſe, that my preſent

K   exiſtence exiltence is the ground of the divine knowledge, that I exift ? If this be not denied, it cannot be denied, that certainty or moral neceffity is in order of nature antecedent to the foreknowledge, and much more antecedent to the exiltence, of a moral action.

Dr. Weft will not deny, that any future event foreknown by God, will certainly come to pafs. Then there is a certainty, or it is an infallible truth, that every fuch event will come to pafs, and this certainty now exifts antecedently to the exiftence of the event. But this certainty with regard to moral events, is moral neceffity. Therefore there is a neceffity of the exiftence of all events divinely foreknown, and this neceffity is antecedent to the exiftence of the events. Thus, mere foreknowledge is an infallible proof of antecedent neceffity.

" We frequently fay, It is a pity fuch a perfon did
" fo ; there was no occafion for it ; he might eafily
" have omitted the doing of the thing in the time of
" it, if he would. Why may we not as well fay, A
" man *will certainly* do a particular thing, though he
" will have power to forbear doing it ? There could
" not be the leaft appearance of abfurdity or contra-
" diction in fpeaking in this manner about a future
" action, any more than about a paft action, were it
" not for the great difficulty or fuppofed impoffibility
" of conceiving how a thing can be foreknown, un-
" lefs it be connected with fomething that now ex-
" ifts ; that is, a thing cannot be foreknown, unlefs
" there is a medium, which has a prefent exiftence."
P. 30.——On this paffage I remark,

1. Here again Dr. Weft holds that certainty in things, which he fo abundantly reprobates in Prefident Edwards. He fays, " a man *will certainly* do a particular thing ;" and he doubtlefs means, that it is a certain futurity, the event itfelf is certain, or it is a certain and infallible truth, that the man will do the thing ; and not merely that this truth is known, whether by God or creature. Truth is truth wheth-

er known or not : And this infallible truth is the very certainty in the things themfelves, of which Pref- ident Edwards fpeaks.

2. What does Dr. Weft mean, when he fays, " He might eafily have omitted the doing of the thing, " *if he would ?*" Suppofe the thing done was an *in- ternal* act, a volition to go to a debauch : In what fenfe does Dr. Weft mean, that the man could have avoided this volition, *if he would ?* Does he mean, that if he had not had the volition, he would not have had it ? This is an undoubted truth, but does not difprove the neceffity of it. If God had not always fpoken the truth, he would not have fpoken the truth. But it does not hence follow, that God does not al- ways neceffarily fpeak the truth, when he fpeaks at all, or that he can lie. If there had been no God, there would indeed have been no God ; but does it hence follow, that the divine exiftence is not necef- fary ?——To fay, that if a man had chofen not to go to a debauch, he would indeed have chofen not to go to it, is too great trifling to be imputed to Dr. Weft. Yet to fay, that the man could have avoided the *external action* of going to the debauch, if he would, would be equal trifling ; for the queftion be- fore us is concerning the liberty of the *will* or *mind* and not of the body.——On the whole, we have before us one of Dr. Weft's *things hard to be underflood,* and we muft wait for an explanation.

3. When we fay concerning any paft action of a man, " There was no occafion for it ; he might eafi- " ly have omitted the doing of the thing in the time " of it, if he would ;" if we mean, that there was no antecedent certainty, that he would perform that ac- tion, we mean a falfehood. That action was as much from eternity the object of the divine omnifcience, as any action which is now future ; therefore the cer- tainty of its then future exiftence preceded its actual exiftence. And this certainty was as fixed, unalterable and indefeafible, as the divine foreknowledge or the

K 2   divine

divine decree. The foreknowledge and decree of God imply no other kind or degree of neceffity, than the aforefaid abfolute certainty. A futurity that is abfolutely certain is implicd in the divine foreknowledge ; and the addition of a decree cannot increafe that certainty.

4. When we fay, A perfon might eafily have omitted a certain paft action, in the time of it, if he would ; we commonly mean, that he was under no compulfion or coaction, or no *natural* neceffity ; and that he had a *natural power* to omit the action. This undoubtedly every man has with regard to every voluntary action, and this however that action be foreknown or decreed by God. Though Judas betrayed his Mafter, " according to the determinate counfel and " foreknowledge of God ;" yet he was under no *natural* neceffity to betray him, but had a full *natural power* to do otherwife. Now Dr. Weft reconciles foreknowledge with liberty, on the ground that we have ftill *a phyfical* or natural power to do otherwife. On the fame ground we may reconcile abfolute decrees with liberty.

5. In the fame fenfe " we may as well fay, Such a " man will *certainly* do a particular thing, though he " will have power to forbear the doing of it." He may doubtlefs have a *natural* power to forbear ; ftill this does not at all diminifh the *certain futurity* of the action ; and that whether the action be foreknown only, or foreknown and decreed. And a natural power is all the power, which the man will have to forbear the action. Any power oppofed to moral neceffity or the certain futurity of the action, would imply that it is uncertain, whether he will perform that action ; which is contrary to the fuppofition made by Dr. Weft, " that the man *will certainly* do the thing."

6. As to " the great difficulty or fuppofed impoffi- " bility of conceiving, *how* a thing can be foreknown, un- " lefs it be connected with fomething that now exifts;" this is needlefsly brought in here. In this part of the
argument

argument we are under no neceffity of inquiring or fhowing *how* God foreknows future events, but may, fo far as relates to the certain futurity of all events foreknown by God and the antecedency of that certainty to the exiftence of the events, allow, that God forcknows future events in the independent and underived manner, which Dr. Weft maintains. This would equally imply a certainty antecedent to the exiftence of the events foreknown, as a foreknowledge founded on a decree would imply it. Dr. Weft's account of the divine foreknowledge implies, as I have fhown, all that certainty or neceffity, for which we plead. Befide what has been already faid to fhow this, I add, that Dr. Weft grants, that foreknowledge has no caufal influence to bring things into exiftence, or to make their exiftence more certain, than it would be without foreknowledge. " I fuppofe it will be " readily granted on all fides, that even the divine " foreknowledge itfelf has no influence or caufal force, " with regard to the thing foreknown, either to bring " it into exiftence or to hinder its happening ; but " that all things would take place juft in the fame " manner, if they were not foreknown, as they do " now ;" p. 45. Dr. Weft alfo grants, that all future events are foreknown by God, and that all things which are foreknown by him, will certainly and infallibly come to pafs. Now as this certainty is not cauf-ed by foreknowledge, it muft exift independently of it. And as God fees all things as they are ; therefore when he fees them to be certainly future, they *are* certainly future; and this certain futurity, which is the objeft of the divine knowledge, exifted in the order of nature antecedently to the divine knowledge, and much more antecedently to the aftual exiftence of the events themfelves. Otherwife God would fee events to be certainly future, while they are not certainly future.

" The obvious reafon," fays Dr. Weft, p. 31, " why we cannot know things but only by intuition

K 3 " or

" or proof, is becaufe all our knowledge is entircly *ab*
" *extra.*" And does the Doctor believe, that if part
of our knowledge were not *ab extra*, we fhould know
fome things neither by intuition nor by proof ? Whatever is known by intuition is felf-evident ; and whatever is known by proof, is evident by the medium of
fomething elfe. And whatever is known at all, is either evident by itfelf immediately, or is evident by
fomething elfe mediately. Therefore Dr. Weft, in
fuppofing, that if our knowledge were not all *ab extra*,
we fhould know fome things neither by intuition nor
by proof, fuppofes that fome things would be evident
to us, neither immediately nor mediately, neither by
themfelves nor by any thing elfe : And what kind of
a fource of knowledge we fhould then have, I leave
the Doctor to explain.

" If previous certainty in things themfelves means
" nothing diftinct from the things themfelves, then all
" that can be meant by this previous certainty in things
" themfelves, upon which the divine knowledge is
" founded, is only this, that the Deity cannot know
" that things will exift, which he knows never will ex-
" ift. And therefore to fay, that there is a previous
" certainty in things themfelves, upon which the di-
" vine knowledge is founded, is only faying in other
" words, that the divine knowledge is founded on the
" divine knowledge ;" p. 34. By certainty in things
themfelves I have already explained myfelf to mean
the *truth* and *reality* of things themfelves, or the truth
of the propofition which afferts their exiftence or relation : And *previous* certainty of things themfelves
means nothing different from the truth of the propofition, which afferts their future exiftence, or its being
a real truth, that thofe things will exift. Now, whether to fay, that the divine foreknowledge of an event,
is founded on the truth, that the event will come into
exiftence, be the fame as to fay, " that the divine fore-
" knowledge is founded on the divine foreknowledge,"
I am willing any candid perfon fhould judge.

The

The Doctor says, p. 34, " That knowledge in the " Deity muft mean the fame thing with certainty." No doubt knowledge in the Deity is the fame thing with *fubjective* certainty or certain knowledge ; but it is not the fame with *objective* certainty, or the truth which is the objeft of the divine knowledge.

The Doctor grants, p. 41, " That the future vo- " litions of moral agents are fo infallibly and indiffo- " lubly connected with the divine foreknowledge, " which has had exiftence from all eternity, that it is " impoffible, that the Deity fhould be deceived ; and " therefore thefe volitions will moft *certainly* take " place. For by *neceffary* here he" [Prefident Ed- wards] " can ——— mean nothing diftinct from *in-* " *fallible certainty.* But how does their being neceffa- " ry in this fenfe, *i. e. infallibly certain*, prove that the " volitions of moral agents are effects produced by an " *extrinfic* caufe."——Undoubtedly by neceffity in this cafe Prefident Edwards means nothing diftinct from infallible certainty. This is the very thing which he abundantly declares himfelf to mean. " And as " the divine foreknowledge," by Dr. Weft's confef- fion, " has had exiftence from eternity ;" and as " the " volitions of moral agents are indiffolubly connected " with that foreknowledge," and " thofe volitions will " moft certainly take place ;" of courfe there was an infallible eternal certainty, that all human volitions would come into exiftence juft as they do exift, and Dr. Weft grants all that we hold on this head. What then becomes of liberty *to either fide, to act or not act ?* For inftance, it is now divinely foreknown, that *Gog* and *Magog* will rife and compafs the camp of the faints. Therefore when *Gog* and *Magog* fhall come into exiftence, they will no more have a liberty *to act or not act*, as to this inftance of their conduct, than they would have, on the fuppofition that the fame conduct were decreed.——It is true, there would be this difference in the cafes, that the decree would *caufe* the certain futurity of that conduct, but the

K 4 foreknowledge

foreknowledge would not *cause* it : Nor is it of any importance as to liberty, by whom or by what this certain futurity is caufed, or whether it be without caufe. If a prifon when built, be no obftruction to liberty, then the agency of the mafon and carpenter who built it was nothing oppofed to liberty. So if *certain futurity*, when eftablifhed, be not inconfiftent with liberty ; then the divine decree, by which it is eftablifhed, is not inconfiftent with liberty.

If it fhould be faid, that God forefees, that *Gog* and *Magog* will influence themfelves to the conduct juft now mentioned ; be it fo ; then it is now infallibly certain, that *Gog* and *Magog* will influence themfelves to that conduct. Where then is their liberty to act or not act ? It is not left loofe and undetermined, whether they fhall influence themfelves to that conduct ; but it is previoufly certain, that they will influence themfelves to it.

The Doctor in the laft quotation, afks, " How " does their being infallibly certain, prove that the " volitions of moral agents are effects produced by " an *extrinfic* caufe ?"——Suppofe they are not effects of an *extrinfic* caufe, but are effected by the fubject of thofe volitions, if that were poffible ; yet if it be previoufly and from all eternity certain, that the fubject will produce thefe volitions in himfelf ; ftill there is no *liberty to either fide, to act or not act ;* but he is limited to produce in himfelf thofe very definite volitions, which are divinely forefeen, and therefore he is confined *to one fide,* is confined *to act* and that definitely.

Or fuppofe thefe volitions are produced by no caufe whatever, then God forefees that they are about to happen abfolutely without caufe and by mere chance ; ftill there is in this cafe no liberty to either fide, but the volitions are without caufe confined to one fide only.

It is abundantly pleaded by Dr. Weft and others, that the circumftance that the divine foreknowledge is not the efficient caufe of human volitions, renders

that

that foreknowledge entirely confiftent with their idea of liberty, even as the divine knowledge of a volition in prefent exiftence is confiftent with the liberty of that volition.——If by liberty in this cafe they mean felf-determination or the caufation of volition by the fubject himfelf ; I grant, that the moft abfolute foreknowledge is perfectly confiftent with this idea of liberty : And fo is an abfolute decree as confiftent with it. If God were abfolutely to decree, that a particular man fhall caufe in himfelf a particular volition, the man would accordingly caufe that volition in himfelf, and therefore according to the definition of liberty now given, he would be free.——But if by liberty in this cafe be meant, what the writers to whom I am oppofed, call *a liberty to either fide*, and *a power to act or not act*, as oppofed to moral neceffity ; the divine foreknowledge of a volition is utterly inconfiftent with the liberty of that volition. For according to this definition, liberty implies, that the volition is not fixed or determined, and therefore it is uncertain what it will be, or whether it will be at all. But divine foreknowledge implies, that it is abfolutely certain, that a volition foreknown will be, and what it will be, as Dr. Weft grants.

The circumftance, that foreknowledge does not efficiently *caufe* an event to be certainly future, is nothing to the prefent purpofe. We are not now inquiring what *caufes* an event to be certainly future, but whether it *be* certainly future. If it be certainly future it is neceffary, in the fenfe in which we ufe the word *neceffity*, let what will be the caufe of that futurity, or if the futurity be uncaufed. Divine prophecy is not the caufe of the futurity of the event foretold, yet no man will fay, that it does not prove the certain futurity of that event. But prophecy no more implies or proves the certain futurity of the event foretold, than the divine foreknowledge implies and proves the certain futurity of the event foreknown.——To fay, that a divine decree is inconfiftent with liberty,

ty, becaufe it *makes* the action certainly future, when
the certain futurity itfelf is allowed to be confiftent
with liberty, is very ftrange ! What if it does make it
certainly future ? That certain futurity, when made,
is not inconfiftent with liberty. So long as this is
granted, to hold that the divine decree as making or
producing that certain futurity is inconfiftent with
liberty, is as abfurd as to grant that a free circulation
of the fluids in the animal conftitution is confiftent
with health ; and yet to hold, that exercife *as producing* and merely becaufe it produces that free circulation, is inconfiftent with health.

I grant, that divine foreknowledge is as confiftent
with liberty, as the divine knowledge of a prefent
volition is. If by liberty be meant the caufation of
volition by the fubject, God may undoubtedly as
well forefee this, as fee it prefent. But if by liberty
be meant a liberty to either fide, a liberty to act or
not act, as oppofed to moral neceffity ; fince this implies, with regard to an act now in exiftence, uncertainty whether the act does exift, and with regard to
a future act, uncertainty in the nature of things and
in the divine mind, whether it will exift ; I fay, no
fuch uncertainty is or can be with regard either to
an act feen by God to be now in exiftence, or an act
divinely forefeen. As therefore the divine knowledge
of the prefent exiftence of an act, is utterly inconfiftent with this kind of liberty in that act ; we need not
and we do not pretend, that the divine foreknowledge
of an act is more inconfiftent with the fame kind of
liberty in the act foreknown.——There is this difference however in the cafes ; knowledge of a prefent
act does not imply, that the act was certain *previoufly* to its exiftence. But the foreknowledge of an
act does imply this. This difference ought carefully
to be noticed, or we fhall run into great errour. If,
when it is faid, that foreknowledge no more proves
a neceffity of the act foreknown, than the knowledge
of an act at prefent exifting, proves the neceffity of
this

this act, the meaning be, that foreknowledge no more proves, that the future act foreknown is certainly future *previously* to the existence of it, than the knowledge of a present act proves, that this act was certainly future *previously* to its existence ; the truth of this proposition is by no means allowed. Foreknowledge by the very term respects a future event ; of course the foreknowledge exists before the event. And as it is granted on all hands, that foreknowledge implies a certainty of the event foreknown ; it follows, that there is a certainty of the future existence of every event foreknown, and this certainty is previous to the existence of the event. But the knowledge of a present event may not exist before the event itself ; if it does, it is then *foreknowledge*. And as it does not, so far as it is the bare knowledge of a present event, exist before the event ; it does not imply a *previous* certainty, that the event would come into existence.

My seeing a man perform an action does not prove, that it was certain beforehand, that he could perform it. But if a prophet under inspiration see, that a man will tomorrow perform a certain action, this does prove, that it is beforehand certain, that he will perform it. And surely the foresight of a prophet no more proves this, than the foreknowledge of God.——— Suppose the act foreknown by God, is about to be self-originated, still it is as necessary or certain beforehand, as if it were not to be self-originated ; because the foreknowledge is from eternity and therefore precedes the existence of the act out of the divine mind. For though all things are always present *in the divine mind ;* yet all things are not always in present existence *out of the divine mind,* any more than all creatures existed from eternity.——— Be it so, that in the divine foreknowledge all things are present ; then all human volitions are from eternity as fixed and certain, as if they existed from eternity not only in the divine mind, but out of the divine mind, and are as incapable of not existing, as the divine mind is incapable of delusion or errour.

" Bare

" Bare *certainty*, that an agent will do fuch a thing,
" does not imply in it, that he had not in himfelf a
" *power* to refrain from doing it ;" p. 45. This depends on the meaning of the word *power* to refrain.
If this mean *natural* power, as it has been explained,
it is granted, that ever fo great certainty and even a
divine abfolute decree, that an agent fhall do fuch a
thing, does not imply in it, that he has not in himfelf
a power to refrain from doing it. But if by *power*
to refrain be meant *moral* power, or a power oppofite
to moral neceffity, which is the bare certainty of a
moral action, it is abfurd and felf-contradictory to
fay, that the bare certainty that an agent will do fuch
a thing, does not imply in it, that he has not a power
to refrain from doing it. It is the very fame abfurdity and contradiction, as to fay, that a bare certainty,
that an agent will do fuch a particular thing, does not
imply in it a certainty, that he will do it.

In the fame page the Doctor tells us, " The only
" queftion is, whether fuppofing it to be foreknown,
" that an agent will conduct in fuch a manner, at
" fuch a time, it will be any contradiction to affirm,
" that the faid agent will have a power, at the fame
" time, to act in a different manner." If it be foreknown, that an agent will act in a particular manner,
at a particular time : it will be granted, that there is
a certainty, that he will act in that particular. But
certainty of moral action is *moral neceffity*, and moral
inability of the contrary. And to affert, that an agent
is under a moral inability to act in a different manner, and yet has a moral power to act in a different
manner, is a direct contradiction.

The Doctor fays, p. 29, " That infallible fore-
" knowledge in the Deity does not prove, that events
" take place in confequence of an antecedent or pre-
" vious neceffity ; that it only proves a *logical* necef-
" fity or a neceffity *of confequence ;* i. e. it being *cer-*
" *tain*, that a thing will take place, it follows, that to
" affert that it will not take place, muft be falfe and
" cannot

" cannot be true."——As the Doctor makes much
of this, which he calls a *logical* neceffity, or a neceffity *of confequence*, let us examine it.

The foreknowledge of God is here faid to prove a
logical neceffity only, or a neceffity of confequence ;
which is faid to be this, that " it being certain, that a
" thing will take place, it follows, that to affert that
" it will not take place, muft be falfe and cannot be
" true." Here one thing is faid to follow from another, by a logical neceffity or a neceffity of confequence. Let us take an example : It is a certain
truth that the dead will rife ; and does it hence *follow*, that it is a falfehood, that the dead will not rife ?
No, the latter is no more a confequence from the
former, than the former is a confequence from the
latter ; or than that twice two are not unequal to four,
is a confequence from this propofition, that twice two
are equal to four ; or than from its being true, that a
thing *is*, it follows as a confequence that it is not true,
that it *is not*. The one is no confequence from the
other, but is precifely the fame thing expreffed in different words, which convey the very fame idea. You
might as well fay, that if a man be *kind*, it follows as
a confequence, that he is *benevolent* ; or that if a
man be *bufy*, it follows as a confequence, that he is
employed in *bufinefs*. Thus we may argue and draw
confequences all day long, yet make no more progrefs,
than the foldier who marches without gaining ground.

Dr. Weft fays, p. 32, " No neceffity is implied in
" divine prefcience, except merely a logical one ;
" but this ——— is in the nature of things *fubfequent*
" to the infallible foreknowledge of the exiftence of
" the thing foreknown." But does Dr. Weft mean, that
in foreknowledge God forefees an event as uncertain,
and that in confequence of this forefight the event
becomes certain ? Surely the Doctor did not well
confider the fubject, if this be his meaning. To foreknow is certainly to forefee : And certainly to forefee, is to fee a future event as certainly about to be.
This

This certainty of its futurity is fuppofed and implied in foreknowledge, and is not the *confequence* of it. Dr. Weft fays, " It will be readily granted on all fides, " that even the divine foreknowledge itfelf has no in- " fluence nor caufal force, with regard to the thing " foreknown, either to bring it into exiftence, or to ". hinder its happening." Therefore it has no influence to make its exiftence certain or neceffary ; how then is the neceffity *fubfequent* to.foreknowledge? The certainty of its exiftence is *antecedent* in the order of nature to the foreknowledge, and is the ground or the objeft of it. This alfo is abundantly implied in va- rious paffages of Dr. Weft's book, as has been fhown above. In p. 53, the Doftor fpeaks of his logical neceffity as " only a *confequence founded* upon the " certainty of the thing foreknown." But this cer- tainty of moral aftions is the very moral neceffity, for which we plead. If the Doftor mean this by his log- ical neceffity, it is prefumed, that the reader fees the abfurdity of faying, that this neceffity is *confequent* on the divine foreknowledge ; and alfo the abfurdity of faying that it is *founded on* the certainty of the thing foreknown. A thing is not confequent on itfelf nor on that which is founded on itfelf, as foreknowledge is founded on the certainty of the thing foreknown. If the Doftor mean any thing elfe by his logical ne- ceffity, I wifh to be informed how he means any thing to the purpofe of oppofing that moral neceffity of hu- man aftions, which Prefident Edwards had advanced, and by which he explained himfelf to mean the certain- ty of moral aftions. A logical neceffity confequent on that certainty is a different thing from the certainty itfelf.

But allowing, what Dr. Weft holds, That fore- knowledge proves a neceffity confequential to fore- knowledge ; this neceffity would be as inconfiftent with liberty, as one that is antecedent to foreknowl- edge ; becaufe the neceffity would exift antecedently to the aftions of creatures, as it follows immediately from foreknowledge.

The

The Doctor, in his Second Part, p. 92, says, " Mr.
" Edwards had raifed a fpectre, which he could not
" lay. With him neceffity was neceffity ; and with
" him it was all one, whether the neceffity was previ-
" ous to the thing in queftion, or a confequence drawn
" from the fuppofition of its having taken place."
This is an injurious reprefentation. The neceffity
for which Prefident Edwards pleads, is " previous to
" the thing in queftion," and he never pleads for a neceffity which is " a confequence drawn from the mere
" fuppofition of its having taken place." The neceffity for which he pleads, is that which is implied in divine foreknowledge ; and as this exifts before the
event foreknown, fo the neceffity which is implied in
it and proved by it, is alfo previous to that event, and
does not follow or begin to exift in confequence even
of that foreknowledge, and much lefs in confequence
of the fuppofition, that the thing foreknown has taken
place. The only thing, fo far as I know, which could
give occafion for this reprefentation by Dr. Weft is,
that Prefident Edwards calls this neceffity *a neceffity
of confequence,* and fays, that a thing neceffary in its
own nature, or one that has already come into exiftence, being fuppofed, another thing neceffarily connected with either of the former, and the neceffity of
whofe exiftence is in queftion, certainly follows ; i. e.
the neceffity of this laft thing certainly follows from
the exiftence or fuppofition of the exiftence, of either
of the former. For inftance, when the divine decree
or foreknowledge of an event is fuppofed, the exiftence of the event decreed or foreknown will certainly follow. But the neceffity, which Dr. Weft inju-
rioufly imputes to Prefident Edwards, is not the neceffary exiftence of *one thing,* implied in the fuppofed
exiftence of *another ;* but the neceffary exiftence of
one and the fame thing, fo long as it is fuppofed to exift ; and this neceffary exiftence amounts to no more
than the mere identical, trifling propofition, that *what
is. is.* Of fuch trifling Prefident Edwards was incapable,

pable, and the implicit imputation, that he has written an octavo volume in support of a proposition so
insignificant, ought either never to have been made,
or to have been better supported, than by mere affertion.

In the latter part of his third essay, the Doctor has
spent a number of pages to show, that a certainty that
a man will perform particular actions does not imply
that he is under a necessity of performing them, or
that he has no power to avoid them. But all this is
labour lost, and is easily answered by making the diftinction between natural and moral inability; or it
all depends on the ambiguity of words and is mere
logomachy.

Dr. Clarke endeavours to evade the argument for
moral necessity drawn from the divine foreknowledge,
by saying, that foreknowledge no more implies necef-
sity, than the truth of a proposition asserting some future event implies necessity. This may be granted.
If a proposition asserting some future event, be a real and absolute truth, there is an absolute certainty of
the event; such absolute certainty is all that is implied in the divine foreknowledge; and all the moral
necessity for which we plead. And though this certainty is consistent with a physical or natural ability to
do otherwise, it is not consistent with the contingence
or uncertainty of the event. So that there is no liberty of contingence in the case, no liberty to either
side, to act or not act, no liberty inconsistent with
previous certainty of moral action, which is moral
necessity.

Dr. West strenuously opposes the doctrine, that the
divine decrees are the foundation of God's foreknowledge. As I have already observed, this question
seems to be foreign from the dispute concerning liberty; therefore I do not wish to bring it in here;
otherwise I should have no objection to entering on
the discussion of it. But suppose the contrary were
true, that foreknowledge is the foundation of decrees;

L

I prefume it would be granted, that decrees immediately follow foreknowledge. Therefore all events are decreed before they come to pafs. And as decrees eftablifh, or imply an eftablifhment of the events decreed, and this antecedently to their exiftence; therefore on this plan there is an abfolute certainty of all events and moral actions, and that antecedently to the exiftence of thofe actions; becaufe they are all abfolutely decreed by God immediately on his foreknowledge of them and before they come into exiftence.

" If this does not imply, that foreknowledge is not " an effential, attribute, I am under a great miftake;" p. 35. Be it fo, that Dr. Weft is under a great miftake; what follows? Is it impoffible, that he fhould be under a great miftake? If foreknowledge be an effential attribute, it doubtlefs exifts antecedently to human actions, and therefore implies a certainty of them antecedent to their exiftence. The truth, is, that the foreknowledge of any particular event is no more an effential attribute of God, than the knowledge of any prefent or paft event. Knowledge in general is an effential attribute; but any particular perception of the divine mind is no more an effential attribute, than any particular act of the divine will, or any one decree of God. Will in general is an effential attribute; but Dr. Weft will not pretend, that every act of the divine will is an effential attribute. Or if it be, doubtlefs every inftance of foreknowledge is an effential attribute. By the fame argument by which Dr. Weft proves, that according to our ideas of decrees and foreknowledge, knowledge is not an effential attribute; it may be proved, that according to Dr. Weft's ideas of thofe fubjects, will is not an effential attribute of God. The Doctor, p. 36, tells us, " That the divine determinations are the Deity decreeing and willing;" i. e. they are the will of God. But according to him the divine determinations or decrees are founded on foreknowledge. There-

L

fore the divine will is founded on God's foreknowledge and is not an effential attribute of God, but is
felf-created, or a creature of the divine underftanding.

The advocates for liberty to act or not act, " pre-
" tend not to be able to folve the difficulty arifing from
" divine prefcience." This is an honeft confeffion.
Yet with this acknowledged infuperable difficulty
attending this favourite doctrine, they are determined
to adhere to it. This confeffion Dr. Price in particular
makes in the following words; " The foreknowledge of a
" contingent event carrying the appearance of a contra-
" diction, is indeed a difficulty; and I do not pretend to
" be capable of removing it." Correfpondence with
Prieftley, p. 175.——If this be a fufficient apology for
holding a doctrine, which cannot be reconciled with
an acknowledged truth, it will be eafy to apologize for
holding any doctrine whatever; e. g. the doctrine of
tranfubftantiation. It is only neceffary to fay, " That
a body fhould be turned into flefh, and yet retain all
the fenfible qualities of bread, as it carries the appearance of a contradiction, is indeed a difficulty;
and we do not pretend to be capable of removing it.

Dr. Weft holds, p. 53, that what is foreknown by
God, is *eternal truth*; yet, p. 33, he holds, that " there
" is no antecedent certainty in things themfelves, on
" which divine prefcience is founded:" *i. e.* God
knows a propofition to be a certain truth, before it is
a certain truth, and after his knowledge of it, it becomes
a certain and eternal truth; yet the divine knowledge
has no caufal influence to make it a truth.——He
ftrenuoufly oppofes the idea, that human moral actions
are certainly future antecedently to the divine foreknowledge of them; at the fame time, he grants, that
they are not *made* certainly future by the divine foreknowledge; and yet holds, that as foreknown by
God, they are *eternal truths*. If they be eternal truths,
doubtlefs the propofitions which affert them, were
certainly true from eternity, and therefore in the divine foreknowledge of them God perceived that eter-

nal

nal truth and certainty, and that certainty was the object and so the ground of the divine foreknowledge,
and therefore there was " an antecedent certainty in
" things themselves, on which the divine prescience is
" founded."——Besides, as the Doctor grants that
foreknowledge has no influence to cause that certainty, I ask, By what is it caused ? Is it caused by nothing ? According to the Doctor the certain futurity of
the things foreknown by God, does not exist antecedently to foreknowledge, and is not caused by it ; yet
it exists from eternity ; and it is that very eternal truth
which there is in all things foreknown by God.

In page 45, he grants, " that all things would take
" place just in the same manner, if they were not fore-
" known, as they do now." Then all things and all e-
vents are fixed and established independently of foreknowledge and antecedently to it, and were independently of foreknowledge certainly about to be. With
what consistency then does Dr. West deny a certainty
in things themselves antecedent to foreknowledge.
And on what ground can he oppose the doctrine of divine decrees, which represents those decrees as antecedent in the order of nature to foreknowledge ?

If God from all eternity knew events to be future,
they were future, and future in the order of nature
before foreknowledge, and were future by the divine
agency or by the agency of some other cause, or of no
cause at all. If they were future by the agency of
God, that is all that the doctrine of absolute decrees implies. If they were future by the agency of any other cause, this supposes another eternal cause. If they
were future by no cause, they may and will come into existence by no cause ; which is absurd. To imagine, that they are from eternity future by the agency of human free will, is to suppose, that human free
will either existed from eternity, or could and did produce effects eternal ages before it existed.

It is said, that there is properly no foreknowledge
in God, that all his knowledge is present knowledge,

and

and that paſt, preſent and future, are now all preſent in the divine mind.——Still God does not view all *poſſible* things as preſent. The *exiſtence* of ſome things is preſent to God ; only the poſſibility of other things is preſent to him. Whence ariſes this difference ? What gives ſome things a preſent exiſtence in the divine mind, when other things have only a poſſible exiſtence in the ſame mind ? This difference is an effect ; otherwiſe all real exiſtences and events are neceſſary exiſtences, or thoſe which are not neceſſary, become future, and finally come into exiſtence, without a cauſe. The difference between poſſible and future volitions cannot be the effect of the mind of the creature ; becauſe it exiſted before that mind exiſted.

By all things being preſent in the divine mind, is meant not that God now ſees them to be preſent to creatures and in their view ; but that his view of all things, ſo far as relates to himſelf, is the ſame as it will be, when they ſhall have come into exiſtence in the view of creatures. He ſees them not to be in exiſtence as to us, but ſees their exiſtence to be as to us future. And this is all that we mean by foreknowledge. So that ſaying, that all knowledge in God is preſent knowledge, does not ſhow, that there is no foreknowledge in him. A knowledge of things as future with reſpect to creatures, is foreknowledge : And the whole objection, that the divine knowledge is all preſent knowledge, is founded on the ambiguity of words, or of the phraſe, *all things are preſent in the divine mind,* or this, that, *all the divine knowledge is preſent knowledge.* If the meaning of that phraſe be, that God ſees now, that certain things will at ſome future time be in exiſtence in the view of creatures ; this is granted on all hands ; and what follows from it ? Surely not that there is no certainty previous to the exiſtence of thoſe things in the view of creatures, that they will thus be in exiſtence ; but, that there is ſuch a certainty. Therefore in this ſenſe of the phraſe it is not at all oppoſed to, but implies the doctrine of previous certainty

and

and moral neceffity, which we maintain. If that phrafe mean, that God now fees all events, which ever take place, to have a prefent exiftence in the view of crea-tures; this is not true and will not be pretended by our opponents. Yet this is the only fenfe of the phrafe, which oppofes the doctrine of previous certain-ty as argued from the divine foreknowledge. That all things are prefent in the divine mind, can mean no more, than that all things are now feen by God, and that there is no paft nor future with him. Still he views fome things to be paft, and other things to be future, with refpect to creatures : And his view of fome things as future with refpect to creatures, is what we mean by the divine foreknowledge ; not that he views things as future with refpect to himfelf. If therefore God now fees, that certain volitions-will hereafter take place in the minds of *Gog* and *Ma-gog*, according to prophecy, they will *certainly* take place, and there is a moral neceffity of it, and a moral neceffity *now exifting* ages before thofe volitions will have an exiftence in the minds of thofe men. The confideration, that all things are prefent with God, does, as before obferved, not at all prove, that there is not now a previous certainty or moral neceffity, that thofe volitions will come into exiftence ; but ev-idently proves that there is fuch certainty, and that in two refpects ; (1.) A certainty previous in order of time to the exiftence of thofe volitions in the minds of *Gog* and *Magog*. (2.) A certainty previous in the order of nature to the divine foreknowledge itfelf, and which is the foundation of that foreknowledge.

Moft or all the objections brought againft moral neceffity, may be brought with equal force againft di-vine foreknowledge. For example ; " If there be " an abfolute moral neceffity, that John go on in fin, and " be finally damned, there is no poffibility that he be " faved. Then why fhould he or any other perfon ufe " any endeavours toward his falvation ?"——If there be force in this objection, it is equally forcible againft

L 3   divine

divine foreknowledge : Thus, If God foreknow, that John will go on in fin and be finally damned, there is an abfolute certainty or moral neceffity of it. Therefore there is no poffibility of John's falvation ; and why fhould he or any other perfon put forth any endeavours toward it ? This and all objeffions of the kind imply, that all moral events are left in a ftate of perfeft uncertainty, till they come to pafs, that they come to pafs by mere chance, and that they are not, and cannot poffibly be, the objeffs of foreknowledge.

It has been already obferved, that though divine foreknowledge is not the efficient caufe of the certain futurity of any event ; yet it implies, that the event is certainly future, and this certainty, let it be caufed by what it will, or though it be uncaufed, is with refpeff to a moral event, moral neceffity, and equally confiftent or inconfiftent with liberty, as if it were caufed by foreknowledge. I now obferve further, that this certain futurity undoubtedly is caufed *by fomething*. It is equally abfurd to imagine, that an event may become *future* without a caufe, as that it may come *into exiftence* without a caufe. Certain futurity implies, that the aftual exiftence of the event is fecured to take place in due time. And whatever is able thus to fecure the event, is able to bring it into exiftence. If it may be fecured without a caufe, it may be brought into exiftence without a caufe. This certain futurity of all events from eternity is an effeff, and cannot be the effeff of any creature, becaufe no creature exifted from eternity. It muft therefore be the effeff of the Creator, who alone exifted from eternity, and who alone therefore could from eternity give futurity to any event.

Therefore however frightened Dr. Weft and other writers be at the idea, that moral affions fhould be the effeff of a caufe extrinfic to the fubjeff of thofe affions, we feem to be neceffitated to give into this idea, from the confideration, that all moral affions of creatures were from eternity foreknown and therefore were certainly future. This eternal futurity muft be

an

an effect of a caufe extrinfic to all creatures. This
extrinfic caufe fecures their exiftence, and in due
time actually brings them into exiftence.

It is faid, that God knows all things from eternity,
as we know things prefently exifting before our eyes.
Now the actual exiftence of things out of our minds
is the foundation of our knowledge in the cafe. But
it will not be faid, that all things exifted from eternity
out of the divine mind, and that this exiftence of
them is the foundation of the divine eternal knowledge of them or of their exiftence in the divine mind.
If they did eternally exift out of the divine mind,
they were neceffarily exiftent in the fame fenfe in
which God is ; and confequently none of our actions
are caufed by ourfelves or by our felf-determining
power : They are as uncaufed, as neceffary and as
eternal, as the divine exiftence.

Dr. Clarke in his remarks on Collins, p. 39, fays,
that " in the argument drawn againft liberty from the
" divine prefcience, or power of judging infallibly con-
" cerning free events, it muft be proved, that things
" otherwife fuppofed free, will thereby unavoidably
" become neceffary." On this I remark, (1.) That
if by the word *free* the Doctor mean any thing oppofite to the moft abfolute moral neceffity, he muft
mean *contingent, uncertain, not certainly future*. But
nothing is in this fenfe fuppofed, or allowed, to be
free.——(2.) We do not pretend from the divine
prefcience to prove, that " thereby things unavoidably *become* neceffary," or certainly future. But we
do pretend from prefcience to prove, that all events
were certainly future, in the order of nature, antecedently to the prefcience ; and that they are certainly
future, in the order of time, antecedently to their exiftence.

Dr. Clarke in his *Being and Attributes,* p. 95, &c.
grants, that all things are and were certain from eternity, and yet fuppofes, p. 97, that an univerfal fatality would be inconfiftent with morality. But it feems,

L 4

that

that according to the Doctor an univerfal and eternal
certainty of all things is not inconfiftent with morality ; and if by fatality he meant any thing different
from certainty, he oppofes whac nobody holds.———
Ibid, p. 98, the Doctor fays, " mere certainty of
" event does not imply neceffity." But mere certainty of event doubtlefs implies itfelf, and that is all
the neceffity, for which we plead. The Doctor's argument to prove, that certainty does not imply neceffity, is, that foreknowledge implies no more certainty,
than would exift without it. At the fame time he
grants, that there is " the fame certainty of event in
" every one of man's actions, as if they were never fo
" fatal and neceffary." Now any other certainty or neceffity than this we do not pretend to be implied in
foreknowledge. And as the Doctor himfelf grants
this neceffity to exift, whether there be or be not foreknowledge ; then in either cafe all that neceffity, for
which we plead, is granted to exift.

Dr. Weft, in p. 20, 21, Part II, thinks Prefident
Edwards inconfiftent with himfelf, in denying, that
the divine decrees are founded on foreknowledge, and
yet holding, that " the perfection of his underftanding
" is the foundation of his decrees." The Doctor argues, that " If foreknowledge in the Deity, is part of
" the perfection of the divine underftanding. Then is it
" the foundation of his wife purpofes and decrees ;
" and fo his objection lies juft as ftrong againft him,
" as againft us." Doubtlefs the perfection of the divine underftanding ; i. .e God's perfect view of the
fitnefs of certain things to certain ufes and ends, is the
reafon why he decrees and appoints thofe things to
thofe ufes and ends. But this is very different from
fuppofing that foreknowledge is the foundation of decrees, and that God firft forefees certain events about
to take place, and then decrees to permit them to take
place. And the inconclufivenefs of Dr. Weft's argument juft quoted, may appear thus ; If after-knowledge,
cr a knowledge, that events have taken place, be a part
of

of the divine underftanding ; then it is the foundation of his wife purpofes and decrees. But it will not be pretended, that the confequent in this cafe juftly follows from the antecedent. Yet it follows as juftly as in the argument of the Doctor. Not every perception which belongs to the divine underftanding is the foundation of God's decrees univerfally or generally : Befide the inftance already mentioned, I might mention God's perfect knowledge of geometry, mechanics, &c. The divine perfect knowledge of thofe fciences is not the foundation of all God's decrees : No more is God's foreknowledge.

CHAPTER

CHAPTER VII.

Objections considered.

1. IT is argued, that we are poffeffed of a felf-determining power and a liberty to either fide, becaufe we find, that we have a power to confider and
examine an action propofed to us, and to *fufpend* our
determination upon it, till we fhall have duly confidered it.——But as the determination to fufpend and
examine is a voluntary act, it no more appears to
be without motive or without moral neceffity than
any other voluntary act.——Sufpenfion is either a voluntary act or not. If it be a voluntary act, it no
more appears to be without motive and moral neceffity, than any other voluntary act. If it be not a voluntary act, it is not a *free* act, nor is any liberty exercifed
in it ; and therefore it is nothing to the prefent purpofe.

To argue, that we have a power of felf-determination, becaufe we have a power to fufpend an action,
is as groundlefs, as to argue, that we have a power of
felf-determination, becaufe we have a power to choofe
to act, or becaufe we have a power of will. Sufpenfion is a voluntary act or a volition, and the argument
under confideration is this ; A man has a volition, not
at prefent to determine in a certain cafe ; therefore
he has a power efficiently to caufe volition in himfelf. This argument is juft as conclufive as the following ; A man has a volition at prefent to determine
in a certain cafe ; therefore he has a power efficiently
to caufe volition in himfelf : Or as this ; A man has a
a volition, therefore he has a power efficiently to caufe
volition in himfelf.

But if fufpenfion be no voluntary act, but a total
fufpenfion of all volition, it is, if poffible, ftill lefs a
proof of felf-determination. Self-determination is a voluntary act, and fufpenfion is brought as an inftance

of

of felf-determination. But how can that, which is no voluntary act be an inſtance of a voluntary act ? This is as abſurd as to argue ſelf-determination from any intellectual perception, or from the perfect inſenſibility of a dead corpſe.———But this mode of arguing is familiar with Dr. Weſt, who conſtantly argues a ſelf-determining power, from a power to *not act* a power to be perfectly torpid.

2. Self-determination is argued from our own conſciouſneſs and experience. Dr. Weſt ſays, page 26, that " we experience in ourſelves, that in willing " and chooſing we act independently of any extrinſic cauſe." Others hold, that we are *conſcious* of ſelf-determination and an exemption from extrinſic cauſality.———When gentlemen ſpeak of experience and conſciouſneſs, they ought to confine their obſervations to themſelves ; as no man is conſcious of more than paſſes in his own mind, and in ſuch things a man can with certainty tell his own experience only. For my own part, I am not conſcious of either ſelf-cauſation of volition, or an exemption from extrinſic cauſality ; and to be ſure I am not conſcious, that my volitions take place without cauſe and by mere chance. I am conſcious of volitions of various kinds ; but I never yet caught myſelf in the act of *making a volition,* if this mean any thing more than *having* a volition or being the ſubject of it. If any man be conſcious, that he makes his own volitions, he is doubtleſs conſcious of two diſtinct acts in this, one *the act made* by himſelf, another *the act making* or by which he makes *the act made.* Now will any man profeſs to the world, that he is or ever has been conſcious of theſe diſtinct acts ? If not, let him tell the world what he means by being the efficient cauſe of his own volitions. If he mean, that he has volitions, this is no more than the advocates for moral neceſſity are conſcious of, and to grant that this is all that is meant, is to give up the argument. If it be meant, that he cauſes them by *the mind itſelf* or by ſome *power* of the mind and not
by

by any *act* of the mind or of thofe powers ; I appeal
to the reader, whether this be, or can be, a matter of
confcioufnefs. I take it to be univerfally granted,
that no man can be confcious of more than the *acts*
and perceptions of his own mind. The exiftence of
the mind and of its powers, is *inferred* from the acts,
and we are not properly confcious of them. Dr.
Reid may be an authority with the gentlemen, with
whom I am now concerned. " *Power*," fays he, " is
" not an object of any of our external fenfes, nor
" even an object of *confcioufnefs*. That it is not feen,
" nor heard, nor touched, nor tafted, nor fmelt, needs
" no proof. That we are not confcious of it, in the
" proper fenfe of the word, will be no lefs evident, if
" we reflect, that confcioufnefs is that power of the
" mind, by which it has an immediate knowledge of
" its own *operations*. Power is not an operation of
" the mind, and therefore is *no object of confcioufnefs*.
" Indeed every operation of the mind is the exertion
" of fome power of the mind ; but we are confcious
" of the *operation only*, and the power lies behind the
" fcene : And though we may juftly *infer* the power
" from the operation, it muft be remembered, that
" *inferring* is not the province of *confcioufnefs*, but of
" *reafon*." *Effays on Active Powers*, p. 7.

If from our confcioufnefs of volitions, it follows,
that we *efficiently caufe* thofe volitions, let a reafon be
given, why it will not equally follow from our confcioufnefs of any perception, *e. g.* the found of thun-
der, that we efficiently caufe that too.

If we be the efficient caufes of our own volitions,
they are effects. But an effect is produced by a previous exertion of the efficient caufe, which act is as
diftinct from the effect, as the divine creating act was
diftinct from the world created. Every effect is paffive with regard to its caufe, and paffive in this refpect,
that the caufal act of the efficient operates upon it :
Therefore the volition is and muft be diftinct from the
act of the efficient by which it is caufed. If a man
be

be the efficient caufe of his own volition and he be confcious of it, he is confcious of an act of his own mind previous to every volition caufed by himfelf, efficiently caufing that volition, and as this caufing act muft be a voluntary act, in order to be a free one, there muft be an infinite feries of voluntary acts caufing one another, or one act before the firft : And of this the man who is fubject, muft have a confcious experience, or elfe he cannot be confcious of felf-determination. Whether any man will profefs to be confcious of all this, we muft wait to fee. It is to be prefumed however, that no man will profefs to have experienced an infinite feries of acts, or one act before the firft act.

As to knowing by confcioufnefs and experience, that our volitions are not the effect of an extrinfic caufe ; this I conceive is an abfolute impoffibility, unlefs we know by experience and are confcious, that we ourfelves efficiently caufe them in the manner juft now defcribed, viz. in an infinite feries, or with one act before the firft. Unlefs we be confcious, that we caufe our own firft volition by a previous act, we cannot be confcious, that we caufe it at all. And if we be not confcious, that we caufe that, we cannot be confcious but that it was caufed extrinfically. If we do not experience that we caufe our volitions by our own previous acts, we do not experience, that we caufe them at all. All we experience is the volitions themfelves, and we have no more evidence, that they are not the effects of an extrinfic caufe, than from the experience of any of our ideas of fenfation, we have evidence that thofe ideas are not excited by an extrinfic caufe.

Let an inftance be taken and I prefume no man will pretend, that he is confcious, that he caufes one volition by another : e. g. a volition to give to the poor. Will any man pretend, that he is confcious, that he caufes in himfelf a volition to give to the poor, by a previous volition ; and that he in the firft place finds,

finds, by confcioufnefs, that he choofes to have a volition to give to the poor before he has it, and that by
this previous choice he becomes willing to give to the
poor ? If no man will pretend this, but every man by
the bare ftating of the cafe fees, that it implies the abfurdity that he is willing before he is willing, furely it
is high time to give up this argument from experience and confcioufnefs.

It has been faid, that we *perceive* no extrinfic influence producing our volitions. Nor do we perceive
any extrinfic influence producing a great part of our
thoughts and perceptions, which yet it will not be pretended, that we ourfelves caufe.

It is impoffible for a man to be confcious of a negative,
otherwife thar as he is either not confcious of it, or is
confcious of the oppofite pofitive. Therefore when it
is faid, that we are confcious, that our volitions are not
the effect of an extrinfic caufe, the meaning muft be either that we are not confcious, that they are the effect of
an extrinfic caufe, or that we are confcious, that we
do efficiently caufe them ourfelves. That we are
not confcious, that our volitions are the effect of an
extrinfic caufe, is no proof, that they are in fact not
the effect of fuch a caufe, becaufe if they were the
effect of fuch a caufe, ftill we fhould not be confcious of it. If whether they be the effect of fuch a
caufe or not, we fhould not be confcious, that they
are the effect of fuch a caufe, then the circumftance
that we are not confcious, that they are the effect of
fuch a caufe, is no proof either way. Nor are we
confcious, that we do efficiently caufe our own volitions, as it is prefumed appears by what has been already faid in this and former chapters.

But if we were confcious, that we do efficiently
caufe our own volitions, this would be no argument
againft the abfolute previous certainty or moral neceffity of all our volitions. Such efficiency may
have been from eternity the object of the divine abfolute foreknowledge or decree. So that to a con-

sciousness of liberty as opposed to moral necessity, it is requisite, that we be conscious not only, that we efficiently cause our own volitions, but that we cause them, with the circumstance, that it was previously uncertain, whether we should cause them or not. But of this circumstance it is impossible, that we should be conscious; it is no act or perception of the mind, and therefore cannot be an object of consciousness.

Archbishop King speaks of a man's being " con- " scious, that it was in his power, to have done other- " wise than he has done." If this mean any thing opposite to moral necessity, it must mean, that a man is conscious, that it was not previously certain, that he would do as he has done. But of this no man can be conscious, for the reason already given.

3. It is further argued, that we act as if we were under no necessity, but at perfect liberty; and that therefore the doctrine of moral necessity is contradicted by all our conduct, and the maxims of it.———— To this I answer, that our conduct does by no means show, that we are not influenced by motives, or that we act without motives, without design, without biases, tastes, appetites or any such principles, and in perfect indifference, insensibility and stupidity. On the other hand, the conduct of all mankind shows, that they are actuated by motives, biases, various passions and appetites, which have as stated and regular an effect on their minds and conduct, as second causes have in the natural world. The conduct of men does by no means show, that their conduct is previously altogether uncertain and left to mere chance. It does indeed show, that they are free agents in the proper sense; i. e. intelligent, voluntary agents, acting upon motives and various principles in human nature, natural and acquired; and therefore we use arguments and motives with one another to influence each other's conduct. All this is perfectly consistent with the scheme of moral necessity for which

which I plead, and is implied in it : And all government civil and domeſtic is not only conſiſtent with
that ſcheme, but is built upon it; otherwiſe in vain
would be all the motives of rewards and puniſhments
exhibited as the means of government, and by which
government is carried into effect.

If moral neceſſity be inconſiſtent with the practice
of mankind, ſo is that previous certainty implied in
the divine foreknowledge; for that, with reſpect to
moral actions, is moral neceſſity.

4. It is objected, that on this plan all agency and
action are deſtroyed or precluded.——Anſwer; If by
agency and action be meant ſelf-determinate or contingent agency and action, I grant that this ſcheme
does preclude them and means to preclude them.
But it is not allowed, that ſuch agency and action are
neceſſary to a rational, moral being, or are at all deſirable or even poſſible : And to take theſe for granted, is to beg the main points in diſpute. Let it be ſhown
that ſuch agency and action are neceſſary, deſirable,
or poſſible, and ſomething to the purpoſe will be done.
But rational voluntary agency or action, ariſing from
motive and principle, and directed to ſome end, is
not precluded, but ſuppoſed and eſtabliſhed by this
ſcheme.

It is ſaid, that on the hypotheſis of a divine agency in all things, there is *but one agent* in the univerſe.
But the Deity is no ſelf-determinate agent : He is no
more the efficient cauſe of his own volitions than he is
of his own exiſtence. If he were, his volitions would
not be from eternity, nor would he be unchangeable.
Therefore with as much reaſon, as it is ſaid, that there
is *but one* agent in the univerſe, it might have been
ſaid, that there is *not one*. Self-efficiency of volition is
either neceſſary to agency and action, or it is not.
If it be neceſſary, God is not an agent. If it be not
neceſſary, we are agents and God too.

It is further ſaid, that on this plan of a moral neceſſity eſtabliſhed by God, all human actions are
nothing

nothing but the operations of God actuating men, as
the foul actuates the body.——If this mean, that God
is the remote and first caufe of all things, and that he
brings to pafs all things and all human actions, either
by an immediate influence, or by the intervention
of fecond caufes, motives, temptations, &c. we allow
it : We firmly believe, that thefe are under the control and at the difpofal of Providence. But becaufe
the devil tempted Eve, it will not be pretended, that
fhe acted nothing, and was merely acted upon by the
devil, as the human body is actuated by the foul ; that
becaufe God fent his prophets to the Ifraelites, to preach
to them, the prophets acted nothing ; that when God
affords the aids of his grace to any man, fo far as he
is influenced by thefe aids to an action, it is no action
of his ; that when the goodnefs of God leadeth a
finner to repentance, the finner does nothing, does
not repent ; but this repentance is the act or exercife of the divine mind, and in it God repents.

If when it is objected, the fcheme of moral neceffity
precludes action, action mean volition ; the objection
is groundlefs : We hold as ftrenuoufly as our opponents,
that we all have action in this fenfe. But if by action
they mean any thing elfe, they muft mean fomething
in which there is no volition. But that any fuch thing
fhould be an action is abfurd and what they will not
pretend. The circumftance, that a man caufes his
own volitions, if it were poffible, would not imply a-
gency or action, unlefs the caufation or caufing act
were a volition.   For inftance, if a man in a convulfion, having a fword in his hand, involuntarily thruft
it into his friend's bofom, this is not agency : Yet the
man caufes the thruft and the wound. But if the caufing
act be a volition, it runs into the abfurdity of an infinite feries of volitions caufing one another.

Dr. Weft, in Part II, p. 8, fays, " If the Deity is the
" proper efficient caufe of volition, then the mind is
" entirely paffive in all its volitions, and confequently
" cannot be in any *proper* fenfe *an agent.*" We grant,

M   that

that the Deity is the primary efficient cauſe of all things, and that he produces volitions in the human mind by ſuch ſecond cauſes as motives, appetites, biaſes, &c. and the human mind, in being the ſubject of the divine agency whether mediate or immediate, is paſſive. Still we hold, that volition is *an action*, as has been already explained. Nor is there the leaſt abſurdity in the ſuppoſition, that an action ſhould be the effect of a divine or other extrinſic agency, unleſs by action or volition be meant a ſelf-cauſed or an uncauſed action or volition. But for Dr. Weſt in the preſent caſe to mean this *by action in the proper ſenſe*, is to beg the queſtion. The very queſtion is, whether action in the proper ſenſe of the word, be ſelf-cauſed or uncauſed. And if, when he ſays, " If the Deity is the effi-
" cient cauſe of volition, the mind cannot be in any
" *proper* ſenſe an agent ;" he mean an agent, who efficiently produces an act of will in himſelf, or who is the ſubject of a volition which is uncauſed ; I grant, that the mind cannot be ſuch an agent ; I believe, that ſuch agency is an abſurdity and impoſſibilty, and call on Dr. Weſt to clear it of the abſurdity and impoſſibility, which has long ſince been pointed out to be implied in it.

Beſides ; the Doctor's reaſoning may be retorted, thus ; If the mind itſelf be the proper efficient cauſe of volition, then the mind is entirely paſſive in its volitions, and conſequently in volition cannot be in any proper ſenſe an agent. For every effect muſt be paſſive, ſeeing it cannot contribute any thing towards its own exiſtence. Volition or the mind acting is either an effect, or it exiſted from eternity, or it came into exiſtence without cauſe. Neither of the two laſt will be pretended. Therefore it is an effect ; and as every effect is paſſive, the mind in volition is, on the ground of Dr. Weſt's argument, in no proper ſenſe an agent in volition.

The Doctor proceeds, ibid, p. 8, " Either volition is
" only the immediate action of the Deity on the mind,
" or

" or it is diftinct from it. If volition is diftinct from
" the action of the Deity on the mind, then the action
" of the Deity on the mind, is only to produce all the
" requifites for action ; and confequently there is no
" abfurdity in fuppofing, that when all thefe requifites
" have taken place, the mind is then only put in a ca-
" pacity for acting."——On this I remark, Volition
is granted to be entirely diftinct from the action of
the Deity, as diftinct from it, as the motion of a planet is. But it is not granted to follow hence, that the
action of the Deity does no more than produce all
the neceffary requifites for action. Dr. Weft will
grant, that when the Deity caufes a planet to move, he
does more than to produce the requifites for its motion, unlefs in requifites for its motion be compre-
hended the actual production of its motion. If this
be his meaning with regard to the action of the mind,
there is an abfurdity in fuppofing, that when all thofe
requifites have taken place, the mind is only put into
a capacity for acting or not acting. And whatever be
his meaning in producing requifites, I do not allow
they do or can put the mind into a capacity of *not*
acting, i. e. of finking itfelf into perfect torpitude.

What immediately follows the laft quotation is, " If
" befides prefenting to the mind the requifites for ac-
" tion, the Deity does produce a certain modification
" of the mind called volition, in which modification the
" mind is wholly paffive, then there is no action, but on-
" ly the immediate action of the Deity on the mind; and
" volition is nothing diftinct from the immediate action of
" the Deity." The very fame mode of reafoning will prove,
that bodily motion is nothing diftinct from the action of
the Deity ; thus, If befides producing the requifites for
motion, the Deity produce a certain modification of
matter, called motion, in which matter is wholly paffive, then there is only the immediate action of the Deity
on matter, and motion is nothing diftinct from the immediate action of the Deity.——Yet it is prefumed, that Dr.
Weft will not pretend, that when God caufes a plan-

M 2   et

et to move round in its orbit, the Deity himself and
he only moves round in that orbit ; or that the motion of the planet is nothing diftinct from the action
of the Deity. Now volition, though caufed by the
Deity, is as diftinct from the action of the Deity, by
which it is caufed, as the motion of a planet is from
the action of God by which that is caufed.

The Doctor fays, p. 10, " If when the mind acts on
" any particular object, the Deity produces *a new act*
" or a new operativenefs in the mind, then there muft
" be a change in the mind." Doubtlefs there is fo far a
change, as is implied in the new act : And what then ?
Why the Doctor " upon the clofeft examination can-
" not find any change in the *operativenefs* of his mind."
Be it fo ; yet as it is fuppofed, that his mind is the fubject of a new *act*, he can doubtlefs find a change in
the *act* of his mind ; and if he cannot find a change
in the *operativenefs* of it, it muft be becaufe operativenefs, which is a peculiar and favourite word with the
Doctor, means fomething different from *act*, and therefore is nothing to the prefent purpofe, as the fubject
under confideration is the production of a new act by
the Deity : And we do not pretend, that when the
Deity produces a new *act* in the mind, he produces a
new *operativenefs* too, unlefs act and operativenefs be
the fame. If they be the fame, whenever the Doctor
can perceive a change in the *act* of his mind, he can
doubtlefs perceive a change in this operativenefs of it.

The Doctor thinks he has faid fomething new concerning his favourite word *operativenefs*: But I fee nothing new or important in it, unlefs it be a new word
ufed in an ambiguous manner.

" I fay, that the operativenefs of the mind on
" different objects is always uniformly one and the
" fame thing, and not that there are as many ope-
" rations, as there are objects on which the mind
" acts;" ibid, p. 13. Here it is manifeft, that the
Doctor ufes the word *operativenefs* as fynonymous
with *operation*, otherwife he is guilty of the moft
grofs

grofs equivocation. And is it indeed one and the fame operation of mind to love virtue and love roaft beef? To choofe the fervice of God and choofe a pine apple? This is new indeed: In this, I prefume the Doctor is an original!

5. My actions are *mine*; but in what fenfe can they be properly called *mine*, if I be not the efficient caufe of them?——Anfwer; My thoughts and all my perceptions and feelings are *mine*; yet it will not be pretended, that I am the efficient of them all.

6. It is faid to be felf-evident, that *abfolute neceſſity* is inconfiftent with *liberty*.——Anfwer; This wholly depends on the meaning of the words *liberty* and *neceſſity*. Abfolute *natural* neceffity is allowed to be inconfiftent with liberty; but the fame conceffion is not made with regard to abfolute moral neceffity. All that is requifite to anfwer this and fuch like objections is to explain the words liberty and neceffity. If by *liberty* be meant *uncertainty*, undoubtedly abfolute moral neceffity, which is the certainty of a moral event, is utterly inconfiftent with liberty. But if by liberty be meant exemption from *natural* neceffity, there is not the leaft inconfiftence between the moft abfolute *moral* neceffity and the moft perfect freedom or exemption from natural neceffity. The moft perfect exemption from natural neceffity is confiftent with the moft abfolute previous certainty of a moral action. Judas in betraying his Lord " according to the determinate counfel and foreknowledge of God," was entirely exempted from natural neceffity; yet his conduct was according to an abfolute previous certainty.

7. That we have liberty of felf-determination is argued from our *moral difcernment*, or fenfe of right and wrong and of defert of praife and blame. And fome are fo confident of the fufficiency of this argument againft moral neceffity, that they are willing to reft the whole caufe on this fingle point. It is therefore a very important point. It is faid, that our eftimating the moral character of the man, from his internal dif-

M 3 pofitions

positions and acts, is on the supposition, that these are *within the power of* the man. But the word *power* is equivocal ; if it mean *natural* power, and that the agent is under no *natural* inability, (as before explained) to other dispositions and acts ; it is granted, that in this sense they are in his power. But if it mean, that there was no previous certainty, that he would have those very dispositions and acts ; and that no man will or can reasonably blame himself or another but in case of a perfect previous uncertainty with respect to those dispositions and acts ; this is not granted, nor is it proved.

It is said, that no man ever did commend or blame himself for what he knew to be *necessary* and *unavoidable*, not within his power, or not determined by himself. This stript of the ambiguity of words is this merely ; that no man ever did commend or blame himself for what he knew to be previously certain, and was not entirely casual. But this is manifestly false ; because every man knows or may know, that all things are previously certain, as they are the objects of the infallible foreknowledge of God : And if no man can commend or blame himself for what is previously certain, no man can commend or blame himself for any thing.

Will it be pretended, that we are more blamable for an action, which is previously uncertain and casual, and which we perform by chance without motive, end or design, than for that which is previously certain and future, and which we do from motive, and with an end and design ? Take the instance of Judas's treachery. The fact is, that this treachery was previously certain and infalliby foreknown by God. Now, was Judas less blamable than if his conduct had been previously uncertain, and had taken place by pure chance ? To say, that he was blamable, if this conduct proceeded from self-determination, affords no satisfaction, unless this self-determination were by chance. For otherwise the self-determining act was previously certain and morally necessary, and therefore liable

able to all the objections, which are brought againſt moral neceſſity in any caſe.

Blameworthineſs is nothing but moral turpitude or odiouſneſs ; praiſeworthineſs is nothing but moral amiableneſs or excellence. But the moral amiableneſs of an action does not depend on the circumſtance, that it is efficiently cauſed by ourſelves ; becauſe this runs into the abſurdity and impoſſibility of an infinite ſeries of actions cauſing one another. Nor does it depend on this circumſtance, that the action is, as Dr. Weſt holds, uncauſed ; for no actions of creatures fall under this deſcription. Either of thoſe hypotheſes would ſhut moral amiableneſs and odiouſneſs out of the world.

That moral neceſſity or previous certainty of moral conduct is conſiſtent with moral diſcernment, may be argued from the caſe of the ſaints and angels in heaven. It will not be pretended, but that there is a certainty, that they will continue in their ſtate of perfect holineſs and happineſs to eternity. Nor will it be pretended, but that they are the ſubjects of moral diſcernment and of that virtue and holineſs which is truly amiable in the moral ſenſe, and the proper object of approbation and reward. Therefore moral neceſſity is not inconſiſtent with praiſe and blame.

I need not inſiſt on the neceſſary holineſs of God and of our Lord Jeſus Chriſt.

The writers in oppoſition to moral neceſſity inſiſt much on its inconſiſtence with accountableneſs. This is really no other than to inſiſt, that it is inconſiſtent with praiſe and blame or with moral agency ; and is the ſame objection, which we have been conſidering. To be accountable is to be liable to be called to an account for an action, and to be the proper ſubject of reward or puniſhment. But this is no other than to be worthy of praiſe or blame, and to deſerve love or hatred, complacency or diſapprobation, on account of moral temper or conduct. So that what has been

M 4

faid

ſaid concerning praiſe and blame, is equally applica‑
ble to accountableneſs.

It has been long ſince ſhown by Preſident Edwards,
that the moral amiableneſs and odiouſneſs of actions,
and their deſert of praiſe or blame, or the eſſence of
virtue and vice, depend not on the circumſtance,
that actions are efficiently cauſed by the ſubject ; but
that the acts themſelves, without any conſideration of
their efficient cauſe, are amiable or odious : As oth‑
erwiſe virtue and vice will be thrown back from the
cauſed act, to the cauſing act, till they are thrown out
of the univerſe. If they conſiſt not in acts of the
will themſelves, but in the acts by which they are
cauſed, as theſe cauſing acts are alſo cauſed, virtue
and vice muſt for the ſame reaſon conſiſt not in them,
but thoſe by which they are cauſed, and ſo on to an
act which is not cauſed. But this being not cauſed
by the ſubject, can, on the principle of our opponents,
have no virtue or vice in it. Thus there would be
no place found in the univerſe for virtue and vice :
Not in the cauſed acts, becauſe virtue and vice con‑
ſiſt not in them, but in their cauſe. Not in any un‑
cauſed act or acts, becauſe they, by the ſuppoſition,
are not cauſed by their ſubject. There is no way to
avoid this conſequence, but to allow that virtue and
vice, deſert of praiſe and blame, conſiſt, in the acts
themſelves and not in their cauſe ; or if there be
any virtue or vice in the cauſe, this is diſtinct from
the virtue or vice, which there is in the acts them‑
ſelves. If I be accountable for any volition, for the
ſole reaſon, that I cauſe it ; then I am accountable
for the act, by which I cauſe it, for the ſole reaſon,
that I cauſe that, and ſo on in an infinite ſeries.

Beſides ; the mere circumſtance, that I cauſe my
own volition, does not on the principles of our oppo‑
nents, make me accountable for it : Becauſe that I
ſhould cauſe it may be a matter of previous certain‑
ty, as it may be foreknown, and even decreed, by
God, that I ſhall cauſe it ; and therefore I cauſe it
not

not freely in the fenfe of our opponents, but neceffarily, under the influence of abfolute moral neceffity.

But Dr. Weft holds, that all our volitions are without caufe. Then they take place by blind fate or chance.
And how, on his principles, are we accountable for them?

The true ground of accountablenefs and of praife
and blame, is not the circumftance, that we ourfelves
efficiently caufe our own volitions; or the circumftance, that they take place without caufe, by mere
chance; but the nature, moral afpect and tendency of
thofe volitions, and of the actions which flow from them.

Our opponents obferve, that we allow, that men
muft be the voluntary caufes of their external actions,
in order to be accountable for them : And then they afk,
why we do not for the fame reafon allow, that we muft
be the voluntary caufes of our acts of will, that we may
be accountable for them ? The anfwer is, that external
actions are not volitions. The volitions of rational
beings, are in their own nature moral acts, and for
that reafon the fubjects of them are accountable for
them. But external actions are not of a moral nature
in themfelves, and therefore the fubjects of them are accountable for them then only, when they are the effects
of volition. Befides; that external actions fhould be the
effects of volition does not run into the abfurdity of
an infinite feries, as is implied in the fuppofition, that
all volitions are the effects of previous volitions.

Dr. Weft fays, " I have already fhown, that necef-
" fity fhuts out all fenfe of vilenefs and unworthinefs ;"
Part II, p. 39. Where he has fhown this, he has not
informed us. If he had, perhaps his readers, on pe-
rufal of the paffage, would not have joined with him in
the opinion, that he had fhown it. For my part, I
cannot find, that he has fhown it in any part of his
two books.———If moral neceffity, which is previous
certain futurity of a moral act, " fhut out all fenfe of
" vilenefs and unworthinefs ;" then it feems, that in order that a man may have any fenfe of vilenefs in fin,
he muft act without any previous certainty in the nature

ture of things, or in divine foreknowledge, what his actions will be ; *i. e.* he muſt act by mere chance.

8. It is objected, that this doctrine of moral neceſ-ſity makes men mere machines.——This objection, which is frequently made by all our opponents, depends on the ſenſe affixed to the word *machine.* If it mean an intelligent voluntary agent, who does not act by perfect contingence or chance, and who does not take one ſtep before his firſt ſtep ; but acts from ſuch motives and purſues ſuch objects, as appear to him moſt eligible ; I grant, that we are machines : And in the ſame ſenſe the ſaints and angels in heaven, and all intelligent beings, are machines. But whether it be not a great abuſe of language, and whether it be not an artifice of our opponents, to excite a popular prejudice and clamour againſt our doctrine, to uſe the word *machine* in this ſenſe ; I leave the reader to judge.——If by *machine* be meant, what is commonly meant by it, a mere material engine, without volition, knowledge or thought in itſelf ; I preſume, that our opponents themſelves will not pretend, that on our principles, men are ſuch machines as this.

Do thoſe who make this objection, hold, that the human underſtanding *is* a *machine ?* Or that, in underſtanding, reaſoning, judging, remembering, &c. man acts mechanically ? Yet all grant, that in theſe things he acts neceſſarily.

If moral neceſſity imply, that we are machines, then whatever induces a moral neceſſity, or actually influences or perſuades us to any conduct, turns us into machines. Now the oppoſers of moral neceſſity often ſpeak of the aids of grace and of the Spirit, as neceſ-ſary and influential to virtue and religion. But if any man become the ſubject of true virtue or piety *by the aids of God's grace,* ſo far he is paſſive, he is wrought upon and governed by an extrinſic cauſe, and his conduct is the effect of that cauſe. But every effect is *neceſſary* with reſpect to its cauſe. Therefore whoever is led by this cauſe to virtue or

piety,

piety, is led neceffarily, and according to the objec
tion now before us, is turned into a mere *machine*.——
On the ground of this objection all finners abandon-
ed by God, all the damned and devils in hell, all the
faints and angels in heaven, the man Chrift Jefus, and
even God himfelf, are mere *machines*.——How neceffary it is, that thofe who make an objection to any
fyftem, fhould confider firft whether the objection be
not equally forcible againft doctrines which they
themfelves hold!

9. It is further objected, that moral neceffity places
men, with refpect to liberty, on a level with brutes.——
If by liberty be meant contingence or previous uncertainty, I grant that the actions of men and brutes
are in this fenfe equally void of liberty ; a previous
certainty attends them equally. Or if it could be
made to appear, that the actions of men are previoufly uncertain ; I fhould maintain, that thofe of
brutes are equally uncertain, and in this fenfe equally
free.——If by liberty be meant exemption from extrinfic caufality of volition ; I grant, that in this
fenfe alfo the actions of men and brutes are equally
void of liberty. Men no more manufacture their
own volitions, than brutes ; and there is no more evidence, that men act without motive or defign, than
that brutes do. But if by liberty be meant *rational*
liberty, the liberty of *a moral* agent, I hold that men
are poffeffed of this, and brutes not. Brutes are no
moral agents ; but it is for the want of reafon and
intelligence, not of any power of will. If Sir Ifaac
Newton's horfe had had as much reafon and knowledge as his mafter, he no doubt would have had as
much moral liberty, and would have been equally a
moral agent and equally accountable. Without reafon and intelligence, though a horfe fhould have a
liberty of perfect uncertainty and act by the pureft
chance ; and though he fhould propagate one volition by another, or without another, with ever fo great
dexterity ; he would be a brute ftill, and no more a
moral

moral agent, than he is now that he acts by motive or appetite. So that the difference between a man and a beaft, as to moral agency, confifts not in liberty of contingence or liberty of felf-determination; but in reafon and knowledge.

We might on this fubject venture to turn the tables on our opponents, and hold, that if a power of felf-determination be liberty, brutes are free as well as men. The afs determining to eat of one of two equally good bundles of hay, is as good an inftance to prove, that fhe has a felf-determining power, as any brought to prove it in men. So that if thofe inftances prove it in men, this proves it in brutes. Self-determining power then is nothing diftinctive between men and brutes.

The capacity of confidering and judging, of diftinguifhing virtue and vice, of deliberating, reafoning, reflecting, and fufpending, have been mentioned as diftinguifhing between men and brutes. But all thefe, except *fufpending*, are acts of the intellect, not of the will: And fufpenfion, though an act of the will, does not appear to imply felf-determination more than any other act of the will. Befides; brutes fufpend, as well as men. A dog in queft of his mafter, will fufpend proceeding in any road, till he is fatisfied, in which his mafter has gone. And fheep, a more ftupid race, on hearing a dog bark, will often fufpend their flight, till they fee from what quarter their enemy is approaching.

It is faid, that external liberty and fpontaneity belong to brutes and mad men, as well as to rational men. Be it fo; yet the power and proper exercife of reafon does not belong to them.——It is faid, that if an action's being voluntary makes it virtuous or vicious; then brutes would be the fubjects of virtue or vice. But merely that an action is voluntary does not conftitute it virtuous or vicious. It muft befides be the action of a rational being.

Dr. Clarke, the greateft champion for the felf-determining power, exprefsly grants that children,

dren, beafts and even every living creature poffefs it.
Remarks on Collins, p. 27. " The actions of *chil-*
" *dren*, and the actions of *every living creature* are
" all of them *effentially free.* The mechanical and
" involuntary motion of their bodies, fuch as the pul-
" fation of the heart and the like, are indeed all nec-
" effary ; but they are none of them *actions.* Every
" *action*, every motion arifing from the *felf-moving*
" *principle*, is effentially *free.* The difference is this
" only, in men this phyfical liberty is joined with a
" fenfe or confcioufnefs of moral good or evil, and
" is therefore eminently called liberty. In beafts
" the fame phyfical liberty or felf-moving power, is
" wholly feparate from a fenfe or confcioufnefs or ca-
" pacity of judging of moral good or evil and is vul-
" garly called fpontaneity. In *children* the fame
" phyfical liberty always is from the very beginning ;
" and in proportion as they increafe in age and in ca-
" pacity of judging, they grow continually *in degree*
" not more *free*, but more *moral*, agents." Thus we
have the Doctor's authority, that children and beafts
poffefs a felf-determining power, as well as men, and
that they are not only as really free as men, but that
their freedom is *in degree* equal to that of men ; and
that what they want to conftitute them *moral* agents,
is not *liberty*, but *reafon* and a capacity of judging.

10. Much has been faid by Dr. Clarke and others after him, concerning the *beginning of motion ;* by
motion meaning *volition*, if they mean any thing to
the purpofe. The argument is, that if motion, *i. e.*
volition, had a beginning, it was begun by God, and
of courfe he had a felf-moving or felf-determining
power, a power efficiently to caufe volition in himfelf, and actually did thus caufe it. That volition
even in the Deity had a beginning, the Doctor argues thus ; " Motion muft either finally be refolved
" into a firft mover, in whom confequently there is
" liberty of action," *i. e.* felf-determination, " or elfe
" into an infinite chain of caufes and effects without
" any

" any caufe at all ; which is an exprefs contradiction,
" except motion could be neceffarily exiflent in its
" own nature ; which that it is not, is evident, be-
" caufe the idea of relt is no contradiction ; and alfo be-
" caufe there being no motion without a particular
" determination one certain way, and no one deter-
" mination being more neceffary than another, an ef-
" fential and neceffary tendency to motion in all de-
" terminations equally, could never have produced
" any motion at all." *Remarks on Collins*, p. 11, 12.
Motion throughout this quotation means internal motion or volition, or the whole is nothing to the purpofe. I grant that external motion, the motion of
matter, had a beginning, and that after the creation
of matter. But the whole queftion is concerning volition, the act or motion of the mind. That this is
not neceffarily exiftent, and therefore not from eternity, the Doctor argues firft from this, that " the idea
of relt," *i. e.* of an entire abfence or non-exiftence
of volition, " is no contradiction." It is doubtlefs as
much and in the fame fenfe a contradiction, as the
idea of the entire non-exiftence of knowledge or intelligence, or of all being : And if this argument prove,
that volition had a beginning, it will equally prove,
that knowledge or the divine exiftence had a beginning. Volition is juft as neceffarily exiftent as God is ;
without volition he would not be God. It is impoffible, that God fhould from eternity have intelligence
and not from eternity have volition.

The Doctor goes on to argue the beginning of volition thus ; " There being no motion, *i. e.* volition,
" without a particular determination one certain way,
" and no one determination being in nature more
" neceffary than another, an effential and neceffary
" tendency to volition in all determinations equally,
" could never have produced any volition at all."
On this I obferve,——

1. That by the fame argument all intellectual ideas
and perceptions of happinefs in the divine mind have

a beginning ; thus, There being no intellectual idea without a particular determination one way, and no one determination being in nature more necessary than another, an essential and necessary tendency to all determinations of idea equally, could never have produced any idea at all. And with regard to perception of happiness, thus ; There being no perception of happiness or misery without a particular determination one certain way, and no one determination being in nature more necessary than another, an essential and necessary tendency to the perception of happiness or misery in all determinations equally, could never have produced any particular perception of them at all.——The same argument will prove, that God's existence is not eternal and necessary ; thus, There can be no being, who is not a particular, determinate being ; and no particular form or kind of being is in nature more necessary than another. But an essential and necessary tendency to existence in all forms and kinds equally, could never have been the foundation of any particular being at all.

If in these cases it should be objected, that one determination of idea is in nature more necessary than another ; that which is according to truth and fact, is more necessary than that which is contrary to truth ; and that feeling of happiness, and that form of existence which is most complete and perfect, is more necessary, than that which is less perfect : I answer, for the same reason, it must be granted, that the volition which is most rational, wise and holy, is more necessary, than that which is less wise and holy ; and therefore this particular volition or determination of will is necessarily existent in its own nature, and is without beginning.

2. From the supposition, that the volitions of God are not eternal and as necessarily existent as the divine knowledge or divine existence, it follows, that he is very far from an unchangeable being ; that from eternity he existed without any volition or choice of

one

one thing in preference to another ; that when the
eternity *a parte ante,* as it is called, had run out, he
began to will and choose, and from that time he has
been the subject of various acts of will, but never
before, and therefore has been the subject of a very
great change.

That God should from eternity exist without volition, and that in time he should become the subject
of volition, implies not only a very great change in
God, but that from eternity he was not a voluntary
agent, and therefore no agent at all. So that the
very argument which Dr. Clarke uses to prove, that
God is a self-determinate agent, in fact does, directly
contrary to his intention, prove, that he was from eternity no agent at all.

If God began volition in himself, he began it either
voluntarily or involuntarily. If he began it voluntarily,
he would be the subject of an infinite series of volitions
causing one another; which is an absurdity, impossibility and contradiction. If he began it involuntarily, he
did not begin it freely.

In his remarks on Collins, p. 6, Dr. Clarke says,
" To be an agent signifies, to have a power of begin-
" ning motion." *Motion* here, if it be at all to the
purpose, must mean *volition* : And to say, " To be an
" agent signifies to have a power of beginning volition."
is a servile begging of the question, utterly unworthy
of Dr. Clarke.

In the same book, p. 44, he observes, " That if mo-
" tion exist necessarily of itself——with a determina-
" tion one certain way ; then that determination is
" necessary, and consequently all other determina-
" tions impossible ; which is contrary to experience."
And how does it appear by experience, that any other determinations of will are, or ever were, possible
in the divine mind, than that which actually exists in
it ? Did Dr. Clarke experience divine exercises, and
find by that experience, that other volitions are possible in God than what actually exist ? Surely this
was

was written by the Doctor with great inattention!——
If to fave the Doctor it fhould be faid, that this obfervation relates not to volition, but to the motion of
matter; this, if it were the meaning of the Doctor,
would argue equal inattention. Would he have imagined, that becaufe the motion of matter is not from
eternity and neceffarily exiftent; therefore the fame
is true of thought and volition?

11. Self-determination has been argued from the
irregular conduct of mankind, and efpecially from
the confideration, that their *moral exercifes* are fo irregular and out of courfe. But the exercifes and
conduct of men, are not more irregular than the blowing of the wind, or the ftate of man's body often is in
ficknefs. Yet it will not be pretended, that this confideration proves, that ficknefs or the blowing of the
wind is felf-determinate.

12. Dr. Weft objects, that " according to Mr. Ed-
" wards, the mind muft always be governed by chance
" or accident; *i. e.* by fomething unforefeen or not de-
" figned by the mind beforehand. Thus, let a man's mind
" be ever fo ftrongly determined at prefent, to purfue
" any particular object, yet that extrinfic caufe, which
" has the entire command of his will, may the next
" hour fruftrate all his purpofes, and determine him to
" a quite contrary purfuit. If this is not to be gov-
" erned by blind fate and chance, I know not what is."
Part II, p. 31.——On this I obferve,——

1. Whether the Doctor do or do not know,
what it is to be governed by blind fate and chance,
is of no importance to his readers; and what a pity,
that he fhould confume fo much of his own and his
readers' time, in appeals to himfelf as an authority.

2. According to this account, to be under the
governing influence of any extrinfic caufe, is to be
governed by blind fate and chance. Therefore the
planetary fyftem and all the material world are under
the government of blind fate and chance; fo were
the prophets and apoftles, fo far as they were infpired

N   and

and influenced by the Spirit of God. Does Dr. Weft acknowledge this ? If not, muft he not own, that when he wrote the paffage above quoted, he was miftaken in his idea of being governed by blind fate and chance ?

3. Doubtlefs Prefident Edwards holds, that the human mind is often governed by motives " un- " forefeen and not defigned by the mind before- " hand." And as Dr. Weft holds, that the mind never acts without motive, unlefs he hold alfo, that it always forefees beforehand, the motives on which it will in future act, he muft join with Prefident Edwards in the idea, that it acts on, or which is the fame, is governed by motives " unforefeen and not defign- ed by the mind beforehand :" And therefore on the fame ground, on which he charges Prefident Edwards with holding principles, which imply that the mind is governed by blind fate and chance, he may be charg- ed with the fame.

He alfo holds, that God " regulates and governs " all things and fets bounds to the actions of all ra- " tional creatures, to bring about his own purpofes," and that " infallibly." Part II, p. 46, 47. " That " the Deity *governs* free agents as *perfectly* and *makes* " them perform his purpofes as *infallibly*, as though " they had no agency at all." Ibid, p. 67. And that " every thing is *firmly fixed* in the divine mind." Ibid, p. 49. Now the Deity is a caufe extrinfic to the hu- man mind, and by conceffion, he *regulates, governs,* and *overrules* all the actions of intelligent creatures, and *makes* them *infallibly* perform *his purpofes.* There- fore " let a man's mind be ever fo ftrongly determin- " ed at prefent to purfue any particular object, yet " that extrinfic caufe," the Deity, " which has the " entire command of his will, may," and certainly will, " fruftrate all his purpofes," unlefs the object of his purfuit be agreeable to the purpofes of the De- ity. Now then I appeal to the reader, whether Dr. Weft do not as fully hold thofe principles which he fays imply, that men are governed by blind fate and chance, as Prefident Edwards.   CHAPTER

CHAPTER VIII.

*In which is confidered the Objection, that Moral Neceffi
ty implies, that God is the Author of Sin.*

IT is objected to the doctrine of moral neceffity;
that fince this neceffity and the connection between
motives and volitions are eftablifhed by God, he is
the author of all the fin and wickednefs in the univerfe ; that he by the motives which he lays before
creatures, tempts them to fin, and is himfelf anfwera-
ble for all the fin committed by them. And a great
deal of vehement declamation is poured out on this
fubject, well fuited to take hold of the feelings and
paffions of men, but not to inform their underftandings and affift their reafon.

Before we proceed to a more direct and particular
confideration of this objection, it is proper to fhow in
what fenfe the advocates for moral neceffity hold that
the divine agency is concerned in the exiftence of fin.

1. They do hold, that all neceffity and certainty
or certain futurity, whether of natural or moral events,
is eftablifhed by God ; of courfe that the connection
between all caufes and effects, and particularly the
connection between motives and volitions, is eftablifhed by the fame fupreme agent.

2. They hold, that all things, which come to pafs
in time, were certainly foreordained by God from e-
ternity ; that he foreordained them not in confequence
of forefeeing, that the free will of man will bring
them into exiftence ; but the free will of man brings
them into exiftence, in confequence of the divine decree, fo far as that will does at all bring them into exiftence.

3. They hold, that whatever fin takes place among
creatures, takes place not by the bare permiffion or
non-influence of God ; but under his fuperintend-

N 2   ing

ing providence, and in confequence of his difpofing things fo, that fin certainly or with moral neceffity, follows.——Prefident Edwards has explained himfelf fully on this head. Inquiry, p. 254; " If by *the au-* " *thor of fin* be meant the *finner,* the *agent* or *actor* of " fin, or the doer of a wicked thing ; fo it would be " a reproach and blafphemy, to fuppofe God to be *the* " *author of fin.* In this fenfe I utterly deny God to " be the author of fin ; rejecting fuch an imputation " on the Moft High, as what is infinitely to be abhor- " red ; and deny any fuch thing to be the confe- " quence of what I have laid down. But if by *author of* " *fin* is meant the permitter or not hinderer of fin, and " at the fame time, a *difpofer of the ftate of events in fuch* " *a manner,* for wife, holy and moft excellent ends and " purpofes, THAT SIN, if it be permitted and not hinder- " ed, WILL MOST CERTAINLY FOLLOW——I do not " deny, that God is the author of fin——it is no re- " proach for the Moft High to be *thus* the author of fin."

The objections againft fuch an agency of God in the exiftence of fin, as has been now defcribed, are two ; (1) That fuch divine agency is inconfiftent with human liberty, moral agency and accountablenefs : (2) That it is inconfiftent with the perfect holinefs of God.——Before I anfwer thefe objections diftinctly, I wifh it to be obferved, that they are inconfiftent and mutually deftroy each other.

If the divine agency in the eftablifhment of moral neceffity and the connection between motives and vo- litions, be inconfiftent with our liberty and moral a- gency ; then God in eftablifhing fuch a neceffity of any action in us, which we call fin, is not the caufe or author of *fin* ; for his agency fo far from produc- ing fin in us, renders us *incapable* of fin. Suppofe God with moral neceffity influence a man to kill an- other with malice prepenfe ; if this neceffitating influ- ence as really deftroy his moral agency, as if it turn- ed him into a windmill, though the man kills the other, he commits no more fin in it, than if a windmill had

had killed him ; and consequently God is no more the author of fin in this inftance, than if he had influenced the windmill to kill him, or had firft turned the man into a windmill, and this windmill had in the courfe of providence been the inftrument of his death. So that they who hold, that moral neceffity is inconfiftent with moral agency, muft never objeft, that God is *the author of fin*, by eftablifhing that necef fity, and thus afts inconfiftently with his perfeft holinefs.

On the other hand, if God do influence any man to *commit fin*, and thus aft inconfiftently with his perfeft holinefs, the man is a moral agent notwithftanding fuch influence, and there is no foundation to objeft, that the influence is inconfiftent with liberty and moral agency ; and they who objeft that fuch influence implies, that God is the author of *fin*, muft forever be filent concerning the inconfiftency of that influence with human liberty and moral agency.

If moral neceffity be inconfiftent with moral agency, it is abfolutely impoffible and contradiftory for God to difpofe things fo, that fin will certainly or with moral neceffity follow. For on this fuppofition whatever certainly follows fuch a difpofal cannot be fin or any other moral aft, as moral agency is in the cafe deftroyed by the difpofal. Therefore it is impoffible, that God in this way fhould caufe fin, and therefore it is abfurd and felf-contradiftory in thofe who hold, that moral neceffity is inconfiftent with moral agency, to charge us with blafphemy, as they frequently do, becaufe we avow the fentiment, that God fo difpofes events that fin certainly follows.

Yet fo far as I know, all thofe who oppofe moral neceffity, make both the objeftions before mentioned, and thus pull down with one hand, what they build up with the other. This is eminently true of Dr. Weft.

I now proceed to confider thofe objeftions diftinftly.

1. It is objefted, that a divine agency eftablifhing a moral neceffity of fin, is inconfiftent with human liberty,

N 3

liberty, moral agency and accountablenefs.——
Anfwer: The divine agency in this cafe is no
more inconfiftent with human liberty, &c. than the
moral neceffity which it eftablifhes. If this neceffity be
inconfiftent with liberty, be it fo; the divine agency
which caufes it, does not increafe the inconfiftency,
beyond what would be, if that neceffity took place
without fuch agency. A mountain placed acrofs the
channel of a river, may be inconfiftent with the
river's flowing in that channel. But whether it were
placed there by God, were conftructed there by human
art and labour, or happened there without caufe, are
queftions immaterial as to the river's running in that
channel, fo long as the mountain is the very fame.
Therefore let our opponents prove, that moral neceffity or a previous certainty of moral actions, is inconfiftent with moral agency, and that moral agents muft
act by perfect contingence, mere chance and blind fate,
and they will carry their point, without faying a word
concerning the divine agency: And until they prove
this, whatever they may fay concerning the divine
agency, will ferve no good purpofe to their caufe, as
to this part of the argument.

2. It is objected, that for God to eftablifh a moral
neceffity of fin, or as Prefident Edwards expreffes it,
" for God to difpofe of the ftate of events in fuch a
" manner, for wife, holy and moft excellent ends,
" that fin will moft certainly and infallibly follow;"
is inconfiftent with the perfect holinefs of God.——
But in what refpects is it inconfiftent with his holinefs?
Or for what reafons are we to conclude, that it is inconfiftent with his holinefs? So far as I have been
able to collect the reafons from the ableft writers on
that fide of the queftion, they are thefe:

(1) That whatever is in the effect is in the caufe,
and the nature of every caufe may be known by the
effect. Therefore if God fo order things, that fin will
certainly follow, he is the caufe of fin, and therefore
is finful himfelf.——If this argument be good, God

is

is the fubject of pain, ficknefs and death, fince he is
the caufe of them : He is material and is the fubject
of all the properties of matter, extenfion, folidity, mo-
bility, figure, colour, &c. becaufe he created matter
and all its properties. Yea he fuffers the torments of
hell, becaufe he inflicts them.——This argument,
though urged by men of great fame, is too weak and
abfurd to bear infpection !

(2) If God difpofe things fo, that fin will certainly
follow ; he doubtlefs takes pleafure in fin, and this
implies fin in God himfelf.——If God do take a di
rect and immediate complacency in fin, it is granted,
that this would imply fin in God. But if he choofe
the exiftence of fin as a mean of good only, as pain
and ficknefs may be the means of good ; this implies
no fin in God. Nor does it follow from his difpofing
things fo, that fin certainly takes place, that he does
directly delight in fin itfelf abftractly confidered, any
more than it follows from his inflicting ficknefs and
mifery on his creatures, that he takes a direct complacency in thefe. And we do not allow, but utterly
deny, that God from a direct complacencey in fin
difpofes things fo, that it certainly follows. If our opponents believe that a direct complacency of God in
fin is implied in our doctrine, it behoves them to
make it out, and not to take it for granted.

Dr. Weft infifts on this argument, Part II, p. 43.
" If the Deity produces finful volitions——then fin
" is his own work——and then he cannot hate fin,
" but muft love it and delight in it." It feems the
Doctor forefaw that to this argument it would be anfwered that God's producing fin in the manner before
explained, no more implies a direct complacency in
it, than his producing *mifery* implies a direct complacency in that ; and he replies, that " the two cafes
" are by no means parallel——that the Deity is no
" where reprefented as being angry at his creatures,
" becaufe they fuffer pain and diftrefs——whereas
" with regard to moral evil, God is always reprefented

N 4   " as

" as hating it, and punishing the impenitent." To this I rejoin, that the want of parallelism does not appear. For though God is not represented to be angry at *pain* and *misery*, as they are not the proper objects of anger ; yet he is represented to be displeased with them ; and anger is only one kind of displeasure, displeasure at moral evil. And if God do produce a thing, with which he is displeased, why may he not produce a thing with which he is angry, and which he is disposed to punish as it deserves ? Let a reason be given, why he may not do the latter, as well as the former.

(3) God hates sin and doubtless he must hate to bring it into existence ; and therefore he will not so dispose things, that it will certainly come into existence. But God hates the pain, misery and death of his creatures in the same sense, that he hates sin ; yet we find in fact, that he does dispose things so, that they do take place among his creatures.

(4) That God should so dispose of events, that sin is the certain consequence, is doing evil, that good may come of it ; which is contrary to scripture, as well as reason.——This is merely asserting, but not proving what is asserted. How does it appear, that for God so to dispose of events, that sin is the certain consequence, and this to subserve the most wise and holy purposes, is doing evil ? To do evil is to commit sin ; and to say that this is to commit sin, is to beg the question. Let it be proved to imply, that God commits sin, and the point is gained. We assert, that to say, such a disposal implies, that God commits sin, is as groundless a proposition, as to say, that if God so dispose of events, that sickness is the certain consequence, implies, that God himself is sick. I presume, it will not be denied, that God did so dispose of events, that the certain consequence would be that Joseph should be sold into Egypt, and that our Saviour should be crucified. Nor will it be denied, that God made this disposition of events with a holy and

and wife purpofe. And if God may do this in one or two inftances; why may he not do the fame in every inftance, in which fin actually exifts?

(5) That God fhould make an eftablifhment whereby any creature is laid under a moral neceffity of finning is a great injury, both to the creature himfelf, and alfo to the fyftem; as all fin is injurious to the fyftem.——Anfwer: What injury can be pretended to be done to the creature, who is the fubject of the fin, in the cafe defcribed, fo long as his liberty and moral agency remain entire? And they do remain entire by the fuppofition; elfe he would be incapable of fin. A creature which is not, and fo long as it remains to be, not a moral agent, cannot be influenced even by God himfelf to commit fin: It would imply a contradiction. So that there is no foundation for complaint, that the fubject is injured, by being laid under a moral neceffity, or previous certainty, of finning.——Befides; this objection implies, that every moral agent is injured, unlefs it be a matter of perfect uncertainty, what his future actions fhall be, uncertainty not only to himfelf and all creatures, but to God and in the nature of things: i. e. every moral agent is injured, unlefs he be left to act by pure chance.

With regard to injury to the fyftem of intelligent beings, there is, if poffible, ftill lefs foundation for objection on this ground. For it is a part of the doctrine of moral neceffity, that God never eftablifhes it, excepting when it's eftablifhment is fubfervient and neceffary to the general good of that fyftem, implying the divine glory; and to be fure, that God never fo difpofes of events, that fin certainly follows, unlefs fuch a difpenfation is neceffary to the general good: Nor ought the contrary to be taken for granted. If God do in any inftance fo difpofe of events, that fin certainly follows, when the exiftence of that fin is not neceffary to the general good, but injurious to it; I confefs, I fee not how in this cafe, the divine holinefs

can

can be vindicated. But this is nothing peculiar to the introduction of sin. It would also be inconsistent with the divine perfect holiness and wisdom to create matter, or to cause holiness, in such circumstances as to disserve the general good.

(6) It is inquired, Where is the consistence between God's laying a man under a moral necessity of sinning, and then punishing him for that sin ?——I answer,

1. How can God consistently make a man sick, and then apply medicines or any remedy toward his restoration ? Punishment is inflicted to prevent either the subject of the punishment, or others, from falling into the same practice. If there be no inconsistence in bringing sickness on a man, and then healing him by medicine ; where is the inconsistence in bringing sin, which is moral sickness, on a man, and whereby both he and that system are so far morally diseased, and then by punishment healing him or the system ?

2. There is no consistence in the case, if moral necessity be incompatible with moral agency. But if it be entirely compatible with moral agency, there is no inconsistence in the case : For in laying a man under a moral necessity of *sinning*, as he is supposed still to *sin*, nothing is done to impair his moral agency or his desert of punishment. On this supposition it is immaterial as to desert of punishment, who or what is the cause of the moral necessity, whether God or any other being, or whether it happen without cause. Therefore God may as consistently punish a sinner, whom he himself has laid under a moral necessity of sinning, as he may punish him, provided he be laid under the same moral necessity by any other being, or by mere chance. If moral necessity be entirely consistent with desert of punishment, it is as impertinent to ask how God can consistently lay a man under a moral necessity of sinning and then punish him for it, as to ask how God can consistently make a man of a dark complexion or a low stature and then punish him, for any sins, which he may commit. For moral

moral neceffity is no more inconfiftent with fin and defert of punifhment, than a dark complexion or a low ftature. To lay a man under a moral neceffity of finning, is to make it certain, that he will fin : And to afk how God can confiftently make it certain, that he will fin, and then punifh him for that fin, implies that previous certainty is inconfiftent with fin, and that in order to fin a man muft act by mere chance.

It is no more inconfiftent, for God to forbid men to fin, and yet fo difpofe things, that they certainly will commit fin ; than it is to forbid them to fin, and yet voluntarily to fuffer other caufes to lead them into fin. Nay, fince liberty is out of the queftion, as by the very ftatement of the objection, it allows, that not-withftanding the divine difpofal, the man who is the fubject of that difpofal does commit *fin ;* it is no more inconfiftent for God to forbid men to fin, and yet fo difpofe things, that fin will follow, than it is for him to forbid it, and yet voluntarily permit men to fin by felf-determination. For in difpofing things fo that fin follows, when the difpofal is fuppofed to be confiftent with fin and moral agency, nothing can be pretended to be inconfiftent with the prohibition of fin, unlefs it be the divine confent, that fin fhould come into exiftence ; and this equally exifts in the cafe of bare permiffion, as in the cafe of the aforefaid difpofal. The law of God, which forbids all fin, does not imply, that God will prevent fin, by introducing the greater evil of deftroying moral agency. Nor does it imply, that he will not confent in his own mind, that it be committed by men or other moral agents, rather than the faid greater evil or other as great evil fhould take place. Therefore rather than that the fame or as great an evil fhould take place, the Deity may not only confent to the exift-ence of fin, but may confent, that fecond caufes, mo-tives, temptations, &c. fhould do whatever they can do, toward the introduction of it, confiftently with the freedom of the creature. He may do all this without inconfiftence

inconfiftence and infincerity. The prohibition of fin
in the law does not imply a wifh or choice of the divine mind, all things confidered, that fin fhould not
be committed. It barely points out our duty, but
reveals nothing of God's defign, whether or not to permit it, or to difpofe things fo, that it will follow.
Therefore there is no inconfiftence between this prohibition and fuch a difpofal in providence, as will be
followed by fin.——A good mafter may ftrictly forbid his fervant to fteal ; yet convinced, that he does
fteal, the mafter may in a particular cafe, wifh him to
fteal, and even leave money expofed to him, that he
may fteal, and ultimately with a defign that an advantage may be put into the mafter's hand, to convict, punifh and reform his fervant. There is no inconfiftence
in the mafter's thus forbidding theft, and yet from the
motive before mentioned wifhing to have it committed.

(7) It is faid, that if God choofe that the finfulnefs
of volitions fhould come into exiftence, and if he fo
difpofe events, that it will certainly come into exiftence ; there is no difference between this, and God's
being himfelf the fubject of finful volitions.——I anfwer, there is the fame difference in this cafe, as there
is between God's choofing that a man fhould be fick,
and being the fubject of ficknefs himfelf ; as there is
between creating matter, and being himfelf material ;
and as there is between willing and caufing the damnation of a finner, and being himfelf the fubject of damnation. It will not be pretended, that if God difpofe
events and circumftances in fuch a manner, that repentance, godly forrow, faith in a Redeemer, fubmif-
fion and holy fear, take place in the heart of a man,
God himfelf is the fubject of thofe exercifes.

If, though human liberty be left entire, God cannot fo difpofe things, that fin will certainly follow,
without being himfelf the fubject of a difpofition
friendly to fin ; he cannot without the fame implication choofe, that fin fhould take place, rather than a
greater evil. But our opponents allow, that God did
choofe,

choose, that sin should take place, rather than a great. er evil ; they allow, that he had a perfect foreknowl- edge, that if he should create man with a self-deter- mining power, and leave him to the free exercise of that power, the consequence would be, that he would commit sin. Therefore they allow, that God chose, that sin should come into existence, rather than hu- man liberty should be destroyed, and rather than free agents should not be brought into existence. So that in the same sense, in which we hold, that God chose or was willing, that sin should come into existence, our opponents hold the same. We hold, that God chose that sin should take place, rather than a greater evil ; and therefore disposed of events consistently with human liberty, so that it certainly followed. They hold, that God chose, that sin should take place, rather than a greater evil, and therefore disposed of events, consistently with human liberty, so that it cer- cainly followed, and when God certainly foresaw, that it would follow.

In that our opponents charge us with holding prin- ciples, which imply, that God is *the author of sin*, they allow, that whatever God does according to our prin- ciples toward the introduction of sin, is consistent with free agency in the subject of sin. This must be con- ceded by them ; else their charge is perfectly incon- sistent and self-contradictory, as has been shown. Therefore since it is allowed, that whatever God has done toward the existence of sin, is consistent with the creature's free agency, the only question remain- ing, is, whether he have acted in this affair, with a holy and wise design, a design to promote the gener- al good : And we argue from the essential perfections of God, that whatever he has done in this, as well as in every other instance, must have been done with such a design.

If it be said, that sin cannot even by the Deity, be made subservient to good ; the question will arise, why then did he so dispose circumstances that it did
come

come into exiftence, and this when he forefaw the confequence ? To anfwer, that he could not, confiftently with free agency, keep it out of exiftence, is on the prefent fuppofition groundlefs. It is now fuppofed, that God did bring it into exiftence, confiftently with free agency ; and therefore he could doubtlefs keep it out of exiftence, confiftently with the fame free agency.

If the exiftence of fin be ultimately made fubfervient to good, or if it be neceffary to the prevention of greater evil ; what reafon in the world, can be given, why God fhould not bring it into exiftence, in a way confiftent with human free agency ? In this way it muft be brought into exiftence, if at all.——Our opponents themfelves allow, as has been obferved, that the exiftence of it was neceffary to the prevention of greater evil, the evil of deftroying human liberty, or of the non-exiftence of free agents : And for God in this view to confent to the exiftence of fin, as our opponents grant that he did, is as inconfiftent with his moral character, as to give the fame confent and to put forth any exertion toward its exiftence, confiftent with human liberty. So long as the exertion is confiftent with liberty, it cannot be pretended, that there is any thing in it more oppofite to the moral character of God or more friendly to fin, than there is in the confent implied in that permiffion of fin, which our opponents hold. Therefore their plan is in this refpect equally liable to the fame objection of being inconfiftent with the moral character of God, as our's.

(8) Dr. Weft argues, that if the Deity order things fo that finful volition follow, " he muft place the ob-" ject in fuch a view before the mind, as to make it " appear the greateft good under prefent circumftan-" ces ; which implies, that he prefents the object in " a falfe point of light, and effectually deceives the " mind;" and " the apoftle was under a great miftake, " when he faid, it was impoffible for God to lie ;" and to lie is fin. The Doctor, as ufual, tells us, " I
" can

" can have no idea, that the Deity can produce a fin-
" ful volition in the human mind, in any other way,
" than what I have now defcribed ;" Part II, p.
41.———On this I remark ;

1. It is very immaterial to others, what Dr. Weft
can, and what he cannot, have an idea of. Does the
Doctor mean this as an argument, that no other perfon can have an idea of it, or that it cannot be true ?

2. If when he fpeaks of God's making fin appear
the greateft good, he mean, that he makes it appear
fo to a man's unbiafed reafon, this is not true, nor is
it pretended by any man.

3. When fin appears to any man the greateft
good, it is in confequence of the influence of his corrupt appetites, and not by the dictates of his unbiafed
reafon. How a man becomes the fubject of corrupt
appetite, I do not undertake to fay any further than
Prefident Edwards has faid already, that God has difpofed things fo, that it takes place as an infallible confequence. But if God fo difpofe things, that an inordi-
nate appetite for ftrong drink take place in the mind
of a man, and by the influence of fuch appetite ftrong
drink appear to him the greateft good ; does it hence
follow, that God is a liar ? Will Dr. Weft affert it ?
If not, the ground of his argument fails.

The Doctor further obferves, that " if God is the
" author of men's lufts, he deceives them, by caufing
" them to view things through the falfe medium of
" their lufts ;" ibid, p. 42, 43.———The expreffion,
" God is the author of men's lufts," is the Doctor's, not
Prefident Edwards's. It tends to miflead, and cannot
be admitted, without explanation and qualifying.
Suppofe a man by leading his neighbour frequently
into the immoderate ufe of ftrong drink, fhould produce an appetite for it in his neighbour, fo that hence-
forward ftrong drink fhould appear to him the greateft
good ; is the man, who does this, a liar ? Whether
he be guilty of other fin, than lying, is nothing to the
prefent purpofe ; for Dr. Weft's argument is, that
God

God by producing luſt in men, deceives the man in ſuch
a ſenſe, as to diſprove the words of the apoſtle, *that
God cannot lie.* If the man above ſuppoſed be not
guilty of lying, neither is the Deity in ſo diſpoſing
things, that luſt infallibly follows.

(9) " If the Deity be the poſitive efficient cauſe of
" ſin, then there can be no foundation for repentance :
" For how can a man repent or be ſorry, that he is juſt
" ſuch a creature, in every reſpeƈt, as the Almighty has
" been pleaſed to make him?" Ibid, p. 44.———With the
ſame objeƈtion to the expreſſion, " poſitive efficient
cauſe of *ſin*," I obſerve, that this argument is equally
good with reſpeƈt to pain, ſickneſs and calamity : and
will prove that no man ought to be ſorry for any calamity
befalling himſelf or others : For " how can a man be
ſorry, that he is juſt ſuch a creature," juſt as miſera-
ble, " as God has made him ?" If the Doƈtor ſay, that
though calamity in itſelf is an evil and therefore to
be regretted ; yet as God ſends it, he will overrule it
for good, and that in that view it is not to be regretted ; the ſame obſervations are applicable to the exiſtence of ſin. Sin in itſelf conſidered is infinitely
vile and abominable, and proper matter of ſorrow and
repentance. But conſidering that it no more came
into exiſtence without the deſign and providence of
God, than calamity did ; and conſidering, that its exiſtence will be certainly overruled for final good ; its
exiſtence is no more to be regretted, than the exiſtence of calamity and miſery, eſpecially extreme and
eternal miſery.

The Doƈtor proceeds ; " What remorſe of con-
" ſcience can there be, when the ſinner believes that
" every ſinful volition was formed in him by the De-
" ity ?" Ibid. Sinful volitions proceed from ſome cauſe,
or no cauſe. If they proceed from no cauſe, what
remorſe of conſcience can there be, when the ſinner
believes and knows, that every ſinful volition happened in him by pure chance ? If ſinful volitions proceed from ſome cauſe, that cauſe is either the ſinner
himſelf

himfelf or fome extrinfic caufe. If they proceed from any other extrinfic caufe, befide the Deity, the fame difficulty will arife, and it may be afked with the fame pertinency, as the above queftion is afked by Dr. Weft, What remorfe of confcience can there be, when the finner believes, that every finful volition was formed in him by an extrinfic caufe? If the efficient caufe be the finner himfelf, then " felf acts on felf and produces volition," which the Doctor denies. And if he did not deny it, it is abfurd and impoffible, as it runs into an infinite feries of volitions propagating one another, and yet all this feries would really amount to but one fingle volition, and this, as there would not then be a preceding caufal volition, would not be efficiently, voluntarily and freely caufed by the fubject himfelf.

Befides ; if the fubject efficiently caufe his own volitions, he either caufes them under the influence of motives or not. If he caufe them under the influence of motives, he caufes them neceffarily, and acts neceffarily in caufing them ; and Dr. Weft fays, " Where " neceffity begins, liberty ends ;" ibid, p. 19. Therefore if a man efficiently caufe his own volitions fo as to be free from neceffity, he muft caufe them without motive, aim or end ; i. e. he muft caufe them in perfect ftupidity, and in the exercife of Dr. Weft's torpid liberty of *not acting.* And then I afk, what remorfe of confcience can there be, when the finner believes, that he himfelf caufed every finful volition in himfelf, as involuntarily as a man in a convulfion ftrikes his friend, and as ftupidly and unmeaningly as a door turns on its hinges ?

Remorfe of confcience is a fenfe of having done wrong ; and whenever a perfon has done wrong, there is a foundation for remorfe of confcience ; and to take it for granted, that there can be no remorfe of confcience, unlefs we determine our own volitions, is to take it for granted, that without felf-determination we can do no wrong and are no moral agents ; which is to beg the main queftion in this controverfy. Let it

O   be be fhown, that without felf-determination, we are not moral agents, and one important ftep will be taken toward fettling this controverfy. Yet even this ftep will not be decifive : It muft be alfo fhown, that our felf-determination was not previoufly certain, but is exercifed by mere chance : For if it be previoufly certain, it is morally neceffary.

(10) If God have fo difpofed of events, that fin certainly follows, it is his work ; and to be oppofed to fin is " to be oppofed to God's work, and to be oppofed to God ;" ibid.——So calamity is the work of God, and to be oppofed to that, is to be oppofed to God's work, and to be oppofed to God. And will Dr. Weft admit that every one who wifhes to efcape any calamity, is in a criminal manner oppofing God ?

(11) " If the Deity has formed finful volitions in a " man, becaufe his glory could not be promoted " without it ; then furely the finner, if he loves God, " muft love him becaufe he has made him a finful crea " ture, and ought to thank him for all the fins, which " he has committed ;" ibid.——The difficulty attending moft of Dr. Weft's arguments, is, that if they prove any thing, they prove too much, and confute principles and facts, which he will not dare to deny. So with refpect to this argument. The Doctor will not deny, that pain and calamity are the work of God. " And if the Deity has" fent pain and calamity " on " a man, becaufe his glory could not be promoted " without them ; then furely the finner, if he loves " God, muft love him, becaufe he has made him a" miferable " creature, and ought to thank him for all" the calamity and mifery, which he fuffers, for all his ficknefs and dangers, for the death of his wife, children, &c. &c. And if a man ought to thank God for thefe things, no doubt, " a finner ought to thank God " for damnation." If thefe confequences do not inevitably follow from the principle of Dr. Weft's argument, let the contrary be fhown, and not merely afferted.———Again ; " If we are to thank God for

all

all the calamities and miferies which we do or fhall fuffer ; " this will imply, that" calamity and mifery " are bleffings or favours; and confequently, if the " finner is to thank God for damnation, then damna- " tion is a bleffing and favour——Hence finners who " believe this doƈrine, will be apt to conclude, that " it is a matter of no confequence, whether they be " faved or damned ; feeing upon either fuppofition, " they are fure that whatever they receive from God " will be fuch a bleffing, that they ought to be thank- " ful for it." Ibid, p. 45.——Thus may the Doƈor's arguments be retorted againft himfelf.

If the Doƈor fhould anfwer, Though calamity and mifery in themfelves are no bleffings, yet when they are overruled by God to the good of thofe who fuffer them, or to the general good, they become bleffings ; I acknowledge the fufficiency of the anfwer. But the fame anfwer may with equal truth and force be made to his obfervations concerning fin. The Doctor grants, that the wickednefs of the vicious fhall be overruled to the glory of God and the advancement of the happinefs of the righteous; ibid, p. 49. Though wickednefs is in itfelf no bleffing and no matter of thankfulnefs ; yet when God overrules it to good, greater good than could have been effeƈed in any other way ; in this conneƈion it is in the fame fenfe a bleffing, and matter of thankfulnefs, as calamity and mifery are.

(12) On the plan of moral neceffity, God tempts mankind to fin.——If the meaning of this be, that God eftablifhes a conneƈion between motives and volitions, and a previous certainty of thofe volitions ; and in the courfe of his providence brings into the view of men motives which aƈually influence them to fin ; I grant, that God does in this fenfe tempt mankind to fin ; as he did our firft parents, Judas, &c. Nor is there any ground, on which this can be denied, unlefs it be allowed, that this previous certainty is eftablifhed by fome other caufe than the Deity, or that it exifts without caufe, or that volitions

O 2   are

are not previoufly certain, but happen by chance. To hold that the previous certainty of all volitions is eftablifhed by fome other caufe than God, is to run into the Manichean fcheme of two Gods, and at the fame time to hold, that the fecond God is an involuntary agent and is the caufe of all the volitions of the voluntary God, as well as of all creatures. If we fay, this previous certainty of all volitions is uncaufed, we may as well fay, that every thing elfe is uncaufed. If we fay, that volitions are not previoufly certain, but happen by mere chance, we may as well fay, that every thing elfe happens by chance.

But if by *tempting* be meant foliciting or enticing to fin, as the devil tempts men, we deny that this is implied in our doctrine.

Dr. Weft makes fome remarks, Part II, p. 75, &c. on Jam. i. 13——16, which appear to be remarkable.——1. He tells us, that " a man is tempted, when " he confents to the gratification of his own luft ; *i. e.* " when he commits fin." Indeed! Is no man tempted, but he who actually commits fin in confequence of the temptation ? The apoftle Paul declares, Acts xx. 19, that he " ferved the Lord with all humility " of mind, and with many tears and *temptations*, which " befel him by the lying in wait of the Jews." And were all thefe temptations fuccefsful with the apoftle ? The very text implies the contrary. Gal. iv. 14. " And my temptation, which was in my flefh, ye def- " pifed not nor rejected, but received me as an angel " of God, even as Chrift Jefus." Jam. i. 2. " Count " it all joy, when ye fall into divers temptations." V. 12. " Bleffed is the man, that endureth temptation : For when he is tried, he fhall receive the crown of life."

Or if Dr. Weft fhall allow, that a man is or may be tempted without falling into fin, this will fpoil his argument. His words immediately following thofe laft quoted from him, are, " This proves, that when it is " faid, neither tempteth he any man, the fenfe is, " God caufeth no man to fin." But if a man may be
tempted

tempted without committing fin, then God may tempt a man, without caufing him to fin.

2. He obferves from *Leigh*, that the Greek verb πειραζω, ufed in the paffage in James now under confideration, fignifies to *make trial*, *i. e. to try* a perfon. But becaufe James fays of God, *neither tempteth he any man*, will Dr. Weft adventure to fay, that God never *tries* any man ? and particularly that he did not try Abraham ?

3. Becaufe this text declares, that God does not *tempt*, *i. e.* according to the Doctor's explanation, *try* any man, he infers that God " does not caufe them to " fin." This confequence follows not from the principle premifed. Whether God do or do not, try men, he may fo difpofe things that fin will be the certain confequence ; and this may be done not to *try* any man.

4. He fays, that " a voluntary confent to indulge or " gratify luft, is fin." Yet in the next fentence he fays, " the apoftle makes every fin to be the *effect* of " a confent to gratify fome particular luft :" *i. e.* every fin is the effect of fin.

5. The whole force of this text, to prove, that God does not difpofe things fo, that fin is the certain confequence, if it prove any thing to this effect, lies in thefe words, " Neither tempteth he any man." The Doctor fays, " thefe muft mean, Neither caufeth he " any man to fin ;" ibid, p. 75.——But if " the Deity " infallibly and perfectly regulate, govern and fet " bounds to the actions of all rational creatures, and " overrule all thofe actions to accomplifh his pur- " pofes," if he *make* them perform his purpofes infallibly ; as Dr. Weft fays ; then every thing which they in fact do, and every fin which they commit, was God's purpofe and he *makes* them perform it. Is he then in no fenfe the caufe of their fin ? Does he not at leaft fo difpofe things, that fin is the certain confequence?

Dr. Weft abundantly afferts thofe things which neceffarily imply both abfolute decrees and fuch dif-

pofal

poſal of God, that ſin certainly and infallibly follows,
" The creature," ſays he, " in every moment of its
" exiſtence, is ſubjeƈt to the divine *control ;* conſe-
" quently *no aƈt can take place,* but what the Deity
" foreſaw and *determined* from all eternity to *overrule*
" to his own glory and the general good. If the Dei-
" ty foreſaw, that a creature ———— would do that
" which could not be overruled to the divine glory
" and the general good ———— he would *reſtrain* him
" from doing that ;" Part II, p. 22. " He who has
" made all things ———— does *regulate* and *govern*
" all things, and *ſets bounds to the aƈtions of all ration-*
" *al creatures.*———The Deity, by his permiſſive de-
" cree, *ſuperintends* and *governs all the aƈtions* of his
" creatures to accompliſh *his own purpoſes, in as ſtrong*
" *a ſenſe, as though he brought them to paſs by his poſ-*
" *itive efficiency ;"* ibid, p. 46. " We believe, that
" the Deity *governs* and overrules the aƈtions of theſe
" beings" [rational creatures] " to bring about his own
" purpoſes and deſigns *as infallibly,* ——— as though
" they were *mere paſſive* beings ;" ibid, p. 47.

Now if theſe things be ſo ; no aƈt of the creature
can take place, but what God determined from all e-
ternity, to overrule to his own glory. If God *re-*
ſtrain the creature from the contrary ; if he *overrule*
all thoſe aƈtions to accompliſh his purpoſes, in as
ſtrong a ſenſe, as though he brought them to paſs by his
poſitive efficiency, and as infallibly as though they
were mere paſſive beings ; then certainly he does
diſpoſe things ſo, that all thoſe aƈtions do infallibly take
place. To be ſubjeƈt to the *control* of our Creator
in every moment of our exiſtence, ſo that no aƈt *can*
take place in us, but what God from eternity *deter-*
mined ; to be *regulated* and *governed* by God in *all things ;*
if he ſet bounds to *all* our aƈtions ; and if he *govern*
and *overrule* all our aƈtions in as ſtrong a ſenſe as
if he brought them to paſs by his *poſitive efficiency,* and
as *infallibly* as though they were mere *paſſive beings :*
ſurely all this implies, that God does ſo diſpoſe of e-
vents,

vents, that fin certainly follows. And on this plan, where is felf-determination? Where is liberty to either fide? liberty to act or not act? All the actions of rational creatures are limited, bounded and reftrained to certain definite objects and purpofes, which God from eternity had in view. They are therefore fhut up to act one way only, and cannot act otherwife. They can act in fuch a manner only, as God from all eternity faw would accomplifh his glorious purpofes, *i. e.* his glorious *decrees.* Therefore all the actions of creatures are decreed from eternity to be precifely what they are, and all creatures are as infallibly reftrained from acting contrary to the decrees of God, as if he brought their actions to pafs by his pofitive efficiency, and as though they were mere paffive beings.

If it fhould be faid, that though God bounds and reftrains his creatures from acting in a manner which is oppofite to his purpofes and decrees; yet he does not neceffitate them to act at all, but leaves them at liberty to act or not act :—On this I obferve,

1. As I have already faid, whenever any thing is propofed to any intelligent being, as the object of his choice, it is, as Mr. Locke has long fince *fo* ught, abfolutely impoffible for that being not to act. He may indeed either choofe or refufe the object. But to refufe it is to act, equally as to choofe it. In either cafe the being acts and cannot avoid acting, unlefs he be funk into a ftate of perfect unfeeling ftupidity.

2. If it were poffible for a creature to act or not act; ftill according to Dr. Weft he could do neither the one nor the other, unlefs it were fubfervient to the glorious purpofes of God. For if God will infallibly reftrain creatures from acting in all inftances, in which their acting is not fubfervient to his purpofes; will he not reftrain them from *not acting, i. e.* prevent their finking into unfeeling ftupidity, and excite them to action, in all inftances in which not acting would not in like manner be fubfervient to his

O 4 purpofes?

purpoſes ? If not, let a reaſon be given ; a reaſon why God will not prevent creatures from counteract-ing his purpoſes by *not acting*, as well as by *acting*. Surely it will not be pretended, that to excite by ra-tional motives and conſiderations, a creature to ac-tion, is more inconſiſtent with liberty, than infallibly to reſtrain, whether by motives or without motives, the ſame creature from action.

3. I appeal to the reader, whether the Doctor have not in the paſſages above quoted, given up the whole queſtion both with reſpect to liberty as oppoſed to infallible moral neceſſity or certainty of moral action, and with reſpect to abſolute decrees. If all men be limited and bounded by God, to act in all caſes according to his purpoſes ; if they be ſhut up to this way of acting, and cannot voluntarily refuſe to act in this way, as that would be to act contrary to God's purpoſe ; if they cannot abſolutely ceaſe from all action when an object is propoſed to their choice, but muſt either chooſe or refuſe, and that according to God's purpoſe ; if, as Doctor Weſt expreſsly declares to be according to his ſentiments, " Every thing is as firmly fixed in the " divine mind, by his permiſſive decree, and ſhall be " as infallibly accompliſhed, as though he was the im-" mediate author or efficient cauſe of all the actions " of creatures ;" ibid, p. 49. Let the candid reader judge, whether the Doctor do not grant both abſo-lute neceſſity and abſolute decrees.

He as we have ſeen in his Part II, p. 22, allows, that God permits and overrules ſin to his own glory and the general good ; but thinks this a demon-ſtrative proof of ſelf-determination. Let us conſider what he ſays on this ſubject.—Ibid, p. 34 ; " If the " doctrine of neceſſity be true, and we are not ſelf-" determined, then it will follow, that we are conſtant-" ly determined by the poſitive efficiency of the Deity." If it be true, as the Doctor holds, that God *regulates* " and *governs* all things, and *ſets bounds* to the actions " of *all* rational creatures, to bring about *infallibly*
" his

" his own purpofes ;" if he " *govern* free agents *as*
" *perfectly* and *make them perform* his purpofes as in-
" fallibly, *as if they had no agency at all ;*" I leave the
reader to judge, whether we, in all our actions, be
not, mediately or immediately, determined by the pofitive efficiency of the Deity. " If God make them
perform his purpofes *infallibly,*" it feems he muft by
his pofitive efficiency determine them to the perform-
ance ; for what is it *to make* men perform a purpofe,
but to put forth pofitive exertions to this end ? This
is alfo by pofitive efficiency to abolifh all liberty of
felf-determination.———If thefe things be denied, and
it be affirmed, that ftill the man is at liberty to act in
that particular manner, which is fubfervient to the divine purpofe, or not to act at all, and thus there is
room for felf-determination ; I anfwer,

1. It is not allowed, that a man on a propofal to
act, can poffibly *not act at all ;* and this ought not to
be taken for granted.

2. Then God does not infallibly make men comply with his purpofe, but leaves them to comply or
not ; which is directly contrary to Dr. Weft himfelf,
in the quotations made above.

3. If the Deity by his pofitive efficiency prevent
his creature from every action, but that which is
agreeable to his purpofe, he will prevent him by his
pofitive efficiency from refufing to comply with that
purpofe, and this is by pofitive efficiency to determine him to comply with that purpofe. And the
Doctor grants, that all the actions of rational creatures
are agreeable to God's purpofes. Therefore all rational creatures in all their actions are determined by
the pofitive efficiency of God. And all thofe which
Dr. Samuel Weft mentions as abfurd confequences
of the fentiments of Dr. Stephen Weft, may be retorted
on the former, thus ; Since God infallibly *makes* and
determines all men to perform his purpofes, in all
their actions, " fin is as much the work of God, as
" any thing that he has made. But that the Deity
" fhould

" fhould have an infinite averfion and an immutable
" hatred to his works, is inconceivable. It is fome-
" times faid, that the tendency of fin is to dethrone
" the Almighty, to kill and utterly to deftroy his ex-
" iftence. But is the Deity eonftantly working to
" deftroy himfelf ? This will make the Deity a ftrange
" contradiction to himfelf, and will conftitute fuch a be-
" ing, as cannot exift in the univerfe. If the Deity
" forms wicked volitions in the human mind, and
" then infinitely hates and abhors thofe very works of
" his, he muft be intinitely miferable and wretched.
" God is faid to rejoice in his own works——If then
" fin is God's work he rejoices in it——God is the
" greateft lover of fin in the univerfe." Whatever
abfurdities thefe be, it concerns Dr. Samuel Weft,
as much as any man, to remove them. As appears,
it is prefumed, by what has been faid already.

Befides ; moft or all thefe objections lie with equal
force againft the divine efficiency of pain, mifery or
death. The Doctor will not deny, that thefe are inflicted by God. Therefore mifery and death " are as
"much the works of God, as any that he has made." Yet
" he does not willingly afflict and grieve the children
" of men." And " he has no pleafure in the death
" of" even " the wicked." Therefore " God has an in-
" finite averfion and an irreconcilable hatred to his own
" works :" And if this be inconceivable to Dr. Weft
he will not deny it to be fact ; and therefore that a thing
is inconceivable to him, is no proof, that it is not
true. And that the Deity fhould hate mifery and
death and yet caufe them, would equally as in the
cafe ftated by Dr. Weft concerning the introduction
of fin, " make the Deity a ftrange contradiction to
" himfelf, and would conftitute fuch a being as can-
" not exift in the univerfe." " If the Deity forms"
mifery and death, " and then infinitely hates and ab-
" hors thefe very works of his hands, he muft be in-
" finitely miferable and wretched. God is faid to re-
" joice in his own works. If then" mifery and death
" be

" be his works, he rejoices in them, and God is the
" greateſt lover" of all the miſery and death " in the
" univerſe." Whenever Dr. Weſt will anſwer theſe
obſervations concerning the divine efficiency of miſery and death, he will furniſh himſelf with an anſwer to
his own ſimilar obſervations concerning the divine
agency in the introduction of moral evil. If he
ſhall ſay, that God does indeed hate miſery and death
in themſelves conſidered, and inflicts them, becauſe
they are neceſſary to greater good, and to the ac-
compliſhment of his own moſt benevolent purpoſes ;
the ſame may be ſaid concerning moral evil.

The Doctor quotes the following paſſage from Dr.
Hopkins ; " If God be the origin or cauſe of moral evil
" this is ſo far from imputing moral evil to him, or
" ſuppoſing, that there is any thing of moral evil in
" him, that it neceſſarily ſuppoſes the contrary :" On
which he remarks, " Conſequently, if God be the or-
" igin and cauſe of holineſs, this by the ſame kind of
" reaſoning, is ſo far from imputing holineſs to him, or
" ſuppoſing, that there is any thing of that nature in
" him, that it neceſſarily ſuppoſes the contrary ; that
" is to ſay, that the Deity has no moral character at
" all." In the above quotation, Dr. Hopkins evidently means, If God be the cauſe of *all* moral evil, or
of the firſt which exiſted in the univerſe. This the
word *origin* implies ; he evidently uſes it to mean *original* cauſe. Now whatever is in God, is uncauſed.
Therefore if there be moral evil in him, neither he
nor any other being is the cauſe of that ; of courſe
whatever moral evil he cauſes, muſt all be out of himſelf; and if he cauſe all moral evil, it muſt all be out
of himſelf and none of it in him. So that Dr. Hopkins's propoſition on this head is manifeſtly true.
Suppoſe the Doctor had ſaid, If God be the cauſe of
all matter, this ſo far from ſuppoſing matter in him, neceſſarily ſuppoſes the contrary ; no doubt Dr. Weſt
himſelf would have acknowledged the truth of the
propoſition : And let a reaſon be given why the former

er propofition, in the fenfe now given of it, is not as true as the latter. As to the confequence which Dr. Weft draws from Dr. Hopkins's propofition, " that " if God be the caufe of holinefs [of *all* holinefs] this " is fo far from fuppofing holinefs in God, that it ne- " ceffarily fuppofes the contrary ;" this is fo far from an abfurdity, as Dr. Weft imagines, that it is a man- feft truth. Holinefs in God is no more caufed or created, than the divine effence. If then there be no other holinefs, than created holinefs, there is and can be none in God.

On a paffage in which Dr. Hopkins afferts, that moral evil and holinefs are equally the confequence of the divine difpofal, but whether by the fame mode of operation he could not tell ; Dr. Weft remarks, " This makes it extremely unhappy for us ; for we " feem to have no way to know a true revelation " from a falfe one, both equally coming from the De- " ity ;" p. 46, Part II. But how this confequence fol- lows from the affertion of Dr. Hopkins, Dr. Weft does not illuftrate. God may fo difpofe things, that fin in- fallibly follows, and yet not be the author of a falfe revelation : And as the Doctor merely afferts, with- out attempting to prove what he afferts, he has no right to expect, that his affertion fhould be received as truth. If the Doctor take it for granted, that if God, in the way which I have explained, introduce fin, he is himfelf as real a finner, as he would be, if he were to give a falfe revelation, he takes for grant- ed the very thing in queftion, which is to be fairly proved, not pitifully begged.

In the fame page, he fays, " According to Dr. " Hopkins will it not follow, that many who are led " by the Spirit of God, are the children of the devil ?" This implies, that whenever God, by means of mo tives or in any other way, fo difpofes of things, that fin infallibly follows, the man who is the fubject of that fin, is in that fin led by the Spirit of God. The principle on which this argument is built, is,

that

that whenever God fo difpofes things, that an action is the certain confequence, in that action the man is led by the Spirit of God. But Dr. Weft will not a-vow and abide by this principle : For he grants, that men always act upon fome motive and never without motive. Nor will he deny, that the conftitution, that men fhould always act upon motive and never with-out, is eftablifhed by God. Yea, the Doctor exprefs-ly afferts, that " God overrules *all the actions of his* " *creatures* to accomplifh his own purpofes in as " ftrong a fenfe as though he brought them to pafs " by his *pofitive efficiency.*" Yet he will not pretend, that in all thofe actions they are led by the Spirit of God.

The Doctor proceeds ; " The Deity is called the " Father of lights, from whom proceeds every good " and perfect gift. But according to thefe principles, " may he not, with as much propriety, be called the " Father of darknefs, from whom proceeds all ma-" lignity and wickednefs ?" Since the Doctor holds, that " The Deity governs free agents as perfectly and " *makes* them perform his purpofe as infallibly, as if " they had no agency at all ;" the queftion which the Doctor here propofes concerning the principles of Dr. Hopkins may with equal propriety be propofed on his own principles. And notwithftanding any agency which God exercifes toward the production of moral evil, he may with the fame truth and propriety be called *the Father of lights,* as he is called *the Father of mercies and the God of all comfort,* although all the pains and miferies, which his creatures fuffer, whether in this world or the future, are inflicted by him.

The Doctor feems to attempt to fcreen himfelf from thofe, which he fuppofes to be abfurd confe-quences of Dr. Hopkins's fcheme, by reprefenting, that he holds, that God barely *permits fin.* But to *fuperintend, govern* and *overrule* the actions of ration-al creatures " as infallibly, as if they were mere paf-" five beings ;" Part II, p. 47 ; and " in as ftrong a fenfe, " as though he brought them to pafs by his pofitive ef-" ficiency ;"

" ficiency ;" ibid, p. 46. " So to fix them, that they
" fhall as infallibly be accomplifhed, as though he was
" the immediate author or efficient caufe of them," ibid,
p. 49. " And to *govern* free agents *as perfectly* and
" to *make* them perform his purpofes *as infallibly*, as
" though they had no agency at all ;" ibid, p. 67 ; is
more than barely to permit free agents to act of themfelves. Barely to permit them to act of themfelves, by
which the Doctor explains himfelf to mean, " ordaining
" things contingently, *i. e.* avoidably, and with a poffi-
" bility of not coming to pafs," ibid, p. 47 ; is not to
govern them at all, but to leave them to govern themfelves ; it is not to overrule their actions, but to leave
them to overrule their own actions ; it is not to *make*
them perform his purpofes, but to leave them loofe to
perform or to omit thofe purpofes. And much lefs is
it to govern and overrule their actions *as infallibly as
if they were mere paffive beings, and in as ftrong a
fenfe as though he brought them to pafs by his pofitive efficiency ; to fix thofe actions as infallibly as though he
was the immediate author of them ; or to govern them
as perfectly and to make them perform his purpofes as
infallibly, as though they had no agency at all.*

Dr. Weft conftantly infifts, that " the Deity has
" communicated to man a felf-moving or felf-active
" principle." But what kind of a felf-moving principle is that, which is always and in all its actions infallibly and perfectly regulated, governed and overruled by an extrinfic caufe ? and which is made by
God as infallibly to perform his purpofes, as if it were
no felf-moving principle at all ? Such a felf-moving
principle as this, is fo like a principle that never moves
itfelf, but is always moved by an extrinfic caufe, that
I requeft Dr. Weft to point out the difference.

The Doctor grants, that " there is a fenfe in which
" God *hardens* the hearts of men," and that this is by
his " taking from *them* what he had granted them, as
" a juft punifhment of their neglect and abufe of the
" advantages which they enjoyed ;" Part II, p. 52. He

grants

grants therefore, that God may confiftently with his
holinefs harden the heart, and caufe fin in men, in
fome cafes ; viz. when they deferve it as a juft punifhment of their fin. But the only reafon, which
renders it confiftent with the divine perfections, to in-
flict this or any other juft punifhment, is, that the glory of God and the general good of his kingdom re
quire it. Now no one pretends, that God ever in
any fenfe caufes fin to take place, unlefs its exiftence be fubfervient to the glory of God and the good
of his kingdcm. And if this reafon will in one cafe
juftify his fo difpofing of things, that fin is the infallible confequence, why not in another ? Until a reafon
is given to the contrary, we may prefume, that whenever the glory of God and the general good of the creation require it, God may and does fo difpofe things,
that fin is the infallible confequence.

"A man's becoming a veffel to honour or difhon-
" our, is in confequence of his own conduct and be-
" haviour." Part II, p. 54. If by becoming a veffel to difhonour the Doctor mean, *being punifhed*, no
doubt it is in confequence of a man's own mifconduct,
and to affert this is to affert nothing very great or
pertinent to the queftion concerning the caufe of fin.
But if he mean by it committing fin ; this is not, nor
can be always in confequence of the finner's own mifconduct ; becaufe this like the felf-determining power,
implies the abfurdity of an infinite feries of actions, in
confequnce of each other ; and that a man is doomed
to commit fin in the firft inftance, in confequence of
a prior fin committed by him.

"God does not harden the hearts of men, by any
" pofitive efficiency in forming or infufing any wick-
" ednefs into their heart, but only taking from them
" thofe things, which were defigned to reftrain them
" from the committing of fin, and by permitting them
" to walk in their own wicked ways ;" ibid, p. 55.
Of all men Dr. Weft fo long as he holds, that God
as perfectly and infallibly regulates, governs and overrules

rules all the actions of free agents, and makes them conform to his purpofes, as perfectly as if they had no agency at all, fhould be the laft to object to the idea of God's pofitive efficiency of fin; as has been already illuftrated. But afide from this, if God by taking from men what is neceffary to reftrain them from fin, lay them under an infallible certainty or abfolute moral neceffity of finning; what advantage is gained by this mode of reprefenting the matter? Is it at all more favourable either to the liberty of men, or to the holinefs of God? To be fure this reprefentation implies all that neceffity, for which Prefident Edwards pleads in the cafe. It is fo to difpofe things, that fin is the infallible confequence. Or if this taking away of reftraints be attended with no certain confequence of fin, how does God by it harden the finner? It feems, that after all he is left in a ftate of uncertainty, *i. e.* Dr. Weft's perfect liberty, whether he will fin or not. Where then is hardnefs of heart? Does it confift in perfect liberty? It is further to be obferved, that if fin, for inftance, an act of malice, envy or inordinate felf-love, fhould come into exiftence, without any pofitive caufation, whether by motive or in fome other way; why may not any other pofitive thing, either fubftance or mode, and even the whole material univerfe, come into exiftence in the fame way?

Dr. Weft remarks on Ifai. lxiii. 17. *O Lord, why haft thou made us to err from thy ways, and hardened our hearts from thy fear?* " Now it is certain from " the texts that have been already examined, that " nothing more is intended, than that God leaves " men to err, and to harden their own hearts;" ibid, p. 51. This pofitive affertion led me to review the Doctor's remarks on thofe texts, and I am very willing the candid fhould judge concerning the Doctor's exhibition of certainty, that nothing more is intended, by God's hardening the hearts of men, than that God leaves them to harden their own hearts. He fays, p. 52, in what fenfe God hardens the heart, our Saviour will

will inform us, Mat. xiii. 14, 15. " This people's
" heart is waxed grofs, and their ears are dull of hear-
" ing, and their eyes *they* have clofed." In anfwer to
this it may be faid with equal force, In what fenfe
God hardens the heart, we are informed in Joh. xii.
40. " *He* hath blinded their minds, and hardened their
" hearts, that they fhould not fee with their eyes," &c.
Whatever right the Doctor has to fuppofe, and without
a reafon to deliver the *opinion* as truth, that Joh. xii.
40, is to be explained by Mat. xiii. 15 ; any other
perfon has the fame right to *fuppofe* and to deliver
the opinion as truth, that Mat. xiii. 15, is to be explained by Joh. xii. 40.

The Doctor conftantly infifts, that " God never hard-
" ens any man or withdraws his fpirit and grace," ibid,
p. 52, but in confequence of his abufe of them. If this
were ever fo true, it would not fettle the queftion
concerning the origin of moral evil. For the queftion is not what is the caufe or fource of fin in fome
particular cafes, as in hardening the heart, in confequence of a former fin or fins; but what is the caufe
of all fin, and particularly of the *firft* fin, whether
in man or in the univerfe. Now to anfwer this queftion by faying, that when a man has " abufed God's
fpirit and grace," God delivers him up to fin, is as abfurd as to anfwer the queftion concerning the origin
of the human race, by faying, that after Adam had
lived a while, he begat a fon.

Although the Doctor thinks it certain from the
texts, which he had examined, that Ifai. lxiii. 17, " in-
" tends nothing more than that God leaves men to
" err and to harden their own hearts ;" he does not
choofe to reft the matter on that foundation ; but obferves, that " Hebrew verbs in Hiphil often fignify only
" permiffion." If this were ever fo true, it would decide nothing concerning Ifai. lxiii. 17. If verbs in
Hiphil do often fignify only permiffion, this implies,
that they often do not fignify that only. Then the
queftion would be, what does it fignify in this text ?

P   Neither

Neither Dr. Weft nor any other Hebraift, will pretend, that a verb in Hiphil *naturally* fignifies permiffion only. If therefore any verb in that conjugation do fignify that only, it muft be for fome other reafon, than merely becaufe it is in that conjugation. If there be any fuch reafon in this cafe, the Doctor has not informed us of it. Nor can I conceive of any, unlefs it be the fuppofed abfurdity of underftanding the text as it is tranflated. But the Doctor muft on reflection be fenfible of the impropriety of taking that fuppofed abfurdity for granted. Let him prove it, and he will oblige us to believe him.

On 1 Sam. xvi. 14, " The fpirit of the Lord de-
" parted from Saul, and an evil fpirit from God troub-
" led him," the Doctor remarks, " *i. e.* he was left
" of God to his own gloomy and frightful imagina-
" tions ;" ibid, p. 57 : But who was the efficient caufe of his own gloomy imaginations? Surely they did not happen out of nothing, like the atheift's world. Nor will the Doctor pretend, that Saul defignedly produced them in his own mind. So that he gives no account of the caufe of thofe imaginations, and no explanation of the text.

" If then the Deity creates fin, in the fenfe in which
" he creates darknefs, it will follow, that as darknefs is
" the confequence of God's withdrawing light, fo the
" confequence of God's withdrawing his fpirit and
" grace from any perfon, is fin ; which will fall in
" exactly with our fenfe of God's hardening the heart."
If fin in no inftance take place, but in confequence of God's withdrawing his fpirit and grace from a perfon ; then God's fpirit and grace are fometimes withdrawn from a perfon, antecedently to his finning : And in thofe cafes they are not withdrawn in righteous judgment, and as a juft punifhment of fin ; becaufe the perfon, by the fuppofition, has been guilty of no antecedent fin. Yet the Doctor every where confiders the withdrawment of God's fpirit and grace as a juft punifhment of the fin of thofe from whom it is withdrawn •

drawn ; as a juft punifhment of the neglect and abufe of the advantages, which they enjoyed, &c. &c. And on this ground only he attempts to juftify the with-drawment. If on the other hand, fin in any inftance, do take place when there has been no withdrawment of the divine fpirit and grace ; then the Doctor has here given no account of the exiftence of fin in that inftance ; and fuch an inftance there was, when fin firft came into exiftence ; it took place without a withdrawment of grace, in the way of righteous judg-ment.

It may here be added, that though darknefs, a mere non-entity, will take place in confequence of the withdrawment of light ; yet malice, envy and inordi-nate felf-love, pofitive acts of the mind, will no more take place in confequence of mere withdrawment of influence, than benevolence or fupreme love to God, or the whole material creation, would come into ex-iftence in confequence of a mere withdrawment of the influence of God.

" We fee in what fenfe God is faid to move, ftir " up or incline men to evil actions ; viz. by permit-" ting Satan to tempt men to evil, or by permitting " things to take place, which *occafion* men to become "perverfe." Ibid, p. 64. If the Doctor by " *permitting* " things to take place," mean that God fo difpofes things that certain definite events will infallibly fol-low ; this is all for which I plead, and which Prefi-dent Edwards held on this head. And furely the Doctor does not mean, that things are of their own accord and by their own native power, independently of the divine agency, endeavouring to take place, and will effect the object of their endeavour, if they be permitted by the Deity ; as a high mettled fteed, when permitted by his rider, leaps into a race. This would favour too much of atheifm, to be holden by a Chriftian divine. As to the human mind's making one volition by another or without another, I have nothing more to fay ; nor do I wifh to fay any more

concerning

concerning it, till an anfwer is given to what has been already faid.

This text, " I will fend him againft an hypocritical " nation, and againft the people of my wrath will I " give him a charge," Ifai. x. 6 ; Dr. Weft fays, " implies no more than that the Deity meant to pun- " ifh the Jews, by *letting loofe* the King of Affyria upon " them ;" ibid, p. 67. Yet in the fame page he fays, that the king of Affyria " was as much under the " control of the Deity, as the axe and the faw are un- " der the control of the workman." Yet this control over that king implies no more, it feems, than that God let him loofe on the Jews. And is no more implied in the control which the workman has over the axe and the faw, than that he *lets them loofe* on the timber ? I appeal to the reader, whether if the king of Affyria " was as much under the control of the Deity, as the " axe and the faw are under the control of the work- " man ;" a pofitive and efficacious influence, and not a *bare permiffion*, be not implied in fuch con- trol.

On Rev. xvii. 17, " For God hath put in their " hearts to fulfil his will, and to agree and give their " kingdom unto the beaft, until the words of God " fhall be fulfilled ;" the Doctor remarks, " Thefe " ten kings are to agree ——— in giving their kingdom " to the beaft, that by his protection and affiftance, " they may be able ——— entirely to deftroy the whore, " by whom they have been long oppreffed." Ibid, p. 68. Thus the Doctor fuppofes, that the end, for which thefe ten kings give their power to the beaft, is that by his affiftance they may deftroy the great whore. But this is a mere *fuppofition*, unfupported by any thing in the text or context ; nor does the Doctor give any reafon toward its fupport. Befides, what advantage is there in this fuppofition ? Is the beaft mentioned a friend to virtue and religion ? And did thofe kings do their duty in giving their power into his hands ? If they did not ; of courfe they did wrong ; and

and then the difficulty of God's putting it into their hearts to do this wrong ſtill remains.

On quoting Iſai. v. 4; " What could have been " done more to my vineyard, that I have not done " in it ? Wherefore, when I looked, that it ſhould " bring forth grapes, brought it forth wild grapes ?" the Doctor adds, " according to the ſcheme I am " oppoſing, all that the Deity has done to his vine- " yard, was to make it bring forth wild grapes. How " could he then appeal to the men of Judah and the " inhabitants of Jeruſalem, to judge between him and " his vineyard ?" Ibid, p. 71, &c. Now this and all the reſt that the Doctor adds in his remarks on that text, lies equally againſt the ſcheme of a permiſſive decree " perfectly and infallibly bounding," " reſtrain- " ing," " marking out" and " fixing bounds to the ac- " tions of men, beyond which they cannot paſs." For " according to this ſcheme" of the Doctor, " all that " the Deity has done to his vineyard was" by re- ſtraining them from all other actions, by bounding them to thoſe very actions which they have perform- ed, and by fixing ſuch bounds as they could not paſs, " to make them bring forth wild grapes. How then " could he appeal to the men of Judah and Jeruſalem " to judge, between him and his vineyard ? Will " it be ſaid, that the means uſed with them were ſuch, " that if they had been rightly improved they would " have enabled them to have brought forth good " grapes ? The anſwer —— is very eaſy ; theſe means " could have no effect but ſuch as the Deity deſigned " them to have;" becauſe " the Deity fixed their bounds, " beyond which they could not paſs," " and they " muſt produce either good or bad grapes, according " to the" bounds fixed by the Deity.——And ſo on through the ſame and following page. But I need not republiſh Dr. Weſt's book by way of retortion.

The Doctor in his 4th eſſay, Part II, (and in his Poſtſcript) on 1 Kings xxii. 23, " Now therefore, be- " hold, the Lord hath put a lying ſpirit in the mouth

" of

" of all thefe thy prophets ;" fays, " 'The word tranſ-
" lated *put* ought to have been tranſlated, The Lord
" hath *permitted* or *fuffered* a lying ſpirit, &c. for the
" verb here tranſlated *put*, frequently ſignifies to *per-*
" *mit* or *fuffer*. For the truth of this I appeal to
" every good Hebrician. Thus in Ezek. xx. 25,
" inſtead of, I *gave* them ſtatutes that were not good,
" it ſhould be, I *fuffered* them to have ſtatutes that
" were not good ;" p 66. It is always a ſufficient
anſwer to a mere confident aſſertion, as confidently to
deny it. Therefore my anſwer is, " The verb here
" tranſlated *put*," which is נתן does not " frequently ſignify *permit* or *fuffer* ;" and in Ezek. xx. 25, " Inſtead
" of, I *gave* them ſtatutes that were not good, it ſhould"
not " be, I *fuffered* them to have ſtatutes that were not
" good." Dr. Weſt for the confirmation of his criticiſm " appeals to every good Hebrician." Whom he
would acknowledge as a good Hebrician, is very uncertain. Therefore, inſtead of appealing to ſo uncertain a judge, I call on the Doctor himſelf, or any other Hebrician good or bad, to point out the inſtances,
whether frequent or unfrequent, in which נתן ſignifies merely to *permit* or *fuffer*. Beſide this, ſufficient
reaſons muſt be given to convince the candid and ju-
dicious, that it is uſed in this ſenſe, in the text now
under conſideration, and reaſons which do not beg
the main point, that God can do nothing toward the
exiſtence of ſin, but barely to permit it. When theſe
things ſhall have been done, we ſhall have better
ground, on which to believe the Doctor's criticiſm,
than his mere round aſſertion.

CONCLUSION.

CONCLUSION.

I HAVE now finifhed my remarks on Dr. Weft's *Effays on Liberty and Neceffity.* If he fhall think proper to write again on thofe fubjeɛts and to reply to thefe remarks, I requeft him to attend to thofe points only, which are material and affeɛt the merits of the caufe. If I have expofed myfelf by ever fo many inadvertencies, which do not affeɛt the merits of the caufe, to take up his own time and that of his readers, to exhibit them, feems not worth while. In difputes of this kind fuch inadvertencies are frequent. Alfo fuch difputes are apt to degenerate into mifreprefenta-tions, perfonal refleɛtions and logomachy. How far I have fallen into any of thefe, it is not proper for me to fay. However, I may fay, that I have endeavour-ed to avoid them. I hope the Doɛtor will be fuccefs-ful in the fame endeavour.

If he fhall write again, I requeft him to inform us more clearly, what he means by felf determination. If he mean no more than he hitherto profeffes to mean, " that we ourfelves determine ;" he will in-form us, wherein on that head he differs from Prefi-dent Edwards or any other man ; and whether it be his opinion, that we determine our own volitions in any other fenfe, than we determine all our perceptions and feelings.—— If he fhall be of the opinion, that we efficiently caufe our own volitions ; I requeft him to inform us, how we do or can do this otherwife than by antecedent volitions. If he fhall grant, that this is the way, in which we caufe them ; he will pleafe to remove the abfurdities fuppofea to attend that fuppo-fition ; and alfo decide whether or not we caufe them without any reftraint by previous certainty, *i. e.* wheth-er we caufe them by mere chance, and at hap hazard.

If he fhall ftill be of the opinion, that volition is no effeɛt ; he will pleafe to inform us how to recon-cile

cile that with the idea, that it proceeds from an intrinfic caufe and is originated by him who is the fubjeƈt
of it. If volition have a caufe, whether intrinfic or
extrinfic, it is of courfe an effeƈt.—He will alfo be
fo kind as to inform us, whether every human volition
exifted from eternity, or whether it came into exiftence
without caufe.

If he ftill maintain, that with refpeƈt to praife and
blame, there is no difference between natural and moral neceffity ; I wifh him to inform us, whether Judas
were as blamelefs in betraying his Lord, becaufe it
was previoufly certain and certainly foretold, that he
would do it, as he was for being attached to the fur-
face of the earth, and not afcending to heaven as Eli-
jah did.

I hope the Doƈtor will explain himfelf concerning
antecedent and confequent neceffity. If he mean,
that before the exiftence of any human aƈtion, there
was no certainty, that it would exift ; he will pleafe
to reconcile this both with divine foreknowledge, and
with the prophecies of fcripture. If by antecedent
neceffity, he mean any thing elfe than antecedent certainty, he will pleafe to fhow how it is to the purpofe,
or how it oppofes what we mean by antecedent neceffity.

I requeft him to fhow the confiftency between thefe
two propofitions, that motive is neceffary to every
volition ; and that men do not always aƈt on the
ftrongeft motive. He will of courfe fhow, what the
motive is which perfuades a man to pafs by the ftrongeft motive, and to aƈt on a weaker.

It is to be wifhed, that the Doƈtor would explain
his favourite power *to aƈt or not aƈt*. If he fhall own,
that he means a power to choofe or refufe merely, it
is prefumed, that his candour will lead him to own alfo, that he means nothing on this head different from
Prefident Edwards, unlefs by *power* he mean previous
uncertainty, and by a man's power to choofe or refufe,
he mean, that it is in itfelf and in the divine view *un-*
certain,

certain, whether he will choofe or refufe : And if he mean this, I wifh him to avow it.

I hope he will not fpend time in difcuffing quef, tions, which are merely verbal, fuch as whether mo- tive be the *caufe* or the *occafion* of volition. All that Prefident Edwards means by *caufe* in this cafe, is *ftat- ed occafion* or *antecedent*.

Perhaps the Doctor will find his book to be no lefs ufeful, if he fhall confine himfelf more to *argument*, and indulge himfelf lefs in *hiftory*. Narratives, how- ever true and accurate, of his own opinion without his reafons, and of his ability or inability whether to do or to conceive, are very uninterefting to thofe who think for themfelves, and do not depend on the Doc- tor as an authority. If he had hitherto fpared all fuch narratives, his books had been confiderably fhorter and no lefs demonftrative.

I hope the Doctor will be very explicit in commu- nicating his idea of liberty. I prefume he will join with me in the opinion, that the whole controverfy turns on this. If the liberty neceffary to moral ac- tion be an exemption from all extrinfic influence, we hold that the certain confequence is that either we caufe one volition by another ; or that our volitions come into exiftence without caufe and by mere chance. Therefore the Doctor will pleafe to fhow, that nei- ther of thefe confequences follows ; or will avow whichever he believes does follow.

He fuppofes felf-determination is free action. Now I wifh him to inform us, whether felf-determination, that is limited, bounded, governed and overruled, to a conformity to the divine purpofe, as he afferts all the actions of rational creatures to be, is free action. If it be, I requeft him to inform us, why an action decreed to be conformed to the fame divine purpofe, is not alfo free.

I rejoice, that this important fubject has been tak- en up by fo able an advocate as Dr. Weft. From his high character we have a right to expect, that if

the

the cauſe which he has undertaken, be capable of ſupport, it will be ſupported by the Doctor. I wiſh the other ſide of the queſtion had an advocate able to do it juſtice. However, ſince I have embarked in the cauſe, I ſhall, ſo long as important matter is brought forward, do as well as I can, till I ſhall either be convinced that the cauſe is a bad one, or find myſelf unable to reply : And I doubt not, that my failure will draw forth to the ſupport of the truth, ſome more able advocate, who now through modeſty or ſome other cauſe, does not appear for its defence.

I think it is but fair, that Dr. Weſt, and all others who write againſt moral neceſſity, ſhould take the explanations, which we give of moral and natural neceſſity and inability, and all other important terms in this diſquiſition. And ſo far as they oppoſe any doctrine which we hold, they ought to oppoſe it in the ſenſe in which we hold it, and not in a ſenſe which they may find it convenient to impute to us, becauſe they can more eaſily confute it. Such a management of any queſtion as the laſt mentioned, will never bring it to an iſſue, and beſides is exceedingly diſingenuous, and gives reaſon to ſuſpect the goodneſs of the cauſe, in favour of which it is employed.

As this queſtion concerning liberty and neceſſity affects the moſt important ſubjects of morality and religion ; it is to be wiſhed, that the diſcuſſion of it may finally conduce to the more clear underſtanding and the more ſincere and cheerful practice of virtue and piety, and to the glory of our God and Redeemer.

F I N I S.

E R R A T A.

THE Reader is requested to correct the following Errors, moſt of which eſcaped the Author, in preparing the Manuſcript for the Preſs.

Page 8, line 21, for *the*, read *ſome*.

37, 17, for *freedom*, read *power*.

50, 11, read, it does *it*.

65, 7, read, why it is *as it is*.

84, 20, for *then*, read *than*.

105, 14, for *Johnſon*, read *Jackſon*.

140, 17, read, which *do not* happen

143, 31, read, judge *the world*.

164, 11, read, *without* a cauſe.

180, 28, for *this*, read *the*.

215, 23, for *thought*, read *taught*.